C

Representation
 in Contemporary
French Fiction

Representation
in Contemporary
French Fiction

Dina Sherzer

University of Nebraska Press
Lincoln and London

Library of Congress
Cataloging in Publication Data

Sherzer, Dina.
   Representation in
   contemporary French fiction.
   Bibliography: p.
   1. French fiction—20th century—
History and criticism.
2. Fiction—Technique.
I. Title.
PQ671.S45   1986
843'.914'09   85-5882
ISBN 0-8032-4158-5
(alk. paper)

Publication of this book
was aided by a grant from
The Andrew W. Mellon Foundation.

Contents

Acknowledgments

The research for this book was made possible in part by a grant from the University of Texas Research Institute. I began working along the lines I propose here in two articles, which have been considerably revised for this study: "*Circus*: An Exercise in Semiotics," which appeared in *Sub-Stance* 17 (1977) (copyright 1977 by the Regents of the University of Wisconsin), and "Serial Constructs in the *Nouveau Roman*," which appeared in *Poetics Today* 1, (no. 3 1980). I thank both journals for permitting me to use this material.

Much of the thinking that has gone into this book is the result of discussions and experiences I have shared with Joel Sherzer. I have benefited from his expertise in linguistics and his research dealing with the rich oral traditions of South American Indians.

1

*Toute science crée
une nouvelle ignorance.
(Any science creates
a new ignorance.)*
Henri Michaux

Must we mean what we say?
Lewis Carroll

Toward a Thick Description of Polyvalent Texts

This book explores the diversity, the singularity, the boldness, and also the intriguing familiarity of contemporary French fiction. The authors of the works considered here—some very well known, others less so—have all been both productive and inventive, and during their careers they have modified their techniques while maintaining certain idiosyncratic features. My aim is not to present each writer by means of his or her most representative work but, rather, to study particular modes of textual organization as they are actualized in different works. Modes of discourse and modes of representation, not authors, are the subject of this book. For this reason I highlight the four modes of representation that I consider to be most salient: serial constructs, multimedia montages, reflexivities, and postmodern feminist fiction.

Representation is not a mirror image copying a preexisting reality but a fiction in which it is possible to visualize and to imagine actions, spaces, places, characters, and objects. As Jean Ricardou writes: "While a scene in daily life provides things to be seen, a scene which is described is a set of signs to be visualized."[1] Representation in any work of art, then, is a construction that has a reference in that it represents something for the reader/observer; however it may have no referent in that it does not necessarily reproduce anything actual in the real world. At times, elements within a text evoke scenes, situations, and persons that exist in the world as we know it, but even those that happen to be congruent with reality are renderings and transpositions of strips of experience. It is for this reason that literary texts in general and these texts in particular are uncanny and powerful machines devised to create meaning by representing experience. In fact, they propose a multiplicity of idiosyncratic ways of ordering experience and patterns of sense-making. In them the only true reality is that of the text itself.

What can be said about the texts chosen here? What justifies my grouping them together in this study? What do they have in common? Their titles—the thresholds, the doors where the fiction begins, announcing, introducing, and opening the works—display features that are very revealing. No proper names designating a person are used. Some titles—*H, L'Innommable,* and *Quelqu'un*—are abstract; they refer to nothing definite. Others refer to a system of elements: *Fugue, Mobile,* and *Triptyque.* (Similar abstract and formalistic titles are used by contemporary composers and painters: *Octandre* by Varese, *Points on a Line* by Berio, *VP-108* by Vasarely, *Impasse III* by Sima, for example.) Place names are utilized, but they connote polyvalence. *L'Observatoire de Cannes* announces seeing, searching, observing; *La Maison de rendez-vous* suggests a multiplicity of meetings in an illicit place; and *Circus* connotes the multifaceted and heterogeneous activities of the Big Top. The titles of the women's texts reflect other types of preoccupation. *Souffles* and *L'Amour* evoke a set of positive connotations having to do with the body, with life, birth, breath, murmurs, and sensuality. *Les Guérillères* makes the reader anticipate violent action by mingling *querrières* (female warriors) and *guerillas* (guerrilla fighters) in a portmanteau word. Instead of leading the reader into a specific historical or emotional setting, most of the titles are ambiguous, and most are both underdetermined and overdetermined, exactly like the works they subsume.[2]

These texts, written during what is called the postmodern era, span a period of roughly thirty years. They display the characteristics of Postmodernism: randomness, pluralism, heterogeneity, multiplicity, dispersion, and indeterminacy rather than univocity, totality, wholeness, hierarchy, and polarity.[3] In Roland Barthes's terms, these are *scriptibles* (writerly) texts, which he defines as "the novelistic without the novel, poetry without the poem, the essay without the dissertation, production without product, structuration without structure."[4]

Developing this pithy statement, we can say than these works are open texts that contain no narrative; as François Lyotard writes, in the postmodern era narrative is in crisis.[5] These texts are verbal configurations that seem to begin and end arbitrarily. It is as if readers were suddenly connected to an ongoing flow of words, which after a while is abruptly interrupted. The originator of the text, the source of meaning, is both present and absent; that is, somebody writes or speaks, but his or her identity is not thematized in the text — or if it is, its status changes constantly.

In the early 1960s, Butor could write that the novel is the laboratory of the narrative.[6] And it is true that in their early works such writers as Butor, Robbe-Grillet, Simon, and Sollers experimented with chronology, point of view, and characters — the traditional components of narrative — forming a school or a movement that has come to be known as the *nouveau roman.* These writers, the *nouveaux romanciers,* then developed their experimentations still further, attempting more radical manipulations of linguistic and textual components: the *nouveau roman* became the *nouveau nouveau roman.* I consider that the texts dealt with here belong to the *nouveau nouveau roman* or to Postmodernism, regardless of their date of publication and regardless of whether or not their authors call themselves new new novelists, Postmodernists, or feminist writers.

These texts are constructed out of fragments that are linked by differences and dissimilarities; they have no reference to a unified totality and do not result in a unified totality. Their hallmark is discontinuity, achieved through fragmentation and heterogeneity and through various linguistic and typographical manipulations. As a consequence, their representation is not linear but spatial, achronic, and nonhierarchical; because of these characteristics it is difficult to decode a referential totality. The texts present not cohesion but dispersion, in which parts are more important than wholes. Since these parts are simply juxtaposed without connecting links, parataxis is the principle by which they are organized.

Because of their particular properties, the texts I consider here both interact with and play off against the backdrop of two traditions. On the one hand, there is the linear novel with a plot, be it psychological or sociological, a love story or a detective story, a travel account or the expression of a personal experience—essentially, the nineteenth-century novelistic model. On the other hand, there is the modernist novel, which presents a subject whose experiences—intellectual, psychological, and physical as well as sociological—are explored while narrative techniques and language are manipulated. Proust, Joyce, and Mann are paradigms. Postmodern texts involve a conscious interplay with these two traditions. Postmodern writers—each in an individual way—deviate, exaggerate, or parody elements of these two traditions. These works, like all works of art, develop out of their predecessors and create a dialogue with them. There is a continuous development out of the past, rather than a break with it.

A famous slogan of the 1960s states that new novels are no longer the writing of adventures but the adventures of writing. The texts discussed here definitely stage adventures of writing and, more generally, adventures of language. They are the production of writers who are logophiles, who show confidence in the lexical, syntactic, and discursive resources and possibilities of language. *H, Circus,* and *Souffles* display a pleasure in crafting and in manipulating language by their puns, their portmanteau words, and their parodies. *Mobile, Circus, H, Souffles,* and *Les Guérillères* present a heterogeneous verbal texture with several styles, registers of language, and intertextual material. *Mobile* and *Les Guérillères* stand out for their idiosyncratic accumulation of names and nouns. *L'Observatoire de Cannes, Triptyque,* and *La Maison de rendez-vous* contain descriptions that are semantically interesting because of the ways in which they privilege shapes. *Fugue* offers an exploration of metaphors, and *L'Innommable* spins torrents of words that create a striking aural experience.

In these texts, language does not serve only to channel information or to transmit referential meaning; on the contrary, its intrinsic properties are always foregrounded. In addition, these works attract attention by means of the organization of words, letters, and shapes on their pages and by their printing styles, typography, and symbols. Instead of successions of sentences broken by paragraph indentations and chapter headings, the pages present less conventional spatial arrangements, ranging from a dense, unpunctuated flow of words (*H*) to poemlike units (*L'Amour, Les Guérillères*), to a very sparse presence of words (*Mobile*), to completely blank pages (*Circus*).

This diversity of presentation requires different types of reading: sometimes a slow movement of the eye from word to word, sometimes a more relaxed decoding of a few words on a page. The reader's eye movement must also change direction, proceeding not only horizontally from left to right but also vertically and diagonally, in order to decode various units displayed in the form of columns, squares, or rectangular blocks of printed material. Writing in its graphic materiality is constantly placed in the foreground.

A notion that captures the textual and verbal strategies utilized in these texts is that of play. Play is understood in the sense of altering and experimenting with modes of representation, language, cultural references, reminiscences, allusions, quotes, and typography. It involves invention, unexpected and incongruous juxtapositions, jugglings, permutations, and reframings. It results in constant disruptions and its modes are both serious and ludic.

Given the nature of the texts I have chosen my analysis cannot be limited to content (themes, images, symbols) or to form (grammar, style, narrative and discourse organization) but must involve both. Or, to put it in terms of different schools of criticism, it is not desirable to operate with the prestructuralist emphasis on signifieds or with both structuralist and poststructuralist emphasis on signifiers; rather, it is necessary to examine both signifiers and signified with the understanding that there is not a one-to-one relationship between them but that both generate meaning independently of each other.

In these texts everything is meaningful; meaning is expresssed not only by the semantic or referential content of language but also in the various modes of communication. The manipulations affecting language and typography are not merely ludic behavior or adornment. They signify, because language and signs express meaning not only by what they say but also by what they are and where they are. Space, letters, and the page also signify by the relationships established among them. It is no longer possible to subscribe to Saussure's idea that language and writing are two distinct systems of signs, the unique raison d'être of the latter being to represent the former. What is special about the texts I deal with here is precisely the fact that they exploit both the potentials and the limits of language, with regard to all its elements, features, and aspects from sounds to meanings, from syntax to typography. And the difficulty and novelty in these texts are that they highlight and display the extremely complicated and heterogeneous nature of language, its involvement in many activities, and its various functions.

"It must be understood literally and in all ways," answers Rimbaud to his mother, who is perplexed after reading his *Une Saison en enfer*. This same attitude is called for by the texts under consideration here. They are verbal constructs capable of being scrutinized from different vantage points and with different critical tools. They are configurations out of which meanings have to be constructed. In each chapter, I begin with a textual reading during which the following questions are asked. What is the representation about; that is, what are the topics or the themes? By whom is this representation encoded; that is, who is the narrator? How does the narrator manifest, or not, her or his presence? Given the lack of temporality and causality, how is the representation organized? What kinds of linguistic, discursive, and typographical resources are utilized, and what are their effects? Once such components have been identified, it is still only the obvious, manifest content, only the surface organization of the text, that has been decoded. As many students of language and communication would remind us, and as we know from our daily experience with language and objects, in addition to their denotation and referential meanings, words, units of words, images, and objects have connotations that constitute one or more added levels and layers of meaning, embedded, contained, and indexed in discourse or objects and actualized by the reader of a text or the perceiver of an object.[7] While anyone analyzing a conventional text, which tends to emphasize its plot and its narrative content, would have to discuss the connotations of the verbal material, in the texts presented here it is necessary to pay attention to the connotations of the visual components—the manipulation of space and typography—as well. Connotations depend on one's social, cultural, and intellectual background, awareness, and knowledge. The point of view adopted here is that of a native speaker of French, raised within French culture and attuned to the French intellectual life of the last two decades.

For several years such scholars as Julia Kristeva, Michael Riffatterre, and Gérard Genette have made us aware of various manifestations of what Genette calls *transtextuality.*[8] That is, texts do not exist in a vacuum; they are not autonomous entities but rather are related in many ways to other texts, and these different manifestations of transtextuality are important features that produce effects of meaning.

Intertextuality is one type of transtextuality that I examine. Intertextuality takes many forms: direct quotations, references, alterations, inversions, transpositions, and "graftings" of portions of other texts.[9] In addition to these different processes, intertextual manipulations in these texts are particularly remarkable because of the wide variety of material they involve. One recognizes not only other literary texts but also popular literature, anthropological, psychoanalytical, and philosophical texts, and everyday noises, voices, advertisements, songs, and iconic representations.

Architextuality is another type of transtextuality particularly relevant for these texts. Architextuality, according to Genette, is a question of label, of taxonomy, or of genre. A text may belong to the architext of the novel genre, to that of poem, or to that of play. Then, more specifically, a text may be a realistic or psychological novel, an epic or lyric poem, a tragedy or a comedy. However, the texts chosen here deliberately flout this notion of architext by mingling the characteristics of several genres and / or by using particular characteristics of a well-defined genre. Thus *Les Guérillères* has characteristics found both in a utopia and in an oral myth from a preliterate society. *Mobile* incorporates forms of discourse characteristic of a catalog or a tourist guide. These features are significant for the message they convey, because utopia, myth, catalog, and guide are very marked genres that carry cultural and textual denotations and connotations.

In addition to intertextual and architextual components, I propose to examine two other forms of transtextuality. The first is what Boris Uspenski calls *structural isomorphisms,* the presence of the same shape or organization in two different forms of expression. Uspenski gives the following examples:

7

The first person in the endings (the "I" of the narrator) can be compared with the self-portrait of the artist in the periphery of a picture, with the precantor on the stage (who often symbolizes the author—narrators), etc. The second person (the "you" of the spectator, reader) can be compared with the function of the chorus in the dramas of Antiquity. . . .

Thus, the general text of a narrative can be divided into a complex of ever smaller microdescriptions, all organized according to the same principle (i.e., having special frames indicated by alternations of the external and internal positions of the author).

The same principle is also found in the spatial organization of Pre-Renaissance painting (using the point of view of the "internal" observer). The general space of the painting is divided here into discrete microspaces, all organized in the same way as the whole represented space. [10]

The term "isomorphism" is not commonly used in literary studies, even though the process itself has frequently been noted. Imbrie Buffum, in his introduction to *Studies in the Baroque from Montaigne to Rotrou,* states that "it has been my aim, wherever possible, to illustrate my literary examples through pertinent comparisons drawn from painting, sculpture, and architecture"; Mario Praz, in his *Mnemosyne: The Parallel between Literature and the Visual Arts,* has a chapter entitled "Sameness of structure in a Variety of Media."[11] In the texts I discuss here, isomorphisms are created in various ways. In Sollers's *H,* they are created by means of language: one finds forms of speech play that are typical of children's linguistic behavior. In Laporte's *Fugue,* isomorphisms are created by means of textual organization: the text is divided into units or sequences recalling mystic works in which there are several stages and phases. In *Triptyque,* Simon creates isomorphisms by means of groupings of elements analogous to mathematical set theory.

The other form of transtextuality I deal with involves the presence of *harmonics* between two different modes of expression. I borrow the term from Roger Laporte, who in his *Carnets* discusses *Fugue* as follows: "Nothing resembles *Fugue* and *Fugue* resembles nothing, neither in literature, nor in music, etc., although for particular aspects, as far as certain situations are concerned, it is possible to find harmonics: I think not only about certain works quoted above (*Destroyed Country* by Klee, *Man Who Walks II* by Giacometti) but about certain works by Lardera, about Kowalski, and even more about *Memory* by Vieira da Silva."[12] Harmonics are a similarity of moods, a consonance, or a resonance that is felt to be present between two works of art. Thus, in Duras's *L'Amour,* the violence of a shout and the features of the landscape where this shout is uttered bring to mind the painting by Edvard Munch entitled *The Cry.* The tone and the mood of the prose of Sollers's *H* share characteristics with Balinese gamelan music.

These various types of transtextual relationships establish explicit and implicit, objective and subjective forms of dialogisms between texts and other texts and between texts and such other forms of expression as music or painting. And it is fascinating to note how various writers, by their deliberate and conscious use of allusions, references, and forms of discourse, place themselves in a network involving other authors—thus creating, as Borges would say, precursors for themselves. It is also fascinating to examine the following questions: Which texts of the past are reworked? Which texts of the present are utilized? And which systems of value and ideologies are considered worth bringing to the fore, legitimized, contested, or subverted? The possibility of finding harmonics points to the efficacy of these texts and to their capacity to stimulate and challenge the minds and the culture of readers. Thus in the texts of Beckett, Cixous, Duras, Laporte, Pinget, Ricardou, Robbe-Grillet, Roche, Simon, and Wittig there is present an impressive list of such artists, thinkers, scientists, and writers as Adami, Bruno, Derrida, Freud, Glass, Joyce, Lacan, Munch, Pascal, Rabelais, Thom, and Warhol. Strange bedfellows indeed, a surrealist list underscoring both the novelty and the conventionality of these texts.

Denotations, connotations, intertextual and architextual components, isomorphisms, and harmonics overlap and intersect in these texts, creating staggered or multilayered systems of meaning.[13] My contribution is to study these systems of meaning by combining text-centered criticism and reader's criticism. For no single model—linguistic, literary, or psychoanalytical—can be applied; on the contrary, these texts explicitly and implicitly question and challenge all such models. For this reason I draw on the diversity of approaches developed for the study of language use, discourse, and communication in general as well as for literary texts. When I state that my textual analysis focuses on the content and on the presentation of this content, I am reformulating the tripartite Aristotelian scheme, which advocates the study of *inventio, elocutio,* and *dispositio.* I combine the study of Emile Benveniste's notion of the enunciated (what is said, written) and of the enunication (how is it written, by whom). What I propose is also akin to a Hjelmslevian analysis, which advocates the study of the substance and form of the content and the substance and form of the expression.

I am further influenced by Roman Jakobson's concept of the functions of language, which involves not only the referential but also the poetic function: that is, the concrete components of language, including the phonic. Present in my approach as well is the idea of J. L. Austin that words convey meaning not only by what they say but by what they do; Austin's concept of the speech act, as developed by John Searle, is a central unit of linguistic and discourse analysis. The notion of frame as developed by Erving Goffman is utilized in this study, because it attracts attention to the anchoring of strips of experience and because it accounts for how experience, transformed verbally and visually, is displayed in a text. Ever present is the notion of play as advocated by Wittgenstein, who sees language as having many potentialities; by Derrida, who advocates play as *différance,* as a means to avoid stability and to postpone closure; and by Deleuze and Guattari, who see the world, the individual, and society in terms of connecting and overlapping networks that undergo grafts and transformations. [14]

By drawing on the different frameworks, analytical models, and notions that the texts themselves require, my approach aims at arriving at *thick descriptions* of literary texts. This term and method have been proposed by Clifford Geertz for the study of the deep, intricate, and complicated nature of cultures. Instead of reducing an event or a ritual to simple, rudimentary patterns, Geertz argues that any cultural entity is multivalent and inserted into a network of relationships that mesh and intertwine. He writes that the ethnographer is in fact faced with "a multiplicity of conceptual structures, many of them superimposed upon or knotted into one another, which are at once strange, irregular and inexplicit and which he must contrive somehow first to grasp and then to render."[15] Similarly, the texts discussed here display a specific internal organization, but in turn they are also linked to other texts and other forms of experience by the connotations, by the intertextuality they encode, and by the architext they belong to.

One consequence of my method is that I do not follow a strict critical grid requiring me to study systematically each text's denotations, connotations, intertextual and architextual elements, isomorphisms, and harmonics. Rather, each text dictates which critical categories are pertinent and which are not. Also, since my analysis depends on a concrete textual study of each work, illustrative examples are presented and analyzed. In addition to being necessary for my argument, these provide readers with a wide sample of the discursive varieties and typographical specificities of the texts, demonstrating the different rhythms of reading and the different perspectives they require.

The nature of these texts and the bold ways in which they explore the potentials and the possibilities of language and communication challenge not only our methods and modes but even the vocabulary we use for talking about literature. As a result, the reader will notice a particular choice of vocabulary in my text about these texts. In some cases I have followed current conventions, using terms that have come to be accepted for the description and analysis of literary and other— especially contemporary—discourse: thus *text* (rather than *novel*), *inscribe* (rather than *write*), *intertext, différance*, and *deconstruction*. In other cases I have borrowed terms from related disciplines, perspectives, and approaches to language—linguistics, sociolinguistics, philosophy, anthropology, and sociology—adapting them to my study of particular contemporary French texts: thus *register, frame, discourse, speech act, contextualization*, and *thick description*. Still another set of terms is necessary because of the particular nature of the texts I deal with: thus *fragmentation, disorder, nonlinearity, lack of cohesion, atemporal*, and *undecidable*. These terms, in spite of their seemingly negative connotations, should not be understood as implying defects or deviances. Rather, they are the positive organizing principles of the texts I have chosen and of postmodern forms of artistic expression in general.

Obviously, the aim of this book is not to engage in a teleological activity in order to provide the ultimate meaning of the texts but rather to explore how they are written, how they play, how they mean, and how they can be played with and performed by readers. While I write readably about texts that seem often unreadable, I work in the spirit of Postmodernism; in fact I practice postmodern criticism in that I group different modes, I deal with different authors within each mode, and I weave together various critical approaches. In this deliberately eclectic yet integrated study—in presenting different possible manifestations of discontinuity, different types of representation, and different modes of discourse—I propose an experience similar to that of attending an exhibition devoted to a particular school of painting. The viewer can see that while adopting the same general techniques, each painter proposes an individual interpretation and realization of them, a unique choice of subject matter, and a particular color scheme. I intend to show that these discontinuous, dispersed, disorderly, and fragmented verbal structures, which pertain to our time and to our epistemology, are meaningful cacographies[16] that offer contributions to and insights into the nature of signification.

2

Serial Constructs

Jean Ricardou's *L'Observatoire de Cannes*, Alain Robbe-Grillet's *La Maison de rendez-vous*, and Claude Simon's *Triptyque* constitute a type of discontinuous and nonlinear text whose representation can best be characterized by the term *serial constructs*. Seriality can be observed in a variety of phenomena, including mathematics, biology, and music; and it can be organized in different ways. I use it here in its most general sense as a set of three or more items or events involving an identity relationship. In the texts of Ricardou, Robbe-Grillet, and Simon, seriality is established by means of a number of elements that are repeated syntagmatically with some variation. The choice of these three particular texts does not imply that the three authors adopt seriality as a constant technique or that only these writers and only these texts employ it. In his previous works—*Les Gommes, La Jalousie,* and *Dans le labyrinthe*—Robbe-Grillet employs seriality in order to develop and highlight the torments and obsessions of, respectively, a criminal, a jealous person, and a dying man. However, in *La Maison de rendez-vous* there is no such character. The text's seriality is more postmodern. Simon also used seriality in *Orion aveugle* and in *Les Corps conducteurs*. I chose *Triptyque* because in it Simon plays with seriality, complicating his task by establishing recurrences across three different panels that offer three different types of representation. *L'Observatoire de Cannes* is the only novel by Richardou that makes massive use of recurrences and repetitions with variations.

L'Observatoire de Cannes, La Maison de rendez-vous, and *Triptyque* share certain characteristics. They are verbal configurations constructed by the juxtaposition of strips of representation. Chronology and plot—that is, temporality, causality, and logical links—are absent; nevertheless, there is cohesion, due to the recurrence of various elements from strip to strip, creating series that cut across the strips. A range of elements is utilized for the elaboration of these series. The same event can take place in different settings; the same shape and/or color and/or movement can be isolated in different items, animate or inanimate; the same character can appear in different roles and in different settings; the same verb can be used for a group of disparate objects; a succession of different visual experiences can be set up. In these texts, structured as they are by repetition and the variation of formal elements, no strip is granted more prominence than the others; no action, situation, or character is staged as more important. Barthes notices that in Robbe-Grillet's texts "the narrative pressure is rigorously steady";[1] this remark applies to *La Maison de rendez-vous* in particular as well as to Ricardou's *L'Observatoire de Cannes* and Simon's *Triptyque*. Furthermore, the texts are open in that no one referential or morphological component brings about the sense of an ending or a feeling of completion; other variations and repetitions could be added to the existing ones, lengthening the text but not changing it otherwise.

Although they do not purport to copy reality, these texts inscribe places, characters, and actions—a representation that can be visualized. The frame through which the representation is presented constantly changes, since visually and perceptually the anchoring constantly varies. What is represented can be what is observed or imagined by the narrator; it can be the content of a painting, a photograph, a poster, an illustrated magazine, a piece of filmstrip, a sculptured scene, or a scene in a play or a film. This change of frames is not motivated psychologically; it is not a device that reveals or emphasizes particular features of a character or situation but simply a formal manipulation of various visual experiences. In addition, constant references are made to shapes, configurations, volumes, textures, and colors.

The narrator in these texts is neutral and uninvolved. The words emanate from an uncertain originator who does not participate in any way in what he or she inscribes. The text does not specify explicitly or implicitly whether the narrator watches, dreams, or imagines what is written; this component is undecidable. At the same time, in each of the three texts, the narrator sustains the same flow of words and elaborates a detached and precise prose. Standard syntax and formal, standard vocabulary, precise yet not overly technical, are defining stylistic features of their style. Embellishments, improprieties, and slang are avoided. There are no self-conscious interventions by the narrator showing approbation or disapprobation, reinforcing or undermining what is written. As a consequence, these texts are neither euphoric nor dysphoric but neutral and objective. Their neutrality is reinforced by the atemporality created by the present tense, employed to the exclusion of all others.

After these general considerations, I want now to analyze each of the texts successively, to examine how it is organized and what series are constructed in it, and then to discuss the effects of representation in which seriality is the organizing principle.

L'Observatoire de Cannes: Cubist Writing

Cannes, on the French Riviera: its beach, its hotels, its yacht marina, the hill with its observatory overlooking the city, the cable train that permits access to the observatory, the panorama of the town, the sea, and various islands are easily recognizable.[2] Several nameless characters, presumably tourists visiting the town during their summer vacations, are seen in the train, in the observatory, on the beach; at the end of the text someone is watching a striptease show in a nightclub. There is a young blond woman, a newlywed couple constantly holding hands and kissing each other, a middle-aged man who seems to accompany an elderly woman and their grandchild. On the beach people play with a beach ball, and a young man has just caught an octopus.

These characters happen to be at the same place at the same time; except for the newlywed couple and the trio of man, woman, and child, they do not appear to know each other. Besides the fact that the characters look at the Cannes landscape or lie on the beach or watch a striptease, we do not know anything about them, nor do we need to. The interest of the text does not reside in who the characters are or what they do, or in any particular significance given to Cannes and its location. Rather, these elements provide the resources for a different textual action: the characters, the places they are in, what they wear, and the fact that they look at people and landscape constitute semantic material with which different series are formed across the thirty-one sections of the text.

One series is elaborated by means of the reappearance of characters with the same element, such as an item of clothing, a physical detail, or an object they carry. For the blond woman, green-and-white checked material, a beach bag, and sandals are the characteristics mentioned repeatedly. The middle-aged man is bald, carries a camera, wears a raincoat, has a red face, and wipes his forehead with a green-and-white striped handkerchief. The young woman is associated with a pink dress and black hair combed in a chignon. The grandmother is frequently described as being fat or enormous. When there are several characteristics, they are not necessarily all repeated every time the person reappears; one of them is sufficient to connote all the others in the mind of the reader.

The recurrence of the action of looking and observing establishes another series of components: the action of looking itself, the different locations for looking, the different frames that anchor what is looked at, and the different optical apparatuses. In the train, tourists look at each other while they watch the landscape through the windows; in the observatory, they look at the landscape; on the beach, people sun themselves and play ball games but also look at other people and are looked at; the bald man and his wife stand in front of a postcard rack, looking at cards before buying; the blond woman looks at photographs in an album; the bald man takes photographs; somebody watches a striptease show; somebody looks underwater with a mask. Quite often the characters are placed spatially in such a way that they can see better. As the train goes up the hill, the landscape appears gradually. The observatory is on top of a hill dominating the town and the bay. The bald man watches the blond girl on the beach from a wall overlooking that beach. The tourists stand in front of the rack of post-cards, and the striptease show is performed in front of the spectators.

The same strip of representation is frequently presented in at least two different frames. The landscape that is seen from the observatory is also reproduced in a mural painting at the train station. The young husband draws for his wife a sketch similar to the one on the orienta-tion table in the observatory. A blond woman wearing a swimsuit is represented on a postcard; a cover girl wearing the same swimsuit takes the same position as she poses for a professional photographer. Certain optical apparatuses keep reappearing: binoculars at the ob-servatory, a camera, an underwater mask, and eyes.

Several series are created by the reappearance of the same shape in heterogeneous elements. An octagon recurs, actualized in objects that have this shape in nature or in groupings of people or objects that form it. The hand rest, actually a sort of table where the landscape is painted on ceramic tiles in the observatory, is octagonal; the young husband reproduces this octagon on a piece of paper to explain the landscape to his wife; geometrical graffiti on a wall form an octagon; the swivel one has to go through to enter the station platform is octa-gonal; young people make an octagon as they play ball on the beach and undo it when they stop playing; the little girl makes an octagon with her sand cakes; the young woman looks at the concentric octa-gons on the card drawn by her husband.

The triangle is another shape that organizes a series. It appears in the V-neck opening of the girl's blouse; a two-piece swimsuit is de-scribed in terms of three triangles; the blind spots that cannot be seen at the foot of the tower are triangular; the graffiti form upside-down V-shapes and triangles; the scapulas are triangular; legs form an up-side-down V; branches form a V; the sails of the boats in the bay are triangles; the bay is delimited into a triangle by buoys; drawings cre-ate a triangle; clothes of triangular shapes are drying in the sun.

Other forms also group elements into series. The scalloped edge of the girl's swimsuit has the same configuration as the foam on the waves, the festoon of debris on the sand, and the contour of a cloud. Rectangles, squares, circles, straight lines, parallel lines, oblongs, spirals, and cylindrical and conical volumes are isolated everywhere in objects, the landscape, and characters; consequently, the mention of geometrical shapes leads one to visualize also objects and movements that are not explicitly described as such in these terms: houses, windows, roofs, rails, towers, ditches, and wires also become shapes. In expressions such as *braquer un regard* (to fix one's eyes) and *alignés sur les fils* (lined up on the wires), it is the straight line of the look and the horizontality of the wires that are focused on and foregrounded.

The recurrence of the number 8 might incite the reader to think that a symbolic meaning is intended, but in fact this is just a clue that exercises our sagacity, leading nowhere as far as symbolism is concerned. It is one more element that organizes a series, related to but independent of the eight sides of the octagons. A tower is 7 to 8 meters high; the underwater mask permits one to see 7 or 8 meters deep; in the water there are 7 or 8 fish; 7 or 8 men and women are standing in shallow water near the beach; the octopus caught by the boy has 8 tentacles.

Colors, too, combine different elements into series. White and green are the colors of the pants the blond woman wears, of her swimsuit, of the handkerchief of the bald man, and of the shining underwear of the girl who performs the striptease. Red is the color of the swimsuit worn by a fat woman on a postcard and by the fat elderly lady on the beach; the beach ball the young people play with is red. White is the color of the sails of the boats and of the triangles that decorate the ball.

These various series created by means of repetitions and differences are orchestrated to structure *L'Observatoire de Cannes;* they overlap and mingle, making the text a tight and intricate network in which something always echoes something else. This tightness and intricacy is especially apparent in sections where the triangle of the swimsuit keeps recurring: in passages on pages 30, 31, 42, 46, 57, 83–84, 96, 103, 104, 133, 145, 174, and 179, systems of repetitions are set up with the recurrence of the same object—the girl's swimsuit with its checked triangles, which contrast two colors—and of certain words. The expression "le ventre enfoui aux deux tiers" (two-thirds of the belly tucked) appears on pages 30, 57, and 84–86. On page 96 the verb is changed: "le ventre caché aux deux tiers" (two-thirds of the belly hidden). At the same time, variations are deployed: a girl is seen on the beach, in a photograph, swimming in the sea, being photographed, doing a striptease.

These different frames explain the changes that occur in the color or texture of the triangles. They are made of green-and-white cloth when the girl is on the beach or swimming; they are black and white on the photographic paper; they are black-and-white lozenges when the photograph represents the body underwater; and they are shiny green-and-white pieces of strass in the cabaret. The lace that edges the swimsuit is also a pretext for variation. "Liseré de dentelles" (edged with lace) on page 30 becomes "ourlé des minuscules festons de la dentelle blanche" (edged with the thin scallops of the white lace) on page 42; "ourlé d'un mince liseré d'écume" (hemmed with a thin edge of foam) on page 46; "la fine bordure de dentelle blanche" (the thin white lace border) on page 103; "le liseré est une simple frange de mousse" (the edge is a simple fringe of foam) on page 104; "ourlé d'un mince liseré de broderie anglaise" (hemmed with a thin edge of English embroidery) on page 174.

Syntactically, the swimsuit is permuted in different positions: on page 31 it is one element of an enumeration, whereas in the other strips it can be the object or subject. Different verbs are used. Some underscore the swimsuit's function of hiding, of covering, therefore pointing insistently at what is covered and hidden—*enfouir* (to tuck), *cacher* (to hide). Other verbs, on the contrary, suggest a bursting out of forms and a sharp delineation of them—*se détacher* (to stand out), *jaillir* (to jut out), *saillir* (to shoot out). Far from being static repetitions and variations, these strips are the focus of an intense activity or, to borrow a title from Ricardou himself, of "minuscule revolutions."[3] Any element or component—frame, lexicon, or syntax—is available for manipulation and permutation, thus creating modifications in the representation and even reaching a certain climax, since what might be called the adventure of the triangle ends with the removing of the triangles on page 179, revealing what was hidden up to that point and satisfying reader, narrator, and grammar. For one might say that these triangles are there only to be taken away and that the narrator and the reader have been waiting for this. And satisfying the grammar, too, because lexically "to cover" is complemented by its antonym, "to uncover."

Ricardou writes that "novelistic matter is entirely invented through the exercise of description . . . everything is constructed, or if one accepts being less derogatory: everything is written."[4] Indeed, in *L'Observatoire de Cannes* everything is invented, constructed, and carefully and minutely contrived. And because the narrator constantly imposes a geometrical filter upon the representation he inscribes, the text is a formal construction the possible harmonics of which are paintings by Cézanne, Picasso, and Braque, studies in the shapes and volumes of objects, people, and landscapes of the same Mediterranean region described in *L'Observatoire de Cannes.*

Although narrative is definitely absent from *L'Observatoire de Cannes,* many stories might be invented and developed from the elements provided. In fact, one reader wrote to Ricardou, "These are exactly my vacations in Cannes." And one could imagine a mystery or pornographic story in which the bald man with his raincoat and his camera is a voyeur or detective behaving like a friendly grandfather taking pictures. The photographs showing the pieces of clothing scattered on the beach or rolled by the waves would be proofs of a crime. And the constant mention of the triangle, referring to the body of the girl but eroticizing the whole landscape, could signal the obsession of the narrator. *L'Observatoire de Cannes* does not preclude the invention of adventures of a more anthropocentric type, such as those I have suggested, but this would impose a conventional reading on a text that proposes a more challenging experience in the form of adventures in shapes perceived in different settings with different optical apparatuses, a text that sets up minute revolutions with words.

La Maison de rendez-vous: Oriental Frames

Robbe-Grillet is a literary *bricoleur.* By means of seriality he revamps popular culture. By taking advantage of it and by playing with it, he makes fun of it and at the same time stresses how its components derive from ideologies and contemporary myths. *La Jalousie* is a reframing of a love story taking place in an exotic colonial background and involving the triangular relationship of husband-wife-lover. *Projet pour une révolution à New York* is constructed with elements that are the ingredients of detective stories and pornographic novels, with their paraphernalia of violence and sadism.[5] *La Maison de rendez-vous*[6] exploits another vein of popular fiction: Hong Kong, its Oriental women, drugs, money, prostitution, and rich Europeans on the margins of legality are the stereotypes chosen as points of departure. As in *L'Observatoire de Cannes,* these elements, with repetitions and variations, are elaborated into series that structure the text.

Each character and the narrator are the starting points of series, since they reappear in different roles and in different settings. Lady Ava is a hostess receiving her guests at a reception in her house, the Villa Bleue. She is also seen in the same setting ordering a blond woman to dance with a man and showing this man an album of photographs of women. Lady Ava acts in the plays that are staged in her house, in a secret theater to which only intimate friends are invited. In her bedroom she counts little bags of drugs and hides some of them. There, too, she dismisses her servant Kim, a beautiful Eurasian girl, by telling her: "I don't need you tonight. I'm old and tired. . . . You can sleep in your own bed" [p. 72]. Lady Ava is a society woman, the director of a high-class brothel, an actress, a drug dealer or drug addict, and a lesbian.

Edouard Manneret, a rich European friend of Lady Ava, is seen writing at his desk, being visited by the Eurasian girl, performing an experiment on her, talking to Ralph Johnson, and lying assassinated in his office. The scene of Manneret's assassination is also acted on the stage of Lady Ava's theater. Manneret is a drug dealer, a moneylender, an experimenter, the subject of a play, and the father of the twin Eurasian girls, Kim and Lucky.

Kim is Lady Ava's servant; she walks her dogs; she goes to Manneret's house; she is a subject for Manneret's drug experiments; and she performs on Lady Ava's stage. At times an unnamed Eurasian girl is seen walking down a street, riding on a ferry, and maneuvering a sampan. Johnson, Lauren, and Marchand, other characters in the text, play several roles involving drugs, money, and sex in the Villa Bleue and in various places in Hong Kong.

The status of the narrator changes as well. At the beginning of the text, a narrator expresses himself in the first person and talks about his sexual obsessions and fantasies. Next he turns to an impersonal style, describing Hong Kong as a tourist brochure would. Then he seems to describe what he sees around him. Later he becomes a participant, talking to Lady Ava and drinking champagne. Eventually he again becomes an anonymous narrator whose speech is skidding like a needle on a broken record:

> Dans l'attention que Lauren porte à cette délicate opération, la chevelure blonde renversée se déplace et découvre danvantage la nuque qui se courbe et la chair fragile, au duvet plus pàle encore que la chevelure blonde, qui se déplace et découvre davantage la nuque, qui se courbe et la chair fragile au duvet plus pâle que le reste de la nuque qui se courbe et la chair fragile qui se courbe davantage et la chair. [p. 82]

> As she concentrates on this delicate operation, Lauren's blond hair falls forward and further exposes the curved nape of her neck and the delicate skin whose down is even paler than the blond hair, which falls forward and further exposes the curved nape of her neck and the delicate skin whose down is even paler than the rest of the curved nape and the delicate skin which curves further and the skin. [p. 54]

At one point it is written that the story of the brothel in Hong Kong was told by somebody to Lady Ava, who is not Ava or Eva but Jacqueline, born in Belleville, a Paris neighborhood.

Two stereotypes about the Orient—eroticism and drugs—are used in different forms and settings to construct two series. Eroticism is represented by the tight-fitting dress that shapes the body of Eurasian girls, either real or represented ones. It is worn by Kim and by Lucky, by a mannequin in a shop window, by a girl represented in a drawing and on a ring, by a girl traveling on a ferry, by a girl walking along a street, and by a girl maneuvering a sampan.

Drugs are constantly present because there is frequent mention of their substance, of the containers in which they are kept, and of their effects; there are many conversations about drugs and meetings to obtain them. At the reception a servant picks up a little bottle, which must have been emptied with a syringe. A little vial of morphine falls from a pocket. Manneret holds a colorless liquid in a glass. The glass is almost empty, and Manneret looks at the Eurasian girl lying motionless on a bed. A street sweeper picks up a leaflet displaying propaganda against drugs. It shows a woman injecting drugs into her arm, then lying motionless on a disorderly bed. Manneret behaves as if he is under the effects of opium when Johnson comes to ask for money. Kim visits Manneret's house, where she undergoes experiments with drugs. Johnson talks about powerful drugs that are used in some brothels to make women completely submissive and ready for any experiment.

A series is created by the recurrence of duplications, in which a scene or an object is inscribed a second time with some modifications. One category of reduplication combines a scene that is real, where the characters are alive, with one where they are represented by means of different techniques. Thus the scene is which men are drinking in front of tables covered with food at Lady Ava's reception is the same as one printed on a leaflet that a street sweeper looks at. A stuffed dog and a mannequin in a shop window duplicate exactly the girl and the dog standing in front of that window. An image on a ring of a girl wearing a tight-fitting dress is but a miniaturized version of a real woman wearing such a dress. A sculptured scene of a lion tearing up a young girl's clothes is reproduced on Lady Ava's stage; this time a dog performs the tearing. Manneret's death is described as having happened; then it is acted out on Lady Ava's stage. The skin of a woman imagined by the narrator—"la chevelure à demi renversée découvrant la peau fragile et son duvet blond" [p. 11] (her hair, fallen forward, revealing the delicate skin with its blond down [p. 1]—is also Lauren's when she is in the same position [p.82].

In another category of duplication, the recurrence involves slight differences. Kim has a twin sister, Lucky. Kim wears a tight-fitting black silk dress; Lucky wears a tight-fitting white silk dress. The design of Lauren's shoes recalls the designs on Kim's. On the table at the reception there is a red hibiscus flower, and Kim has a red hibiscus flower in her hair. The hair of the dog shines and so does the Eurasian girl's hair.

Words, too, are utilized to form series; in fact they set up series superimposed on existing ones: names of characters, for example, and expressions used to describe the tight-fitting dress are repeated with variations. Lady Ava is called Lady Eva, Eva Bergman, or Jacqueline. Marchand is called Marchant or Marchat. Johnson is called Joneston, Jonestone, or Sir Ralph. And Lauren is Laureen or Lorraine. The tight-fitting dress is "l'étroite jupe entravée, fendue jusqu'aux cuisses des élégantes de Hong Kong" [p. 11] (the narrow hobble skirt, slit to the thighs of the elegant women of Hong Kong [p. 1]); "un fourreau de soie noire" [p. 13] (a black silk sheath [p. 3]); "une robe collante" [p. 34] (a clinging dress [p. 18]); "la fine soie noire de la robe ajustée" [p. 75] (the thin black silk of the clinging dress [p. 49]); "la gorge, la taille, les hanches moulées dans la soie lâche et souple" [p. 104] (her breast, her waist, her hips in the clinging supple silk [p. 71]).

This presentation of its series might suggest that *La Maison de rendez-vous* has a tight structure. It does not. Repetitions, recurrences of shapes and scenes, and transformations of characters make it a controlled but mobile configuration — where unity is created by both differences and similarities and where any strip of representation could be placed anywhere in relation to the others. Objects, characters, and words permuted in different settings, changes of proportion (a miniature of a woman on a ring, a drawing of a woman on paper, a real woman), changes of substance (a mannequin, a real woman), and changes of identities and roles contribute to the creation of a representation which is frozen and alive, static and dizzying at the same time. A formal and contrived configuration, this text retains the paraphernalia of eroticism, exoticism, and illicitness, but instead of developing them it indexes them with a few semantically highly charged components.

La Maison de rendez-vous can be disorienting or puzzling. Yet without the help of chronological, causal, or logical links, it sets up and solves, with its repetitions and variations, the ambiguities of a popular pornographic-detective novel based on the same topic. Indeed, the mysteries are resolved at the end of the text. The house of rendezvous turns out to be Lady Ava's but also Manneret's and Tchang's, where women or drugs can be obtained. Lady Ava, Sir Ralph Johnson, and Manneret turn out to be dealers of drugs and women. And the Eurasian girl described as mysterious (as the stereotype has it) is a servant, a go-between, an experimental subject, and a sexual partner. Eroticism is foregrounded by the constant mention of the tight-fitting dress on the slim bodies of Eurasian girls and by the description of Lauren with her low-necked white dress and her velvety skin or her sexy pajamas. The fact that the characters are made to play different roles is a device used in readerly literary novels, as well as in more popular fiction, where secret roles hidden behind normal and dignified behavior and changes of roles due to circumstances, events, and age are processes that keep the reader interested and in suspense. But in such novels these changes are motivated and explained; in *La Maison de rendez-vous* they are not. Such motivation, *La Maison de rendez-vous* indeed teaches us, is only a novelistic convention, possible but in fact not indispensable. Formal textual relationships such as repetitions and variations can replace psychological and causal ones.

Triptyque: Paronomasia of Things

On the cover of *Triptyque*[7] we find the following statement, presumably written by Simon himself: "In painting, a triptych is a work consisting of three panels. If the actions of the characters depicted can be connected more or less closely [for example, several episodes of a legend] at other times the subjects of each panel are different. But in one way or another, the entire work constitutes an indissociable whole, as much by the unity of construction as by the calculated way in which the different forms and colors match and balance each other." *Triptyque* is a serial construct organized precisely according to this description. It is a fragmented configuration that also contains devices to make it a unified whole. This fragmentation-unification, created by differences and repetitions, characterizes the content and the ways in which this content is presented, both in the overall structure or macrolevel and in the organizational details of the discourse structure, the microlevel of the text.[8]

Simon presents three different settings inhabited by different characters: a prosaic country village, an elegant seaside resort, and a dirty, noisy industrial city. Three different mini-narratives can be reconstructed, but only at the end of the text, because only at that moment is any reason for the presence and behavior of the characters provided. In the village, men come back from hunting. The hunters and others, including a young woman accompanied by a little girl, surround the wild boar that has been killed. The woman looks at one of the hunters, who winks at her. This tells her that they have a rendezvous at the barn where they usually meet. The man leaves on his motorcycle and goes to the barn. The woman, leaving the little girl to play with two boys, joins the hunter. The boys who were supposed to take care of the girl go to the barn and, through a hole in the wooden wall, watch the couple making love. The girl, left unattended, drowns in the river. At the seaside resort, the action takes place in a room of an upper-class hotel. A woman has just made love with an influential man in exchange for the help he might give her son, who has been caught with drugs. In the city, a barmaid is making love in an alley with a young man wearing a tuxedo. Little by little we learn that the man has just been married, that the bride stayed in her room while the bridgroom went drinking with his friends in a bar where the barmaid is his former lover, and that the two have slipped out into the night to make love.

Thus, there are three different settings, three different sets of characters, three different and unrelated units of representation. This referential fragmentation is reinforced by the fact that the three units are not presented successively in the three sections that form the text; rather, each unit is cut up into strips distributed throughout the three sections, so that it is possible to read a strip of representation referring to the village unit, then, without transition—typographical, syntactical, or referential—to find oneself in a strip describing something going on in the city. Fragmentation is also caused by an exuberance of details and by the extreme diversity of juxtaposed entities. Indiscriminately, algae and a trout undulating in a river, the meandering of this river, striations on cow excrement or on wood, the rising tail of a cow, ripples of water, waves of the sea, butterflies on grass, a penis entering a woman's body, people drinking in a bar, buildings and palm trees, and a rabbit lying on a table are described, making the text an inventory of disparate elements.

At the same time, this macro- and microdiversity and discontinuity, set up so carefully with several cumulative devices, are counterbalanced by equally cumulative unifying devices. The same precise, elegant, and objective style is used throughout the three panels. Vocabulary and syntax are the same whether the scene described takes place in the country, in the city, or at the seaside; whether it is about a rabbit, a flower, or male or female anatomy. Various series elaborated with different repeated elements constitute unifying devices. Each of the three sections contains the same topic: illicit lovemaking. In the city, in the countryside, and at the seaside, a woman and her lover make love on the run, hiding in a barn, a hotel room, an alley. In addition, an engraving, the poster of a film in the village, and the film being shot at the seaside are also about lovers meeting clandestinely.[9]

Structurally, in each section, strips of representation referring to the countryside, the seaside, and the city reappear with modifications. With each repetition more information is provided—although essentially the same elements keep coming back, presented in a different angle or with a new detail—until, at the end of the text, it is possible to construct the mini-narratives.

Reduplication is utilized in the text, as in Ricardou's and Robbe-Grillet's, for the elaboration of a series. The actions or features of living characters are filmed or reproduced in paintings, filmstrips, or posters. The scene of the woman and the hunter making love in the barn is also the subject of an engraving representing a maid and a valet making love on bales of hay. The black curly hair and sheeplike face of the man making love in the alley are also the characteristics of a man in a movie poster placed in the village. The scene of a woman lying in bed while she talks to the man standing up in the room overlooking the sea is also a sequence of a film being shot.

The recurrence of the same word placed in different contexts is another technique used to construct series. For instance, the verb *luire* (to gleam) in its present participial form qualifies a man's penis in "son membre luisant" (the gleaming member); the effect of a white shirt in the night is described with the same verb in "le plastron blanc de sa chemise qui luit dans l'ombre" (his white shirtfront gleaming in the shadow); the makeup of a clown shines because of its greasiness in 'la sueur délaye le blanc gras du maquillage qui luit sur ses tempes et ses joues" (sweat thins out the white greasepaint that gleams on his temples and cheeks); the shininess of the blade of a knife and of railroad tracks under the rain is described with this same verb. Colors (brown, black, red, and green) are also utilized repeatedly, thus setting up series as well.

Another series-creating linking device is the recurrence of different types of curves and movements, inscribed massively in the whole text. Here are five short passages (emphases mine):

Une longue falaise de façades blanches, éblouissantes, aux ornements *rococo, s'incurve* doucement en suivant la *courbe* de la baie. [p.7]

A long cliff of blinding white façades, with *rococo* decorations, *follows the curve* of the bay in a *gently sweeping arc.* [p. 1]

27

Le verger s'étend jusqu'à la rivière avant le *coude* qu'elle fait pour se diriger vers le hameau. Peu après le *coude,* son cours est capté en partie par le canal qui passe sous la première *arche* d'un pont de pierre dont la *seconde enjambe* en contre-bas de la murette le scintillement de l'eau libre courant repidement entre des ilôts où poussent des *touffes* d'osier et d'énormes feuilles d'un vert pâle et bleuté en forme d'*entonnoirs* évasés. [p. 8]

The orchard extends as far as the river, just before the *bend* it makes as it heads toward the little village. Just past the *bend,* the current is partially diverted into the millrace, which flows underneath the first *arch* of a stone bridge, the second *arch* of which, downstream from the low wall, spans the sparkling free water flowing rapidly between little islands with *clumps* of water willow and enormous pale bluish green leaves shaped like flaring *funnels.* [p. 2]

Le garçon soulève la feuille. . . . Sous la feuille se trouve, arrachée d'un magazine, la photo d'une fille nue, aux gros *seins,* agenouillée . . . dans les remous *baveux* d'une vague qui vient de se briser et s'étale sur le sable de la plage. Les *seins* pendants ont la forme *galbée* et effilée des *mamelles* d'une chèvre. . . . Des *volutes* écumeuses enserrent les cuisses et forment des *bracelets* autour des poignets. [p. 75]

The boy raises the paper. . . . Underneath the paper is a photograph, torn out of a magazine, of a naked girl with big *breasts,* kneeling down . . . in the *trickling* ebb of a wave that has just broken and is spreading out over the sand of the beach. Her *round* pendulous *breasts* narrow to pointed tips, like the *udders* of a nanny-goat. . . . Foamy *whirls* circle her thighs and form *bracelets* around her wrists. [p. 54]

La silhouette *courbée* s'appuie des deux mains sur la poignée d'un landau d'enfant fait d'une *nacelle* d'osier haut perchée sur les roues. . . . Par instant on voit luire l'acier *recourbé* de la *faux* posée en diagonale sur la *nacelle.* [p. 112]

The *bent* silhouette is leaning with both hands on the handlebar of a baby buggy with a wicker *chassis (nacelle)* perched high on the wheels. . . . From time to time one can see the gleam of the *curved* blade of the *scythe* lying diagonally across the buggy *(nacelle).* [p. 84][10]

L'eau glisse rapidement avec un bruit soyeux, presque imperceptible, agitée de faibles *remous* le long des bords et de *tourbillons* qui *s'enroulent* à la surface. . . . Entre les feuillages sombres reflétés jouent des fragments de ciel, comme des flaques d'argent, *ondulant* à peine. . . . Le clown blanc imprime aux manches de la chambrière de brèves *secousses* qui se transmettent le long de la corde. . . . La fille est affalée en avant, la tête tournée sur le côté, la *joue* frottant contre le drap rugueux et sale de la capote, les *genoux repliés* sous elles, les *fesses* comme collées à la *boule frisée* que forme la chevelure de l'homme couché sous elle. [p. 194]

The water flows along rapidly with a silky, almost imperceptible sound, agitated by faint *eddies* along the edges or little *whirlpools twisting* round and round on its surface. . . . Between the dark reflections of the leaves, little bits of sky gleam like pools of silver, *undulating* slightly. . . . The white clown moves the handle of the whip in a series of sharp *jerks,* which are transmitted like a wave along the entire length of the lash. . . . The girl has flopped forward, her head turned to one side between her arms, her *cheek* rubbing against the rough, dirty cloth of the army overcoat, her *knees bent* beneath her, her *buttocks* seemingly glued to the *curly ball* formed by the hair of the arm lying stretched out underneath her. [p. 147]

These passages construct a series with curves—such as S-forms, meanders, undulations, and curls—which are singled out in many parts of the body, objects, and items of topography. Thus a curve is inscribed by the shape of a scythe, cheeks, breasts, curly hair, a wicker pram, a bay, a cliff made of buildings curving softly, plants grouped in a clump resembling a funnel, a river making a bend. Or a word can connote curves or undulations, as is the case with "rococo" or "foam." Movements also create curves, as when the woman bends over the pram. In the whole text, one is struck by the massive presence of curves created by various movements. Thus one reads about water falling over a wall, cracks forming on cow excrement which has just fallen, jerks agitating the back of a rabbit that has just been killed, tops of trees waving in the wind, shivers of poplars agitated by a breeze, masts of yachts swaying in the wind, concentric ripples formed around an object in a river, the back of a man shaken by spasms as he vomits, movements of lovemaking, and strings of mists undulating in the air. All this is accompanied by an exuberant lexical display suggesting movements and curves. Some examples of verbs are *osciller, onduler, frétiller, serpenter, basculer, balloter, bondir, se voûter, se balancer, se tordre en arc, s'arc-bouter, s'enfler* (to oscillate, to undulate, to wiggle, to meander, to topple over, to bounce, to spring up, to stoop, to swing, to twist in an arc, to lean against, to swell). Nouns such as *craquelures, boursoufflures, sinuosités, ondulations, soubresauts, saccades, secousses, courbures, rides* (cracks, swellings, windings, undulations, jolts, jerks, shakes, curvatures, wrinkles) are constantly used.

Simon says that in *Triptyque* he established correspondences, echoes, interferences, associations, and oppositions.[11] I have shown how such effects are created with colors, shapes, words, situations, and various frames displayed in series that link disparate as well as similar elements, making the text a construct teeming with activity. In *Orion aveugle* and in *Les Corps conducteurs,* the two works preceding *Triptyque,* Simon had already linked such entities as the meandering of a tropical river, the undulating movement of a snake, a piece of string on the floor, a boa (a woman's scarf), a celestial constellation, and the coils and twists of the intestine, thereby unexpectedly relating many different places and entities: the sky, the body, the jungle of South America, and a North American city. In order to explain such a construction, Simon stated that he was interested in mathematical set theory and wanted to apply its principle in a text.[12] He was thus consciously creating a textual ordering isomorphic to a mathematical one. *Triptyque* is an expansion and a generalization of that process, since as in a mathematical set instead of monovalence it focuses on polyvalence, grouping heterogeneous entities according to their shapes, colors, and movements.

I have pointed out that one of the series in *Triptyque* is elaborated by the recurrence of movements creating curves. Such situations I would suggest are isomorphic to what René Thom calls *catastrophes,* which he defines as morphogeneses, or changes, produced in forms by exterior factors—such as those that can be observed in the fall of a leaf, the foam on a glass of beer, the cracks in an old wall, or the shape of a cloud[13]—precisely the kinds of phenomena that Simon describes repeatedly in *Triptyque.* Georges Raillard suggests yet another sort of isomorphism when he writes that in *Triptyque* representation is constructed with the technique of paronomasia, a figure of speech in which two almost identical words are juxtaposed, as in the sentence, "He who *excuses* himself *accuses* himself."[14] In the text of *Triptyque* the effect of paronomasia is achieved by means of the recurrence with slight variation of the same theme, of colors, of shapes, and of movements. Raillard also notes that the paintings of Antonio Tapiès display harmonics with Simon's works because both the writer and the painter juxtapose heterogeneous items to create a representation characterized by its disparity, unexpectedness, and fragmentation.

In his preface to *Orion aveugle,* where he explains how he writes and what writing means for him, Simon speaks of the prodigious power of words that enables them to bring together and to compare what, without them, would remain scattered.[15] Words in *Triptyque* have the singular power of bringing together unrelated but familiar items, animate and inanimate, which thus acquire an uncanny quality.

Effects of Seriality

L'Observatoire de Cannes, La Maison de rendez-vous, and *Triptyque* propose a new representational experience. The neologism *discoherence* describes these texts perfectly, for in them the constant reappearance of elements serves as the basis of unity, and the constant changes serve as the basis of variety. Put another way, every element is self-sufficient and independent, yet all the elements are interdependent. Or again, these texts are the loci of generalized, formal, anaphoric and cataphoric relationships. Discontinuity does not preclude cohesion, for cohesion can be achieved not only by logical, causal, or syntactic links — as is the case with traditional narratives — but also by various types of morphological structuring, such as occur in these serial constructs. Just as in contemporary music, melody and harmony can be superseded by seriality as the formal organizing principle, and just as musical dimensions other than pitch are explored in post-Schoenberg serial compositions, in these texts (although they lack the formal rigor of musical composition) narrative and plot are superseded by series, and any element can be used to create a series.

The recurrence of elements and units of content entails the recurrence of the same words, expressions, and sentences and of slightly different words, expressions, and sentences. These significant variations within similitude constitute, as Jakobson has taught us, the projection of paradigmatic elements onto the syntagmatic axis; that is, they introduce in a prose text an organizing principle characteristic of poetry. [16] The repetitions also have another consequence. Again in Jakobson's terms, the referential function is played down and the repeated elements become units of sounds that structure the texts phonetically. Such phonic structuring is akin to that found in the oral ritual discourse of preliterate societies, in which parallelism is often omnipresent and is intimately related to poetic line structure. [17] In these three texts, the repetitions are not organized in such a systematic and almost predictable way; they do not create the incantatory effects of preliterate discourse. However, the phonic recurrences are definitely foregrounded, and convey rhythm and order to the serial texts of Ricardou, Robbe-Grillet, and Simon.

L'Observatoire de Cannes, La Maison de rendez-vous, and *Triptyque* display a type of writing that explores forms, shapes, and volumes. In fact, they bring to mind the research of D'Arcy Thompson, who, also fascinated by forms, compares the shape of a jellyfish to that created by the diffusion of a drop of ink in water: "The waves of the sea, the little ripples on the shore, the sweeping curve of the dandy beach between the headlands, the outline of the hills, the shape of the clouds are so many riddles of form, so many problems in morphology." [18] These texts are the loci of a semantic innovation in which shape is used as a principle to group many disparate entities.

According to Benjamin Whorf, the grammar of a language filters reality for the speakers of that language. [19] Here the texts, through the filter of the semantic configurations that organize them, offer a representation highlighting the morphological. With such geometrical shapes as the triangles in Ricardou's text, the contour of a woman's silhouette in Robbe-Grillet's, and the curves in Simon's, three different and idiosyncratic ways of inscribing representation are proposed, all focusing on the exterior morphological aspects of objects, characters, and places. Because of this focus on shape, the texts both manipulate and break away from Western linguistic and cultural taxonomic conventions for the grouping of objects. Instead of using principles such as animate and inanimate, mineral and vegetable, or species or families, the use of series organized according to shape permits the grouping of a wide array of entities. These texts thus propose a taxonomic principle akin to those found in many languages and cultures of Asia and native America, in which, for purposes of counting objects or describing states, a form-shape classification is employed: oblong objects, flat objects, round objects, or narrow objects.

Mingling the animate and the inanimate, humans and objects, is a familiar device in novels. Balzac, Flaubert, and Zola invent objects that have metonymic relationships to characters and situations. Sartre in *La Nausée* has Roquentin, assaulted by nausea, perceive objects as alive, disgusting, contingent, and absurd. Sarraute in *Le Planétarium* has objects become tormenting entities for her characters. In Robbe-Grillet's *La Jalousie* objects are part of the obsession of the main character, being associated with the woman whom he is observing and by whom he is tormented. Pérec's *Les Choses* could be interpreted as presenting the effects of the reification of merchandise in the capitalist system, which make the young couple covet items of consumer society.

Such relationships between objects and characters are not found in the three texts discussed here. In them objects are not indexes of social, psychological, emotional, or economical components and factors. Nor is there hierarchical and anthropocentric organization to grant characters and actions more importance than objects. Rather, objects are entities of their own, placed on the same level as the characters. In this sense the three texts participate in a specific trend in twentieth-century aesthetics, which Pierre Francastel describes in discussing *Le Marocain* by Matisse: "[Matisse] absolutely rejects the arbitrary scale that grants more importance to the supposedly direct vision of man than to incidentals . . . it is contemporary art that introduced unity of vision by putting on the same plane the cabbage, the roof and the Moroccan."[20]

Another remarkable characteristic of these texts is the proliferation of spaces they inscribe: beaches, mountains, streets, ports, trains, boats, landscapes, and stages—spaces that are juxtaposed in the different series but not linked by any rapport or motivation due to the displacements, travels, actions, or behavior of the characters. Furthermore, because of the technique of reduplication—whereby a poster, a painting, a postcard, a piece of sculpture, or a mannequin in a store window repeats a scene in which real characters act—representation is organized by means of a multiplicity of frames embedded into other frames. In terms more familiar to students of literature, the device of *mise en abyme* is massively deployed.[21] There is no motivation for these embeddings, and the result is a dizzying interplay of frames creating a movement of *différance,* where no frame is the original and each one is a copy of a copy. With such multiplicity of disconnected spaces and frames, these texts offer a representation in which the homogeneity and order of Euclidean space are subverted.

Twentieth-century French literature tends to give prominence to the visual over the other senses. These three texts are examples par excellence of this tendency. However, what characterizes them is not only their focus on the visual but the way they play with—in the sense of manipulate—different visual experiences. This type of play points to a manifestation of baroque aesthetics, a formal baroque with metatextual consequences. When Ricardou, Robbe-Grillet, and Simon set up repetitions of the same strip of representation in different frames, they specify the medium (theater, photography, striptease, film) or the material (wood, metal, wax, ceramics) being used. In so doing they underscore the fact that these strips of representation are products of skill, technique, work, and props, that therefore they are artificial and contrived constructions, devised to create representation. This play with frames is an implicit metatextual statement reiterating that writing is production and not reproduction.

L'Observatoire de Cannes, La Maison de rendez-vous, and *Triptyque* on the one hand offer an adventure of words comparable to the adventures of characters. At the beginning of each text, a set of unmarked sentences creates representation; then when one color, one shape, a character, or a group of words reappear, each is simple repetition. As all recur, they become verbal events that structure the work; the repetitions and variations set up epiphanies with words and shapes. The reader feels pleasure not because of a landscape or a scene but because of the reappearance of words, of groups of words, permuted and played with. A sense of suspense is also created as the reader wonders which shape is going to recur, what variation is going to be invented, what object is going to be represented and in what form. On the other hand, these repetitions in complete achrony are uncanny, because in Western culture we are programmed by difference. "The strange is located in repetition," writes Derrida rightfully.[22] Yet, paradoxically, repetition provokes satisfaction (*Fort-Da*):[23] pleasure in recognizing, pleasure in formal variation, pleasure in anticipated order.

It is also possible that such a marked morphological orientation (of series, shapes, frames) in the texts' representation is felt to be pathological and thus disturbing to some readers. A sense of frustration might be experienced, too, because despite their present-absent narrators, the texts remain tauntingly and teasingly inconclusive. Seriality and morphology that are used to describe any encounter or situation will fragment representation to the point of preventing or interrupting any possible denouement.

That the texts contain highly charged sociocultural components of eroticism and sexuality is also likely to provoke negative reactions. The triangle and the shape of the dress are suggestive and titillating, at times on the verge of sadism, in *La Maison de rendez-vous* and in *L'Observatorie de Cannes*.[24] The shapes of sexual parts and the positions and movements of bodies making love create an eroticism frankly graphic and anatomic in *Triptyque*. It might be argued that these texts, while innovative in their manipulations of the possibilities of representation, nevertheless retain a very trite conventional component of the novel in general and of pornographic novels in particular: namely, the reification of women from a masculine point of view. Parts of women's bodies and feminine items of clothing are presented as objects of erotic value, and female characters are placed on voyeuresque display and are used and dominated in various ways.[25] It is tempting to reproach these authors for inventing phallocentric narrators.

Both Simon and Robbe-Grillet have explained their emphasis on eroticism and sexuality, in an attempt to absolve themselves of any tendentious, phallocentric stance. Thus Simon writes: "Challenge, fragmentation, repetition, for these are the characteristics of my texts, whether it be a question of leaves, clouds, battles, or sexual matters. As you can see, I treat sexual subjects exactly the same way I treat all the rest. Beginning with Christianity, everything related to matter and the body has given rise to a long series of censorships, to alibis. . . . So I think it would not be a bad idea to strip these sexual subjects of all the religious paraphernalia and write about them as one would write about a trip, a battle, a fish, or a blade of grass. That's what I have tried to do, particularly in *Triptyque.*"[26] Robbe-Grillet, often accused of writing about his own erotic fantasmas, states: "In my latest books fantasmas have been taken as generators; in other words they no longer function as the hidden fantasma of pre-Freudian work but as the designated fantasma of post-Freudian work. From the time when the workings of the psyche were first dismantled by Freud, they belong to a cultural and even quite popular stock, for they are used in publicity, in brochures, in mass-consumption literature."[27] Despite such disclaimers, Ricardou, Robbe-Grillet, and Simon have chosen to manipulate the paraphernalia of eroticism. By reframing it, by presenting it in a morphological and serial key, they parody it and perhaps play down its charge. Nonetheless, they present a male-oriented view of sexuality that contrasts with that of the women's texts I discuss in chapter 5.

Oscar Wilde suggested that people did not see fogs and mists until the Impressionists painted them. Perhaps these serial constructs will make readers more conscious of the formal relationships existing between various entities in everyday life as well as in artistic creation. Ricardou, Robbe-Grillet, and Simon display affinities or establish harmonics with Adami, Escher, Steinberg, and Warhol, also manipulators of frames, repetitions, and discontinuities.[28] Like those artists, these authors defamiliarize the familiar and familiarize the unfamiliar.

3

Multidimensional
Montages

Michel Butor's *Mobile,* Maurice
Roche's *Circus,* and Philippe Sollers's *H* are three heterogeneous
texts each of which in its own way
can be characterized as "le règne de
l'hétérogène sans gêne" (the reign of shameless heterogeneity).[1] There
are many devices for introducing heterogeneity into a text. Genres can
be mingled as in Dante's *Vita nuova,* which one of its translators found
to be a curious work because "it is written in three forms (memoirs,
novel, poem) developed simultaneously."[2] In his famous *Exercices de
style,* Raymond Queneau introduces heterogeneity by using various
registers and styles to describe the same scene. And in *A la recherche du
temps perdu,* Proust weaves into his narrative commentaries, digres-
sions, and dissertations bearing on historical, aesthetic, psychological, philosophical, and metaphysical matters.[3]

Intertextuality is another technique frequently utilized to introduce heterogeneity into a text.[4] Intertextuality can take many forms.
Its most direct and common manifestation is the presence of quotations from other texts that are embedded into and made to function in
the new text; Montaigne's *Essais* are a striking case in point. There are

also texts that contain borrowed portions of others, which, although slightly modified and transformed, are still identifiable, as in Lautréamont's *Les chants de Maldoror* or in Pound's *Cantos*. In another sort of textual borrowing, the semantic content is utilized but the specific style and discourse structure are no longer apparent. Sollers experiments with this kind of grafting in *Nombres*.

Mobile, Circus, and *H* display yet another possibility for creating heterogeneity. Their verbal texture is not one in which fragments of other texts are embedded; rather, each author creates a massive accumulation of textual fragments, including some of his own invention. The textual fragments can be recognized as belonging to a variety of domains: literary and scientific texts, newspapers and catalogs, conversations, or simply utterances associated with particular scenes of everyday life. In Roche's text the heterogeneity is even more extreme, because *Circus* also contains a whole array of signs and symbols.

These fragments of discourse, signs, and symbols—whether they are taken unchanged from identifiable texts, transformed, or invented—are not grafted into a uniform prose but retain their specific lexical, syntactic, and—when applicable—iconic properties. No register or style is granted more importance than any other, and no chronological or hierarchical ordering organizes these fragments: they are simply juxtaposed paratactically. Since they are not developed or correlated but simply assembled, it is impossible to reconstruct a narrative or to find an overall significance.

Often the terms *collage* and *montage* are employed to describe any heterogeneous work of art made up of composite elements. But there is a difference between them. A collage is simply a juxtaposition of disparate elements, whereas a montage groups heterogeneous components so as to create unity and cohesion within diversity.[5] *Mobile, Circus,* and *H* are montages that integrate a wide variety of elements and in which cohesion is created by several devices. Semantically, these texts exploit the resources provided by the existence of semantic fields, of sets of words that are both linked by and link items within a particular theme, or area: thus within its semantic field the notion of education includes school, book, teacher, grade, and exam. In the texts considered here, semantic fields are actualized, exploited, foregrounded, and even created by means of verbal, iconic, and symbolic representations. For instance, the semantic field of death in *Circus* is created by references to a tomb, the presence of the skull-and-bones symbol, and the use of the word "death" itself.[6] The recurrence of units of discourse (portions of sentences, mini-poems, lists, enumerations, groups of nouns or names), of typographical material, and of a certain spatial disposition is also used to create cohesion. Here too, as in the case of serial constructs, techniques are put into play to create continuous discontinuous structures that combine extreme heterogeneity and cohesion.[7]

The individual who is the originator of each of these texts cannot be called the narrator, since he narrates nothing. He can more properly be labeled a postmodern scribe whose activity consists mainly in choosing, compiling, copying, manipulating, and distributing fragments of discourse, signs, and symbols. Consequently, readers' roles are changed, too. Confronted with many verbal styles and a multiplicity of places, characters, situations, and concepts, their task consists mainly in contextualizing what they read—in matching what is on the page with what they have read before, with what they have at their disposal from their personal and cultural experiences.

This chapter could have been entitled "polyphonic texts," or "polytopies," or "polysemiotic texts," or "citationalities." But each of these terms, while adequate, has the disadvantage of emphasizing one aspect of the texts and neglecting others. *Polyphonies* or *polytopies,* implying many voices and many topics, would not account for the visual and multimedia characteristics of these texts. *Polysemiotic* would insist too much on the presence of several systems of communication, which is indeed a striking feature in Roche's *Circus* but exists only in the form of typographical and spatial manipulation in *Mobile* and *H. Citationalities,* a term borrowed from Derrida,[8] would account for the fact that these texts are constructed with quotations from other texts but would focus only on this aspect. Hence the choice of *multidimensional montages,* which expresses the fact that the texts are controlled, disparate, multimedia structures that require the attention of the mind, the memory, the eyes, and the ears because they inscribe material that is intelligible, visible, and audible.

Mobile: An Exercise in Onomastics

Inquiring traveler, avid reader, productive writer, and eclectic critic,

Michel Butor has lived in Australia, Japan, many Mediterranean countries, and the United States. He has written on Donne, Faulkner, Joyce, Pound, Proust, Rabelais, and Rousel, among others. Before the appearance of *Mobile* in 1962, he published several novels that develop a story but also intermingle an extraordinary amount of culture, erudition, and experience. In a sense, Butor has always had a polyphonic mind; he has always been fascinated by the multiplicity of experience.

Mobile,[9] intended to be a study for a representation of a huge country, the United States, is a continuation and an expansion of Butor's previous works. It is a montage that offers an overview, a macrosurvey, or—as Butor himself says—a *remembrement* (a regrouping of land) of the United States.[10] To deal with such a vast subject, choices had to be made and strategies devised regarding the types of information and discourse that would best allow Butor to account for American immensity and multiplicity. Given such a broad topic, it is interesting to examine Butor's treatment of it and the kind of representation he proposes.

The geographic reality of the United States is realized on the pages of *Mobile* by the naming, in alphabetical order, of the fifty states, from Alabama to Wyoming. For each state the names of some of its cities, some of its counties, a few rivers and mountains, and American Indian tribes in the area give factual information of the type provided by an atlas or a geography book.

> GREENVILLE, sur la rivière du Goudron, chef-lieu de Pike, CAROLINE DU NORD. [p. 18]

> GREENVILLE, on the Tar River, county seat of Pike [*sic*] County, NORTH CAROLINA. [p. 18]

> FAIRFIELD, cf. de Wayne, Etat du chêne. [p. 66]

> FAIRFIELD, county seat of Wayne County, the oak tree state. [p. 61]

> HANOVER, Essex, N.J., le plus petit état après le Rhode Island, le Delaware, le Connecticut. [p. 189]

> HANOVER, Essex County, N.J., smallest state after Rhode Island, Delaware, Connecticut. [p. 181]

Details about the landscape, the climate, the fauna and flora of a particular state are presented, not in sentence and paragraph form but in mini-poems consisting of few nouns that capture the essence of a place:

MADISON, FLORIDE (for whites only), —la réserve des Indiens
   Séminoles.
Tornades,
tourbillons de branches,
ponts emportés.

Frégates,
   grives des dunes,
      sternes royaux,
         sternes de Cabot,
      grands hérons blancs,
   petits hérons bleus,
grandes jambes jaunes.

La mer,
   cérithes de Floride,
cônes alphabets,
   buccins poires,
balistes de la reine,
   poissons papillons.
Bigarades,
   mandarines,
      clémentines,
         pomélos,
tamariniers,
   mangliers rouges,
      figuiers étrangleurs,
prunes de coco,
   bois-poisons   [pp. 36–37]

MADISON, FLORIDA (for whites only, —the Seminole Indian Reservation. // Tornadoes, / lashing branches, / bridges washed out. // Frigate birds, / sandpipers, / royal terns, / Cabot terns, / great white herons, / little blue herons, / greater yellowlegs. // The sea, / Florida ceriths, / alphabet cones, / pear whelks, / queen triggerfish, / butterfly fish. / Bigarades, / tangerines, / grapefruit, / pomelos, / tamarinds, / red mangroves, / strangler figs, / coco plum, / poisonwoods   [p. 35]

Several types of discourse, such as impersonal statements, short descriptions, and enumerations, are the linguistic devices used to provide information concerning ethnic groups, personalities, and American objects or entities:

A Lincoln, les Allemands lisent toutes les semaines "Die Welt Post." (p. 57)

In Lincoln, Germans read the weekly *Die Welt Post.* [p. 57]

Le visage illuminé de Jerry Lewis. (p. 103)

The illuminated face of Jerry Lewis. [p. 100]

CONCORD, FLORIDE (. . . whites only), — la réserve des Indiens Séminoles. [p. 17]

CONCORD, FLORIDA [. . . whites only], — the Seminole Indian Reservation. [p. 17]

Various anonymous inscriptions found in everyday American surroundings are reproduced. Even in Butor's French renderings we recognize road signs (60 mph, drive friendly, turn on your lights, welcome to Connecticut) and billboard advertising (did you remember your Kleenex, drive friendly, smile, drink Coca-Cola). Here and there are scattered ordinary, everyday utterances that might be heard anywhere: greetings (Hello Mrs. Davis, Hello Mac), requests on the telephone (Hello I would like Madison, Wisconsin), purchases in a store (a pack of Lucky Strikes), and bits and pieces of conversation (we should buy gas at the next station.

Mingled with the geographical names, details about the fauna and the flora, and the fragments discussed above are longer prose units also belonging to the American past and present. Although translated into French by Butor, these passages retain their distinctive syntax and vocabulary. There are extracts from speeches, letters, trials, treaties, old newspapers, books about politics and history, catalogs, tourist guides, and medical books:

Traité de William Penn, fondateur de la Pennsylvanie, avec les Indiens Delaware en 1682:
"Le Grand Dieu qui est le pouvoir et la sagesse qui vous a faits et qui m'a fait, incline votre amour à la droiture, à l'amour et à la paix. Je vous envoie ceci pour vous assurer de mon amour, et dans le désir que vous aimiez mes amis." [pp. 73–74]

(Treaty of William Penn, founder of Pennyslvania, with the Delaware Indians in 1682:
The Great God who is the power and wisdom that made you and me, incline your hearts to Righteousness, Love and Peace. This I sent to assure you of my Love, and to desire your Love to my friends." [p. 70]

"The New York World," 15 avril 1893:
"Il faut presque toute une vie pour apprendre le savoir-vivre. Dès lors, les gens de Chicago ne peuvent espérer obtenir ces connaissances mondaines sans l'expérience et la fréquentation de ceux qui ont consacré leur vie à l'étude de ces questions. De nos jours, point de bonne société sans chefs français. Celui qui a été habitué aux délicats filets de boeuf, aux tortues, aux pâtés de foie gras, aux dindons truffés, et autres merveilles de ce genre, n'aimerait guère s'asseoir devant un gigot bouilli aux navets." [p. 64]

The New York World, April 15, 1893:
"It takes nearly a lifetime to educate a man how to live. Therefore Chicagoans can't expect to obtain social knowledge without experience and contact with those who have made such things the study of their lives. In these modern days society cannot get along without French chefs. The man who has been accustomed to delicate fillets of beef, terrapin, pâté de foie gras, truffled turkey and things of that sort would not care to sit down to boiled leg of mutton with turnips." [p. 61]

Le peyotl est un cactus ("lophophora williamsii"), de petites dimensions, glabre, en forme de carotte, qui pousse aux confins du Mexique et des Etats-Unis, dans la vallée du Rio Grande. On peut en consommer le bouton frais ou séché au soleil. . . . Ses effets psychophysiologiques les plus remarquables sont un extraordinaire affinement des sens, surtout en ce qui concerne la

perception des couleurs, des formes et des sons; des hallucinations visuelles et auditives, avec quelques désordres de la spère
cénesthésique. [pp. 105–6]

Peyotl is a cactus (*Lophophora williamsii*), small in size, shiny, carrot-
shaped, that grows on the Mexican border of the United States, in the
Rio Grande Valley. It can be eaten raw or sun-dried. . . . Its most
remarkable psychophysiological effects are an extraordinary heighten-
ing of the senses, especially with regard to the perception of colors,
shapes and sounds; visual and auditive hallucinations, with some dis-
orders in the coenesthetic sphere. [p. 101]

Mobile thus presents various aspects of American geography, history, fauna, flora, and forms of discourse. It lists different ethnic
groups, religious sects, objects and customs, and historical figures.
More generally, nature and culture, topography, past and present,
and popular and high culture are the topics chosen to represent the
United States.

The verbal texture of *Mobile* is particularly innovative and
meaningful by virtue of the various items of discourse which are privileged and the ways in which they are displayed grammatically — or,
rather, ungrammatically — and spatially. The text contains a
metatextual comment that describes its own structure: "Mobile is
composed somewhat like a quilt" [p. 29, French; p. 28, English].
Just like a quilt made from patches of material of different colors and
shapes, forming a patterned surface unified in its diversity, *Mobile* is
constructed with fragments that work together to form a composite
yet unified structure. Unity is provided by the recurrence of the same
type of information for each state, by linguistic techniques such as the
massive use of names and nouns, by pointing to the items of the
American reality, and by repetition: each state is represented and concretized by a certain number of cities the names of which recur in the
states that surround it and in those that follow it alphabetically.
Several sets of discourse units reappear throughout the text with only
slight lexical changes: for instance, greetings (Hello Al, Hello Harry,
Hello Mrs. Auburn, Hello Mrs. Greenwood) and statements containing names of cars or of different ethnic groups.

Sur la route, une Oldsmobile grise, très endommagée, qui dépasse largement les soixante miles autorisées, "il faudra prendre de l'essence au prochain Caltex." [p. 19]

On the highway, a battered gray Oldsmobile going much faster than the 60-mile speed limit, "get gas at the next Caltex." [p. 18]

Une Frazer chocolat conduite par un vieux Noir. [p. 77]

A chocolate Frazer driven by an old Negro. [p. 74]

Sur la route, une énorme Studebaker (vitesse limitée la nuit à 60 miles), "il faudra prendre de l'essence au prochain Texaco." [p. 105]

On the highway, a huge Studebaker (speed limit at night 60 miles), "get gas at the next Texaco." [p. 101]

A Saint-Louis, les Allemands lisent toutes les semaines la "Deutsche Wochenschrift," les Hongrois tous les quinze jours le "Saint Louis Es Videke," les Italiens toutes les semaines "Il Pensiero."

In Saint Louis, Germans read the weekly *Deutsche Wochenschrift,* Hungarians the bimonthly *Saint Louis Es Videke,* Italians the weekly *Il Pensiero.* [p. 61]

The result is that a great amount of information is processed in the same types of discursive molds, combining again multiplicity and unity. The spatial disposition of the text is also a component that creates diversity and unity. On each page, words and groups of words are arranged differently in lists, sentences, sprinklings of words, or paragraphs, with white spaces on the right or on the left, and with differing indentation. The same typographical arrangement keeps recurring, mingling uppercase and lowercase letters, italics, bold and normal type.

Mobile is a text in which proper names are *mis en écriture*: they are made to signify not as one of the grammatical components combined with others to form a sentence but as autonomous entities. This singling out of proper names is a minimal and yet a very productive technique, for as Alan Gardiner explains: "The greatest virtue of proper names is that they are the most economical of all words, inasmuch as they make only a very small demand on the eloquence of the speaker, and an equally small demand upon the attention of the listener."[11] By means of proper names, Butor is able to create an inventory of American reality simply by designating it. The reinscription of portions of discourse from history, science, advertising, newspapers, and conversations—rather than descriptions, commentaries, and explanations—is also a very economical way to present information, because it gives quick snapshots of different domains of reality past and present, of different people involved in different activities. The technique works because the readers' competence is put to use; it takes advantage of the readers' ability to contextualize discourse and to place it in its appropriate setting. This process of contextualization in language use must be actualized in the extreme because of the laconic means employed by Butor.

It is also worth noting that *Mobile* is a semiotic catalog. It presents the variety of American but also of Western means of receiving and transmitting communication. It utilizes such written texts as letters, portions of treaties, catalogs, newspapers, and guides; and it contains utterances implying oral communications like those that take place in speechs, sermons, greetings, and face-to-face or telephone conversations. And because it amounts to a long list or catalog of objects and places, *Mobile* is an inventory of America. As such it is akin to the earliest written documents, characteristic of the transition from preliterate to literate societies.[12] So this avant-garde text combines the most ancient and the most modern of scriptive techniques.

Mobile is an open structure. It does not impose any choice on its readers but leaves them free to react according to their feelings and experiences. The alphabetical order of presenting the states is the most neutral, the most unmarked, "a zero degree of classification," says Barthes.[13] It expresses no personal preference and avoids privileging any such aspect as size, location, economy, or demography—each one of which would generate a different and possibly contradictory scheme or classification. Reinforcing this neutrality, the predominant use of paratactical constructions presents facts uncontaminated by the intellect or the subjectivity of a narrator. The discursive device of featuring names of states, countries, cities, mountains, and rivers also contributes to the objectivity of the text, because it takes advantage of the intrinsic properties of names, which John Searle describes in the following terms: "A proper name refers without presupposing any stage setting or any special contextual conditions surrounding the utterance of expression . . . the uniqueness and pragmatic convenience of proper names lie on the fact that they enable us to refer publicly to objects without being forced to raise issues and agree on what descriptive characteristics constitute the identity of the object."[14] Because of its massive use of names, then, *Mobile* focuses attention on topography and toponymy but does not present these aspects of the American reality as being perceived by a specific character.

Another reason why the names and also the great number of nouns help create such an open text is the expansion and systematization of a device that Leo Spitzer notices in analyzing another of Butor's novels, *L'Emploi du temps,* which he calls "dramatic laconism."[15] That is, the names, nouns, and details about geography, fauna, and flora are presented as if they were information about places and settings found in the script of a play, which need to be concretized and actualized in the performance. *Mobile* is like a set of didascalic remarks for future travelers, allowing the readers to invent a story or the adventures that might take place, or letting the possible connotations which might be associated with different places enter into play.[16] And this is all the more possible since, as Butor states elsewhere, "Places always have a historicity, either in relation to universal history or in relation to the biography of the individual."[17] *Mobile* then is a mold or a shell which can be filled.

Because they designate and therefore textually concretize the American topographic and toponymic reality, proper names produce certain effects in *Mobile.* As Proust, also fascinated by names, notes: "Names present persons and cities which they accustom us to believe are unique."[18] And because of this property of names, one can imagine the surprise and perhaps the slight disturbance which might be felt by Europeans in realizing that familiar names do not have a single referent but can have several, in different American states and in Europe. For there is not only Paris, France, but Paris, Texas; there are not only Bristol and Windsor in England and Berlin in Germany but Bristol and Windsor and Berlin across the Atlantic and in many other places as well. These European names also remind readers that emigration and colonization mean not only appropriation and expropriation of lands but also linguistic domination.

Names and nouns are also poetic devices in *Mobile*. Certain names and nouns familiar to the French reader are by themselves banal and commonplace, but their appearance in a literary text remotivates them phonetically and morphologically. In addition, many American—especially American Indian—names are striking because of their non-European phonetic and morphological properties (Chattahoochee, Chihuahua, Susquehanna, Youghiogheny, Kittatinny, Pottawatomies). Names of cars that no longer exist (Studebaker, Hudson), and of past actors (Rita Hayworth, Marilyn Monroe) now belong to the domain of kitsch and exude their own kind of nostalgia and quaintness. Some names of plants and animals are recognizable, but many are unknown to the nonspecialist and sound exotic and strange.

Because of these unusual nouns and its Anglo-Saxon, French, Italian, Chinese, and German names, *Mobile* is a multilingual, multiphonic montage that attracts attention to the properties of signifiers and displays constant contrasts between the familiar and the strange. Geoffrey Hartman writes that the closer the words are to the status of pure signifiers, the closer they are to magic.[19] It would be exaggeration to say that signifiers create a magical atmosphere in *Mobile*, but there is no doubt that for the French reader they contribute to the presentation of an America that is still the land of novelties and mysteries. And it is well known that names, because of their connotations, are a pretext for travel; that they incite individuals to travel to or to dream about distant lands. Even the blasé and disgusted Roquentin in *La Nausée* acknowledges this evocative power of words: "Sometimes, in my story, I happen to pronounce some of these beautiful names you read in atlases, Aranjuez or Canterbury. They engender brand-new pictures in me, like the pictures which people who have never traveled create on the basis of their reading: I dream about words, that's all."[20]

Mobile, with its massive deployment of names and nouns, is a huge reserve of dreams, a stimulus to start exploring. Butor has said that *Mobile* is "the reproduction of a previous itinerary created by an explorer and intended for any amateur traveler."[21] Indeed, it can be read as a travel book, but it is a travel book written by an ethnographer flirting with political issues. It informs the prospective traveler about the diversity of climates, vegetation, and fauna and the great number of racial and ethnic groups. Any French reader who has heard of the Apaches and the Sioux only from cowboy-and-Indian movies is made aware of the existence of a great number of American Indian tribes. *Mobile* also points to cultural differences that give the United States a distinctive flavor. That an American hotel can boast of 2,200 rooms and that the Empire State Building uses 2,000,000 kilowatt-hours of electricity per month underscore the fact that there is a different scale in this country. That language is used differently is evident in the choice of color terms (*une Chevrolet tomate*: a tomato Chevrolet; *une Cadillac mirabelle*: a plum Cadillac; *une Studebaker mangue*: a mango Studebaker) and greetings using the abbreviated form of names (Hello Al) or the last name after Mr. or Mrs. (Hello Mrs. Webster). Other details of American life are surprising to Europeans and introduce them to this different culture — billboards that order individuals to drive friendly or to smile, the listing of many religious sects, the gaudiness of an elderly lady's clothes: "une énorme Plymouth grise conduite par une vieille Blanche très jaune en robe cassis à pois cerise avec un chapeau à fleurs chocolat" [p. 55] (a huge gray Plymouth driven by an old yellowish white woman in a currant-colored dress with cerise polka dots and a hat with chocolate flowers [p. 53]).

Although a travel book, *Mobile* does not belong to the category of tourist guides, which forget that people live in a country where there are certain social conditions determined by the past and ideologies that will determine the present.[22] The greetings, the tiny snatches of conversation, the mention of moving cars, the setting of the scene as day or night do not leave the reader with the impression of a lifeless and deserted land. And although the narrator-traveler does not take a stand on any issue, the simple mention and juxtaposition of certain facts gives the reader an image of a conflict-ridden America rather than an idyllic, mythic America. The repetition of "whites only" can be interpreted as pointing to racism against blacks, Mexicans, and Indians; the various portions of texts written by and about Indians play up the treatment inflicted on them by whites; the Salem witch trials underscore fanaticism; and the enumeration and accumulation of details as in a catalog may be interpreted as a reminder of an American capitalist world view that encourages consumption and exploits the environment.

Mobile is a montage à la Alexander Calder, capable of taking on many different meanings; it displays a unity in diversity à la Jackson Pollock, to whom it is dedicated. It can offer a complex experience yet is without narrative, protagonists, different actions or situations. A spatial polyphony in which historical and geographical spaces mingle, it is elaborated like a long concrete poem in several panels, recycling items of banality, consumer society, and documents from the present and the past. As a result, it is a multidimensional montage— poetry, realism, and kitsch—combining the rudimentary features of the early stages of literacy with experimental postmodernism.

Circus: Postmodern Baroque

Actor, journalist, keen observer of people and of everyday reality, specialist in music, author of a book on Claudio Monteverdi (1960), *bricoleur* with words, letters, drawings, signs, and symbols, Maurice Roche is a most prolific author. He has written *Compact* (1965), *Circus* (1972), *Codex* (1974), *Opéra bouffe* (1975), *Mémoire* (1976), *Macabré* (1979), *Testament* (1979), *Maladie mélodie* (1980), and *Camar(a)de* (1982), all of which are intended to form a single work made up of interdependent panels. I have chosen *Circus* because within this single text are contained all the topics and techniques characteristic of Roche's writing as a whole. Roche, who has discussed his works and his methods in published interviews, explains that for him "the novel is a fiction which on the one hand appropriates language, on the other hand reality."[23] This statement is not a gratuitous remark: it describes Roche's texts, for he speaks to us about the world, the human condition, and our diverse experiences with language and other aspects of communication.

One way to prepare oneself to enter *Circus* is to think of the memorable Dada evenings of the Zurich Cabaret Voltaire. The readings of prose and poetry in several languages; the shaking of bells and the beating of drums; the use of puppets, masks, and costumes; the interest in nonsense; and the mixing of high and low cultures in a setting decorated with works of Picasso and Kandinsky—all these created a multimedia, heterogeneous atmosphere. This is what is found in *Circus*.

Circus mingles fragments of discourse in different languages, as well as in different registers and styles of French. Here are some examples (the translations are mine).[24]

> Some Whites, many years ago, visited the camp of the Indians under the guise of friendship and presented the Indians with whiskey which contained strychnine [p. 90]

could be a passage taken out of a politically oriented American historical document.

> Lawd, cap'n, i's not a singing, i's yes a hollerin' to h'p me wid my wu'k [p. 101]

is a sentence in black English that could be heard in a black revivalist church or a slave or prison work group.

> To be sold a choice cargo of about 250 fine healthy negroes just arrived [p. 97]

is an advertisement of the kind that probably appeared on the billboards of southern American towns before the Civil War.

> Colui che toccava-suonava pianoforte e le donne (he who touched-played the piano and women) [p. 49]

could appear in a bawdy Italian song.

> Es gibt einen Weg zur Freihet eine Meilensteine heissen: Gehorsam, Fleiss, Ehrlichkeit, Ordnung, Sauberkeit, Nüchternheit, Wahrhaftigkeit, Opfersinn und Liebe zum Vaterlande! [p. 108]
>
> There is a way to freedom and some of its milestones are: obedience, diligence, honesty, orderliness, cleanliness, sobriety, veracity, a sense for sacrifice and love for the fatherland!

could be a political slogan or appear in a political speech in German.

> Comment acquérir l'art d'écrire.
> Comment utiliser à son profit le pouvoir magique des mots.
> Comment se faire des amis.
> Comment arriver à devenir riche avec sa plume. [p. 45]
>
> How to acquire the art of writing.
> How to use the magic power of words to one's advantage.

How to make friends.
How to succeed in becoming rich with one's pen.

are elements of advertisements that can be found in contemporary French newspapers.

De sinople surchargé d'un étalage de vanités au globe céleste d'argent accompagné de luth d'or et de basson de sable [p. 59]

Of sinople overloaded with a display of vanities with the silver celestial globe accompanied with a golden lute and a sand bassoon

could appear in a book dealing with heraldry.

Sur toute la circonvolution pariétale ascendante en arrière de la scissure de Rolando se trouve le centre de la sensibilité tactile; cette zone est probablement en rapport avec la sensibilité de la douleur. [p. 22]

On the entire ascending parietal convolution at the back of the rolandic fissure the center of tactile sensitivity is found; this zone is probably associated with the sense of pain.

could be found in a medical book or medical report.

Ta "sorbonne" pleine du sable de villes ensevelies [p. 48]

(Your mind full of the sand of buried cities)

Moyenant roupies couper et naturaliser les roupettes [p. 56]

In exchange for rupees, cut and naturalize the testicles [25]

un pot-pourri de gonzesses [p. 66]

a potpourri of women

are utterances in which *sorbonne, roupettes,* and *gonzesses* are slang expressions for mind, testicles, and women, respectively. I have cited examples in English, Italian, German, and French; one comes across passages in Spanish, Portuguese, and various Asiatic languages as well.

Circus also displays an impressive—indeed incredible—juxtaposition, mixing, and meshing of various types of signs. It is possible to recognize both ancient and modern languages in their original script—Arabic, Chinese, German, Gothic, Aztec glyphs, Egyptian hieroglyphs; artificial languages in their appropriate representation—road signs, chemical formulas, mathematical and physical symbols and formulas, shorthand, proofreading symbols, labels of products, pieces of music, symbols from the Michelin guide, and signs of the zodiac. Furthermore, *Circus* is a typographical festival featuring various kinds of printing: italics, boldface, large and small lowercase and uppercase letters; horizontal, vertical, and sideways writing; passages put in parentheses, brackets, braces, and boxes; underlining, arrows, and oscillograms. Its pages are not an agglomeration of words contained in the white frame of the margins; they are not invaded by a "voracious typography"[26] that eats up their blank space. Rather they are sculpted and designed by varied spacing, print, signs, and symbols.

In addition to exhibiting an extreme heterogeneity created by languages, registers, styles, and signs, *Circus* is a text literally teeming with activity: embedded in the words, fragments, and signs appear other words, other fragments, and other signs. This polysemy is achieved by means of various techniques. *Circus* looks like the manuscript of a book proofread and corrected, ready to be typeset, with the mistakes and their corrections appearing together on the pages and yielding two meanings. Roche calls these *coquilles créatives,* drawing attention to the double meaning of *coquille* as a typographical error and as a shield used by men to protect their genital organs. He also specifies that the typographical error is a blow or a punch below the belt given to the text, which reveals and brings to the fore unsuspected and unconscious meanings.[27] For example:

erᅡ Charnière [p. 58]

in which *charnier* is a charnel house and *charnière* a hinge;

Ecou╳̇ter le Laïus [p. 25]

in which *écouter* means "to listen to," and *écourter* is "to shorten." Typographical resources such as upper- and lowercase letters also permit two simultaneous meanings: the capital L of Laïus makes it a proper name, the father of Oedipus, but juxtaposed with *écouter* or *écourter* it takes on the meaning *laius,* a familiar word for a long-winded speech. The very banal phrase *qu'est-ce-que lettre* turns out to contain the word *squelette* (skeleton) by means of a clever capitalization of selected letters: qu'eSt-ce QUE LETTrE [p. 32]. And two letters shared by three words can superimpose several levels of meaning:

embarquer pour **CY** thère
stite
noque [p. 36]

Cythère is a Greek island where Aphrodite had a temple, inspiring both a painting by Watteau and a poem by Baudelaire; *cystite* is the technical term for an inflammation of the bladder; and *cynoque* is a slang word meaning "crazy" (usually written *cinoque*).

Polysemy is also achieved by means of permutations of letters of the type that we are accustomed to find in the works of Robert Desnos, Marcel Duchamp, Michel Leiris, and Raymond Roussel. Thus "coeur de palchier sur fond d'artimaut" [p. 57] sounds both mysterious and scatological until the normal order of letters is reestablished to yield the culinary specialty "coeur de palmier sur fond d'artichaut" (palm hearts on a canapé of artichokes); François Villon's famous title "Ballade des dames du temps jadis" (Ballad of Ladies of Yesteryear) generates the three following rhymed variations that actually complement it:

> Drames de temps jadis
> Trames d'outrages ourdies
> Dames de tragédies [p. 65]

> Dramas of yesteryear
> Webs of plotted insults
> Ladies of tragedies[28]

It would be possible to cite many other examples, for acrostics, anagrams, spoonerisms, homonyms, paronomasias, and puns abound in *Circus*. At times additional effects of meaning are encoded by the context and the discourse properties of utterances of a particular portion of the text. The following is a typical example:

> Ariane en solde Isole au rabais Béatrice à crédit Didon bon marché Schéhérazade ramenteuse pour dormeur oublié. [p. 66]

> Ariane on sale Isolde on discount Beatrice on credit Dido low price Schéhérazade remembrancer for forgotten sleeper.

This listing of well-known mythological and literary characters, famous women of the past (dames du temps jadis) who have experienced insults and tragedy, points back to the little poem built on Villon's title; at the same time, since the list footnotes a passage containing a portmanteau word, "sa voix de mêlécallass" (mélasse-mêlé-Callas: molasses-mixed-Callas), a direct allusion to the opera singer Maria Callas, these names are also to be understood as being those of famous opera heroines. Furthermore, rhythm and repetitions make this sequence of words sound like a children's counting-out rhyme as well as a line of advertising, and the commercial aspect is also encoded by the terms "on sale," "on discount," and "low price." Thus literature, opera, mythology, children's lore, and modern marketing techniques are collapsed and combined in this short portion of text, showing that Roche makes the words mean more than they say.

Parody is a frequent device employed in *Circus,* so that under one verbal utterance lurks another and well-known verbal utterance. The first line of the Lord's Prayer, "Notre père qui êtes aux cieux," underlies "Notre Père qui êtes aux yeux du monde sans effet."[29] *Foetus* is a deformation of *Faustus* in the following example in French repeated in German:

Et le docteur Foetus, vieux prodige, de practiser et composer avec le dyable (diable)

(Und der doktor Foetus, alter Wunderknabe, mit dern Tyfel (Teufel) [p. 34]

And Doctor Foetus, old prodigy, goes on to associate and compromise with the devil

And "J'ai mon luger à cheveux blancs" [p. 106] (I have my white-haired luger) recalls "Le Révolver à cheveux blancs" (the White-Haired Revolver), a title invented by André Breton for one of his collections of poems.

In these examples, the parody consists in altering the content of a verbal fragment. There are as well transpositions and transformations from one medium to another, an act of transcreation: with the resources of the underlying model, changes are introduced that emphasize certain features of the original. Thus Mademoiselle de Scudéry's *Carte du Tendre,* an illustration of the different steps or phases of a relationship culminating in love, considered by the Précieux as something dangerous and unreasonable, is deciphered and reinterpreted. In his new version Roche introduces an ironic and comical touch by mingling frank anatomical double entendres (*dresser* can mean "to draw a map" and "to have an erection" in this context), with the euphemisms of the original:

> Pays de Tendre en filigrane; sa carte (la dresser) faisant songer à la coupe longitudinale d'un vagin—région impossible!—ou au plan d'une ville aquatique souvenir—son grand canal: le Fleuve Inclination débouchant, après la percée du col de la matrice, dans la Mer dangereuse—Lagune à traverser en gondole funèbre. [p. 37]

> Country of Tendre in filigree; its map [to make / erect it] recalling the longitudinal cut of a vagina—impossible region!—or the map of a souvenir aquatic city—its grand canal: the River Inclination running into, after the opening of the neck of the womb, the Dangerous Sea—Laguna to be crossed with a funeral gondola.

In another visual experience transposed into a verbal one, the spatial disposition of Holbein's famous painting *The Ambassadors* is recreated by the grouping of the words on the page, and the content of the painting is named and interpreted in ways pointing out that the objects there are the instruments used to carry out colonization and Western hegemony in order to achieve domination over others [p. 59].

As its title suggests, in *Circus* we can observe a heterogeneous spectacle similar to one composed of wild animals and their tamers, tightrope walkers, horseback riders, trapeze artists and clowns, all appearing successively in the ring with fast tempo and exhibiting virtuosity and prowess. At this point certain questions come to mind. Is *Circus* a semiotic Babel? Is it just a display of tricks and gimmicks? Is it merely an entertaining linguistic and typographical exhibition?

The pages of *Circus* constitute a semiographic space, a constant visual spectacle, in which a compendium of signs and symbols create a polysemiotic environment, a kind of *intersignalité,* comparable to the one that readers are exposed to every day in their lives. In a sense, then, the representation here is congruent with and mimetic to our reality. But this does not mean that Roche accepts or celebrates this

reality; rather, many aspects of it are denounced—again, as in
Mobile, not by overtly stating a point of view but by choosing and
juxtaposing particular examples. The propaganda and brainwashing
with which we are bombarded daily in our capitalist society are under-
scored in the following example [p. 29]:[30]

Mettre la brique à l'abri: investir dans la valeur la plus sûre, la
pierre (ou le béton)—bref, ce qui ne se déval$_{OR}$isepas.

			r	r
			e	e
			p	p
culture	confort	loisirs	drague	drogue
			s	s

To shelter bricks: to invest in the surest commodity, stone (or concrete)—in short, what does not lose value/get stolen

			GOLD	
culture	comfort	leisure	cruising	drug
			e	e
			p	s
			a	t
			s	
			t	

The portmanteau word used to speak of organized tours, *voyages
orgasmisés* [p. 38], is self-explanatory, and the insertion of the skull-
and-crossbones in the series of Michelin guide symbols [p. 19] leaves
no doubt about what mass tourism is. Other fragments implicitly denounce such forms of exploitation as the treatment of American Indians by whites [p. 90], the slave trade [p. 97], and the attraction and
fascination of electronic objects used to incite men in India to subject
themselves to vasectomy [p. 56]. These are but a few of many examples in the text that refer to the consumer society and to the exploitation of man by man, thus forming two semantic fields.

In addition, four other topics are presented by means of semantic
fields. First, eroticism and sexuality are constantly present; they
appear in the mention of erotic objects, the reference to contracep-
tives, drawings that can be interpreted erotically, and passages in
which a woman's body as a sensual object is named or alluded to. Sexual references or innuendos are present on almost every page. It is in-

teresting to note that Roche, who seems to criticize so caustically many aspects of contemporary society, nonetheless falls into the phallocratic mode when establishing the semantic field of sexuality.

Along with Eros, Thanatos or Death is omnipresent in the pages of *Circus,* with a whole array of paraphernalia that make the text a comic and tragic thanatology and thanatography. The following words appear on many pages: *crâne* (skull), *tombe* (tomb), *mort* (death), mausolée (mausoleum), *épitaphe* (epitaph), *squelette* (skeleton), *charnier* (charnel-house), *ossuaire* (ossuary), and *tzompantli* (the Aztec skull rack).[31] The idea of death is also signified by the sign of the skull-and-crossbones, by a drawing that suggests a skull [p. 72], in a typographical disposition where blank black spaces delineate a skull [p. 68], and in the line that Faust utters looking at a skull: "Was grinsest du mir, hohler Schädel, her?" [p. 33] (Why do you grin at me, you hollow skull?)

In Rabelaisian fashion, drinking is also constantly alluded to by means of several techniques, which include the quoting of portions of drinking songs, the mention of a specific liquor (Vat 69), or the drawing of a bottle.

Eros, Thanatos, and Bacchus—*Circus* is about the pleasures and the torments of the body. But it does not neglect the intellect, which constitutes its fourth semantic field. There are repeated allusions to the head, the memory, and the activity of thinking, deciphering, and reading, accompanied by anatomical references to the head and by drawings suggesting the head. Furthermore, with its many quotes, allusions, and references, *Circus* as a whole is a tribute to and a celebration of memory, knowledge, erudition, and culture.

Again we must ask, what does this all mean? Is it a statement about the human condition? A postmodern way of presenting *carpe diem?* These suggestions are not so farfetched as they might seem, for because of its content and its presentation of this content, *Circus* is akin to or has features that make it isomorphic to the symbolic still life known as the *vanitas.* Like such a painting, *Circus* displays in random fashion on its pages signs or fragments of discourse that symbolize or talk about the activities of human existence—arts, literature, various sciences, politics, economics, and ludic and pleasurable activities—at the same time insisting on the ephemeral character of life by constantly referring to death.[32] *Circus* then, like a *vanitas,* can be interpreted as a reminder of an ontological truth: the human condition is finite and precarious, since all artistic, political, economic, and ludic activities are interrupted by sickness and death. Detachment from and the despising of riches and power of all kinds are thus implicitly advocated.

At this point, were I discussing Pascal or Bossuet, I would have to say that the only possible remedy for such a pessimistic state of affairs is to turn to God. This is not, however, the cure envisaged by Roche. Nor does he opt for Sartrean existentialist *engagement*. Rather, he chooses a derisive mood, for humor, for desacralization of well-known images, sayings, and institutions, and for satirical and parodic fervor, since these are perhaps the only weapons that allow an individual to fight, to protest, to keep alive. Roche says that *"Circus* wants to be the jarring laughter of death, this buffoonery in the ring of a rotten society when our own disintegration is played out."[33]

What is no doubt the most striking aspect of *Circus*—one quite difficult to evaluate—is the material presentation of the text, its constant play with signs, letters, and space, and the facile and irritating play with and on words that creates endless polysemies. It is undeniable that the writing appears overtly as techno-narcissism, exhibitionism, mannerism, contrived exaggeration, and constant fireworks. It is also the production of someone who enjoys mixing, cutting, splicing, and "joycing" (in the sense of James Joyce) words, languages, signs, and symbols. As a consequence, the space of the text is treated as free and utopic: anything is permitted. It is a space taken over by someone who has the free spirit of a child or a carnival reveler, the fantasy of a graffiti scribbler, the diligence of a calligrapher, and the skills of a tattooer, all wrapped in one. *Circus* is a space where play is constantly at work, utilizing erasure, hesitation, overabundance, and excess—backstage behaviors of the writer which have connotations of unfinished work in progress and rough copy but which are here positive creators of meaning, active elements in the visual presentation of the text. Play means revalorizing forms of discourse often considered popular or inferior, such as puns, children's folklore, and wit in the Freudian sense. Play also means indulging in such discredited discourse manipulations as parodies, plagiarisms, and "playgiarisms," which exploit both difference and similarity. And play also means making words, symbols, and signs lose their univocity and become polyreferential units. This practice involves a constant dynamization of signifiers, since each word, sign, or symbol can yield several meanings by being transformed, manipulated, and displaced from its usual context.

"The positive hero of my books is the reader," says Roche.[34] This statement is quite true in many ways, for to read *Circus* is to experience many cognitive potentialities and ways of processing information, as well as to test one's memory and knowledge. Readers are constantly invited and stimulated to look for several layers of meaning because of the text's manipulations and transformations. But readers are also faced with fragments which have no referential meaning for them because they do not comprehend the language or the code necessary for understanding the words and signs. They may, however, recognize these items by their appearance as Chinese, Arabic, Hindi (Devanagari), or hieroglyphs; therefore, such fragments are not meaningless but stand for a specific culture, as well as having a purely visual impact. There are also blank pages. Thus readers come across elements that have an overdetermined referentiality, diacritical elements that are only indexes, and free spaces that they can fill in as they choose, with their own thoughts or their reflections on what they have just read. The cover of the book, under the title *Circus*, states that the text is a *roman(s)*, a novel(s). The plurality indicates that individual readers, according to their own knowledge and experience, will elaborate their own texts by reacting to different cultures and different semiotic systems which they know or do not know.

One passage in *Circus* comments on the reading process in the following way:

Traînant les phrases (n'importe laquelle pouvant signifier n'importe quoi), le regard glisse drainant signes et mots jusqu'à leur terme
        au bas d'une page
                      puis, débordant
sur le drap, continue sur (selon) les plis (les bourrelets du cerveau) [p. 69]

Pulling sentences (any one being able to mean anything), the look slides dragging signs and words until their ends at the bottom of a page, then, overflowing on the sheet, continues on (according to) the pleats (the folds of the brain)

Readers are in fact given maximum freedom by two devices. Many of the passages contain verbs in the infinitive; thus only the raw, semantic notion of the verbs is expressed, without being fixed in time or in aspect, and the reader is open and free and able to escape and avoid specific situations and specific narratives. In addition, the meaning of the text is not invested in one story, told by one narrator expressing himself in either the first or third person; rather, the narrator disappears behind the text formed by the gathering of many texts belonging to many different corpuses written by many writers, mostly anonymous.

While *Circus* allows and indeed encourages each reader to elaborate and to look for new possibilities from total content to a single word, a number of harmonics come to mind that are shared by many readers because they are suggested by techniques and themes used by certain illustrious predecessors of Roche. The multilingualism makes one think of Pound's enterprise; the derisive and satiric mood recalls Swift or Jarry; the play with words is in the tradition of Leiris, Roussel, and Joyce; the obscenities and the praise of wine point to Rabelais; and the many references to death evoke works of Guyot Marchand, Villon, Bossuet, and Michaux. The playful splitting of words and the typographical experimentation existed already in the avant-garde movements of the beginning of the century, in the various Dada manifestations in Europe, and in Italian and Russian futurism. But perhaps closest to *Circus,* and to us as well, and of the same satiric and caustic vein, is *Mad* magazine.

Exuberant, full of tensions; mingling trivialities and refinements, obscenity and elegance; being serious and comic, grotesque and grave, *Circus* is a toy to play with in many different ways, says Roche;[35] it is a potlatch of signs and languages that makes us "étouffer de n'avoir dans sa bouche que sa langue maternelle [p. 35] (choke by having in one's mouth only one's mother tongue).

H: An Opera of Language

Philippe Sollers is founder and editor of *Tel Quel,* an influential Parisian journal which from 1960 to 1983 was at the forefront of literary criticism, avant-garde movements, and new artistic and political trends. Philippe Sollers is also a critic who has written on Artaud, Bataille, Dante, Joyce, Lautréamont, and Sade.[36] He calls these writers "écrivains des limites" (writers of the margins), because they have produced texts considered threatening and subversive in their content or in the ways in which they are written.

At this point the creative works of Sollers himself can be grouped into five phases, constituting five different ways of writing. About *Le Défi* (1957) and *Une Curieuse Solitude* (1958), traditional psychological novels that were praised respectively by Mauriac and Aragon, Sollers makes the arrogantly provocative remark that "the first things I have written should have been refused by a publisher who knew what he was about." He calls *Le Parc* (1961), which is in the style of the early *nouveau roman*, "the first book that I consider as relatively written, although it is not really exciting."[37] *Drame* (1965) and *Nombres* (1968) constitute a third phase which can be considered as belonging to the *nouveau nouveau roman*; they are formal constructs organized and elaborated with very precise grids. *Drame*, a dialogue between "I" and "he," takes place in sixty-four fragments modeled on the *I Ching* and a checkerboard. Within this very formal framework, a narrator reflects about writing as he writes. *Nombres* is composed of one hundred sections which put into play numbers, Chinese characters, the pronouns, *I, he,* and *you,* and the imperfect and present tenses. It contains allusions and references to Artaud, Bataille, Bruno, Mao Zedong, Nietzsche, and Spinoza, among many others. During this formalist phase, Sollers experimented with the production of meaning through language, a strategy to show that representation is not bound by a preexisting reality but can be created artificially with grids and schemes that avoid linearity and narrative.[38]

H (1973)[39] represents, with *Lois* (1972) and *Paradis* (1982), the fourth trend in Sollers's writing career; it is characterized by a preoccupation with the concrete aspects of language and an exploration of its materiality. This preoccupation remains dominant in *Femmes* (1983), a text which for the time being constitutes a fifth phase in which Sollers is also returning to more conventional storytelling techniques and plot. I have chosen to discuss *H* because it is a montage that shares certain structural features with *Mobile* and *Circus* but is nonetheless quite different from them. In an interview following the publication of *H,* Sollers explained:

> The relationship a writer maintains with his senses, that of smell, that of touch, and most of all with his sexuality, is very important. But as far as I am concerned, I would point out that 90% of my work consists of listening. . . . In fact, I always carry a notebook in which I pile up, at cafes, in the street, at home, anytime they come to me, the various bricks that will fall into place in the process of drafting. . . . I was half deaf until *Lois.* . . . It is about 1968 that something happened. Censorship was lifted. That's when I abruptly abandoned searching for a utopian language that could say everything while saying practically nothing.[40]

Concrete and realist rather than utopian language, the body in its materialistic aspects, a focus on aurality and orality—this is what Sollers claims to have written in *H.* My intention here is to examine how he concretizes these topics, what discursive techniques he utilizes, how he exploits the resources of language, how the text means, and how it affects readers.

H is the production of an anonymous narrator whom Sollers defines in the following terms: "It is the upsurge of the subject: or of what I have been calling the subject; the possibility of saying 'I' within, at the heart of language. Language is not neutral, but it needs to be taken over by a subject, a subject I would call illimitable, numberless, rather like in *Finnegans Wake.* This is not a biographical subject, the psychological subject, it is not a 'me.' "[41] The following passage demonstrates what is meant by an illimited subject. Three names, Octave Joyaux (Sollers's father's name), Philippe Joyaux (Sollers's real name), and Philippe Sollers (his literary pseudonym) are unpacked and uncoiled with an extraordinary delirium:

> non tu ne trouversas pas je l'écris octave oui exactement comme in-octavo ce qui lui donnait pour signer ce o tournant sur lui-même suivi d'un point minuscule juste avant le j travaillé brodé genre glaieul clocher clé de sol emportant oyaux en musique o. joyaux . . . le nom lui-même suffisait pour les exciter pourquoi parce qu'on y entend à la fois jeu joie juif jouissance . . . noyau

boyau aloyau ou alors sans x mais non pas joyeux joyaux avec un
x come xylophone . . . philippe joyaux bande de cons . . .
peu importe la ribambelle des rois le hardi l'auguste l'affreux
le merdeux accumulation en espagne donnant l'archipel fémi-
nisé philippines . . . tragédie pour l'alighieri et sollers écho
du surnom d'ulysse de sollus tout entier intact ars ingénieux
terrain travailleur fertile lyrae sollers science de la lyre.
[pp. 10–11]

no you will not find I write it octave yes exactly as in-octavo which
would allow him to sign this o turning on itself followed by a tiny dot
just before the j wrought embroidered gladiola style steeple key of G
carrying off oyaux in music o. joyaux . . . the name itself was enough
to excite them why because in it one hears, play joy jew orgasm . . . a
seed tripe sirloin or else without x but not joyous joyaux with an x like
xylophone . . . philippe joyaux you pack of assholes . . . no matter
the swarm of sovereigns the bold the august the horrible the shitty pile
in spain producing the feminized archipelago philippines . . . tragedy
for the alighieri and sollers echo of the surname of ulysses of sollus all
together intact ars ingenious terrain worker fertile lyrae sollers science
of the lyre[42]

This breaking up, this undoing by means of the play on signifiers
and signifieds of the three names, the biological, the biographical,
and the professional, puts all three of them on the same level and de-
nies any of them any precedence over the other.[43] The three are presented as a crossroad of significations and of sounds, radiate a host of
disparate entities which branch out into history, literature, geography, and mythology as well as biography.

H's unlimited subject, who turns out to be masculine, speaks to us
about language, the body, culture, literature, and writing, and he
recounts experiences that he or someone might have had or retells
what he has heard. David Hayman writes that *H* is a dissemination of
"nodes and knots of allusions or significations.[44] To put this in the
terms I have been using here, *H* is constructed out of fragments of
discourse that can be placed in a number of semantic fields. Reflexive
statements about *H* as a text, comments on the way it is written and
on the act of writing in general, and quotations from what has been
said or might be said about it constitute the semantic field of writing.
Here are a few examples:

mais est-ce qu'on peut mettre le tout en vrac en jet continu personne ne pourra naviguer là-dedans c'est sûr la ponctuation est
nécessaire la ponctuation vieux c'est la métaphysique en personne [p. 14]

but can one throw it all topsy turvy in a steady stream no one will be
able to navigate through it for sure punctuation is necessary punctuation ol' buddy it is metaphysics in person

j'oppose au monologue intérieur le polylogue extérieur [p. 42]

against the interior monologue I pit the exterior polylogue

mais la question reste posée comment dire ça dans quel rythme
comment transformer la langue écrite et parlée dans le sens
d'une respiration [p. 83]

but the question remains how to say this with what rhythm how to
transform written and spoken language into a breathing

il parait que l'ensemble du livre est la description très croustil-
lante d'une gigantesque mêlée sexuelle d'accouplements sans
nombre de caresses . . . vous avez sa fiche de baisage [p. 135]

people say that the whole book is the very spicy description of a gigantic sexual melee of innumerable couplings of caresses . . . you find his
screwing ledger

et maintenant parce que l'un d'eux a dit que toute l'écriture est
de la cochonnerie ils sont persuadés que toute cochonnerie est de
l'écriture [p. 177]

and now because one of them said that all writing is trash they're con-
vinced that all trash is writing

The title *H* is itself the starting point of three semantic fields. Sollers explains: "Take the title *H*, you hear the sound. It cuts. There is
of course Rimbaud's poem. But above all there is hashish."[45]
Thus the letter *H* generates the semantic field of drugs, and their
effects. Rimbaud's poem "H" from *Les Illuminations* is very mysterious, but it is generally agreed that it is about sexuality and adolescence, topics that constitute two more semantic fields in Sollers's *H*.[46]

Sexuality is presented through different types of discourse: jokes, descriptions of lovemaking, descriptions of an experience in a special brothel, references to Sade, conversations regarding the places in the world where it is best to make love, the demands of prostitutes, and childhood and adolescent explorations and experiences of sexuality. Passages in the semantic field of childhood and adolescence include sayings that are uttered to children (to catch a bird, one needs to put salt on its tail [p. 127]), portions of lullabies or nursery rhymes (pp. 84, 164, 177), reminiscences of school days, commands directed at children, and references to games and playful activities with other children.

Sollers also sets up a semantic field of politics by mentioning names of political figures and theoreticians, including Hitler, Lenin, Machiavelli, Mao Zedong, and Marx, or by quoting something they said, wrote, or might have said or written. A semantic field of literature contains writers such as Artaud, Joyce, Montaigne, Nerval, and Pascal, whose names are referred to or whose actual words are directly quoted or modified in a still recognizable way. The semantic field of science, which includes physics, biology, psychoanalysis, and linguistics, is also created by means of citations and quotations. The semantic field of contemporary culture includes items referring to current events, preoccupations, and fads such as the oil scarcity, artificial insemination, women's liberation, the plight of workers, advertisements, and jokes that can be heard in France.

These different semantic fields do not form discrete axes cutting across the text; rather, they are distributed in such a way as to create a network of intersections, meshings, and superpositions, making *H* a montage where again, as in *Circus* and *Mobile,* similarity and diversity combine to form a continuous-discontinuous texture.

From the very beginning of *H*, an explicit relationship is established with the philosophy of Giordano Bruno, whose diagram *Figura Intellectus* appears on the cover and on the first page of the book. Giordano Bruno was burned at the stake in 1600 in Rome because he was considered intellectually subversive. According to his philosophical and metaphysical stance, man, the world, religion, experience, and magic were intimately linked. Bruno devised memory wheels that grouped officially recognized and accepted languages, arts, and sciences with others considered marginal and sinful, such as magic and esotericism. Bruno dared to advocate plurality and multiplicity and the presence of unity in multiplicity, thus deconstructing the Aristotelian system of causality and hierarchy, questioning the power of religion and God and, in fact, of any system of power.[47]

In the particular diagram reproduced in *H*, the intersecting circles represent the intellect, which sees and distributes everything, but there is no main or single organizing principle at the center; rather, many satellites with their own centers are copresent, forming a polygon. *H*'s structure is also precisely that. Through its semantic fields it integrates a multiplicity of domains, many topics, popular as well as high cultures, and many aspects of the experience of individuals in the modern world, including their physical and psychic life and linguistic abilities, their sexuality, and their intellect. These are presented not through the perception of one narrator but through a polylogue of voices and discourses. *H* is a verbal structure isomorphic to Bruno's geometrical structure, and in retrospect one realizes that the diagram at the beginning of the text is meant to orient the reader, that it is the key to what follows. Readers may find such a device too coy or too cute; this is a question of taste. What is certain, however, is that by referring to Giordano Bruno's philosophy, Sollers deliberately implies a desire to subvert conventions, and in this sense the reference must be taken seriously.

In *Logiques,* Sollers writes: "The fundamental aesthetic error consists in believing that language is a simple tool for creating representation."[48] In *H* he utilizes techniques that not only provide a visual and mental experience (as in more traditional novels) but also focus on both the oral and the aural components of language and communication. There are no characters for us to watch speaking; there are only fragments of discourse that require us to imagine a situation in which oral communication is taking place between anonymous and unnamed individuals. These utterances are recognized as representing specific speech acts: insults, commands, declarative statements, nursery talk, and tellings or retellings of personal experiences or jokes. Sollers also presents fragments of anonymous utterances broadcast from a loudspeaker in an airport, on the radio, or on television.[49]

The various instances of oral communication make of *H* an exterior polylogue, as indicated in a metatextual comment in the text itself [p. 42]. But *H* is also an interior polylogue, because it creates for readers a multifaceted aural experience. Since there are no indications why and to whom these utterances are spoken, readers contextualize them — they imagine and in fact internally hear an intonation of the different speech acts according to their own experience of different ways of speaking. Native speakers of French know that a joke involving Gérard and Marie-Chantal must be told in an upper-class intonation and style and that the sentence "une à papa une à maman" is pronounced with a singsong voice. They are aware that a statement about having a sandwich and a beer is uttered in a casual tone, whereas announcements coming from a radio or loudspeaker are emitted in an impersonal tone; that a pornographic joke or a sexual experience is not recounted in the same tone as a request for a loaf of bread.

Aurality is also foregrounded by means of various types of play with sound. There are units in which sounds are juggled: "faudrait pas confondre les *populations laborieuses* du *cap* avec les *copulations laborieuses* du *pape*" [p. 111]; verbal skiddings involving the recurrence of one word in a series of words: "la période où nous vivons a un nom *boul*eversement sans précédent sur la *boule* qui se met en *boule* d'où *boul*on *boul*onner *boul*otter cham*bou*ler sa*bouler* le camp impérialiste" [p. 121]; the repetition of one affix or letter: "nag*eur* travaill*eur,* gland*eur* rêv*eur* et touch*eur* ment*eur* et cherch*eur* [p. 120] or "*formes* sa*crées* *fill*ettes *tri*fouil*l*ant leur *art*" [p. 129];[50] onomatopoeia with familiar French sounds like "crac" and others that do not correspond to French: "après flouc en floc" [p. 143] or "noum toum atoum tefnout shoum" [p. 159].[51] Mentally, as one reads, decasyllables or alexandrines form themselves, and the rhythm accelerates when words are accumulated, as in a list of slang synonyms for the word crazy: "louf maboul dingue siphoné givré" [p. 163], or in the accumulations of three or more nouns: "thalanium librium valium" [p. 150] or "après le vin d'une messe folle exquise assise parlant au poulailler baptisant veaux vaches cochons chenilles enfants vers luisants" [p. 145] (after the wine of a crazy exquisite mass sitting speaking in the henhouse baptizing calves cows sows pigs caterpillars children glowworms); or with the listing of several expressions associated with a particular motion: "ça fait un drôle de cheval ce sujet au pas au trot au galop devant toi derrière toi sous toi et sur toi avancée et recul" [p. 129] (that makes a bizarre horse this subject marching trotting galloping in front of you behind you under you and on you forwards and back-wards).

This foregrounding of the oral and aural aspects of discourse is the result of a conscious effort on the part of Sollers, who explains:

> It is the equivalent of a musical act, an act that I perform after having listened to music: Haydn, Monteverdi, Schoenberg, Stockhausen . . . My dream would be to succeed in creating a sort of opera of language. . . . Thus since *Lois* as I draft I use a tape recorder in order to rework different passages according to their sound effects. It was somewhat like the technique developed by Joyce for *Finnegans Wake*.[52]

H thus provides an instance of "l'écriture à haute voix" that Barthes called for in *Le Plaisir du texte*.[53] Its representation depends on the aural more than on the visual decoding of language.

Because it exploits and foregrounds the various properties and possibilities of language in general, and because of its different speech acts and its various phonic manipulations, *H* mimics the phases of linguistic awareness and performance that individuals experience in their consciousness and unconsciousness. Successions of sounds like "flouc floc" and "noum toum atoum" are like the babble of an infant; successions of words like "oui melissa dorée le miel des abeilles la paillettes ruche cueillie dans les fleurs abeille abeille" [p. 105] are similar to the ludic glossolalia of children, who invent such rhythmic and highly patterned forms of speech play.[54] With these and different forms of adult language expressed in various types of discourse, *H* also mimics different stages in the acquisition of language. Further, the play with sounds, free associations, constant disjunctions, puns, and anagrams found in *H* are characteristic of dreams and hallucinatory states; they are, as Freud and Lacan taught us, manifestations of the unconscious surfacing in signifiers. Sollers in fact explained that he deliberately aimed at achieving this sort of effect: "What does it mean to listen? Well! it means above all to put oneself in an almost musical state of porosity, both voluntary and involuntary, conscious and unconscious, to try and capture what takes place unconsciously in language."[55]

In an article entitled "Dante et la traversée de l'écriture" (Dante and the Traversal of Writing), Sollers writes that Dante "makes of his text a total world designating itself, a comedy of the language and of the distance that a subject can cover in attempting to exhaust it in all of its dimensions in an active discovery."[56] In *H*, similarly, Sollers succeeds in presenting a traversal through language, recreating the linguistic processes by which individuals acquire and live language, in their conscious and psychic lives as well as in their social and cultural experiences.

H is a very concrete and realistic text in the sense that it constitutes a documentation of the knowledge, interests, and experiences of individuals in the last part of the twentieth century. Linguistically, it presents the heterogeneity and variety of the French language, since it utilizes many registers and styles of French — familiar, scientific, slang, and pornographic. It also shows that oral communication is central to our experience in the world, that as individuals we are constantly speaking and listening to others — a situation that might indeed change with the development of a computerized society, which favors solitary communication and dialogue with a screen. Written at a time when Sollers was experimenting with drugs — like Burroughs, Michaux, Sartre, and many others before him — *H* also inscribes the rhythms of a special type of consciousness in which the unconscious is prodded to the surface. Verbally and rhythmically, it represents the alternation of both moments of relaxed and flowing detachment and moments of lucid and disturbing awareness. Paradoxically, while belonging strikingly to our time and inscribing a distinctly Western content, *H* is characterized by a tone and a mood which perhaps have no equivalents in Western culture. Julia Kristeva describes it as follows:

> An unfamiliar, troubling, undefinable laugh. *H*'s laughter does not arise out of the Rabelaisian joy shaking up science and esotericism, marriage and Spirit, based on a full, recovered, promising body — the laughter of gigantic Man. Nor is it Swift's furious, disillusioned, and cruel fit, unearthing hell under social harmony and proving to Man that he is "Lilliputian." Since the Renaissance, the West has laughed only with the Enlightenment (with Voltaire and Diderot, laughter dethrones), or perhaps in the recesses of psychosis, where power

and logic are experienced as ambivalent at first, and broken down in the end (laughter is black with burnt up meaning: Jarry, Roussel, Chaplin . . .). *H* laughs differently.[57]

Indeed one cannot say that *H* is sad, happy, bawdy, aggressive, hostile, or neutral. It is all of these for short moments, since each fragment has a different tone—with the result that the whole text defies classification. It mingles euphoric and dysphoric modes. One form of art that offers a quite similar experience is Balinese music and drama with its continued and sustained fluidity, disturbed here and there by a sudden acceleration or slowing-down of rhythms and its avoidance of dramatic climaxes. In the words of Gregory Bateson: "The music typically has a progression, derived from the logic of its formal structure, and modifications of intensity determined by the duration and progress of the working out of these formal relations. It does not have the sort of rising intensity and climax structure characteristic of modern Occidental music, but rather a formal progression."[58]

Barthes calls *H* a whirlpool of language, a forest of words.[59] Typographically *H* is a thick, dense, continuous flow of words. Rather than a long sentence, it is more appropriate to call it a long clause without interruption. For 185 pages there are no paragraphs, no punctuation marks, no capital letters; the only diacritical elements utilized are accent marks. Because of its spatial and visual presentation, the reader entering *H* feels as one does just before falling asleep or at the moment of waking up. After this initial mental and intellectual blurring, reading becomes performing. As Sollers advises on the book's jacket, "It is therefore necessary to experience its rhythm: dictions, tones, accents, latent punctuation, whirlpool, flux, summons." Reading/performing involves the introduction of punctuation, the feeling of rhythms, the attribution of intonations, and the contextualization of units of discourse. One progresses neither too fast nor too slow, carried by the flow of words in the carnival of rhythms, sounds, references, allusions, and conversations.

As a literary text, *H* is best characterized by a remark that Richard Ellman made about *Finnegans Wake*: "It is a wholly new book based upon the premise that there is nothing new under the sun."[60] Deliberately and consciously, Sollers alludes to, borrows from, imitates, or—in the terms I have been using here—creates harmonics with works that preceded his. *Finnegans Wake* plays an important role. In the interview with David Hayman in *TriQuarterly*, Sollers declares that he considers himself to be working in the wake of the *Wake* and that three aspects of the *Wake* concern him: "its tendency to dissolve linguistic barriers through multilingual puns, the rhythmic qualities through which subjectivity is projected, and the manner in which it telescopes history to create the effect of a unified historical or 'epic' dimension." These comments constitute an excellent critical assessment of both Joyce's and Sollers's work.

Other writers also come to mind as we read *H*, including those whom Sollers presents in *Logiques* or admires because he considers them to be *écrivains des limites*. Sollers's use of popular language and slang recalls Céline; his interest in sexuality recalls Bataille and Sade; his insistence on the body and on bodily functions points to Rabelais; and he shares with Joyce, Beckett, and the contemporary Italian novelist Carlo Emilio Gadda an interest in Giordano Bruno's philosophy.[61] In the wake of other texts, reactivating some of their devices and some of their ideas, *H* also bears the mark of a writer-critic both aware of and influenced by contemporary research in philosophy, psychology, and literary criticism. Derrida's notion of a text where units of meaning are disseminated and where the textual space becomes a space of play is very much present in *H*. Words are treated as ubiquitous entities; multiple possible meanings are allowed and in fact foregrounded. Polyvalence, polysemy, and polyphony are constantly present.

The principle defined by Kristeva as *differentielle significante*,[62] according to which each element of language is a knot of multiple significations that includes synonyms and homonyms in addition to all the mythic and social meanings of which it is susceptible, is evident in *H*—this is exemplified in the passage playing with Sollers's different names (quoted above). The influence of Lacan, in particular his interest in linguistic manipulations, is felt through the massive use of signifieds and signifiers, which are deployed not so much to create one meaning as to create effects of meaning, of sounds, and of intonation.

H succeeds in being old and new, familiar and unusual, Western and Oriental. It brings together the experimental spirit of Postmodernism and the free spirit of Giordano Bruno, drug culture, and extreme intellectualism, while talking about the individual's body and about conscious and unconscious experiences.

Effects of Multidimensionality

Opera, carnival, *fatrasie,* heterotopy, mnenopolis, and creolization—these are the terms that come to mind in analyzing *Mobile, Circus,* and *H.* Decentered montages in which forms of discourse, letters, signs, and symbols are the actors, these texts are highly serious works reflecting the experiences of individuals and the realities around them. Although they do not deal with specific characters in specific situations, the texts speak to us about the individual, not in idealistic terms but in terms of lived experiences. They encode the activities that individuals engage in in order to make sense of their surroundings—seeing, listening, reading, and talking. They mimic the heterogeneity everyone is exposed to—at play, at work, and at home—in a mass-mediated society. They show how individuals' lives are controlled by oral and written discourse and how their perceptions are constantly mediated by this discourse. They concretely demonstrate how political, commercial, and pornographic discourse is used to dominate the individual. These texts, which are contrived and formalistic constructs, are to a certain extent *engagés,* for each in its own way attacks and criticizes the underpinnings of modern society and Western assumptions.

Because of their heterogeneity and fragmentation, *Mobile, Circus,* and *H* propose an alteration of the conventions that govern more traditional literary texts. They bring together poetry and prose, the language of everyday communication and the language of high literature, and the language of pornography and sexuality with the language of many scholarly disciplines. Coexisting in a single text, these forms and types of discourse and signs cut across various levels of culture and establish a continuity between art and non-art, between the artistic and the everyday, between what is immediately useful and what is more esoteric and decorative. By their copresence, juxtaposition, and intermingling, the different forms of discourse and signs subvert the principle of compartmentalization and specialization so characteristic of contemporary Western culture, according to which each entity and each form of discourse is assigned its particular context.

The notion of incompatibility is also subverted by these texts, which gather differences in order to exploit and play with them. Instead of a continuous prose, of sentences connected by logic and causality, these three texts are the loci of fortuitous meetings analogous to Lautréamont's unexpected *rapprochement,* in which he juxtaposes an umbrella and a sewing machine on a dissecting table. They gather and jumble bits and snatches of discourse, signs, and typographies, resulting sometimes in clashes and sometimes in attractions between different forms of rhetoric and different codes, thus forming a space in which hierarchies and priorities are evacuated and in which permeability between and among quite disparate entities is allowed. This practice constitutes a subversion of the tradition of literary works as totalities elaborated by homogeneous units. It is also an implicit counterrhetoric that undermines the traditional tripartite operation of *inventio-dispositio-elocutio.*

Because they displace and reframe forms of discourse and signs, *Mobile, Circus,* and *H* constitute explorations in the possibilities of intertextuality in their display of quotations, transpositions, transcreations, and parodies. As a consequence of these reframings, these texts become the space of general catachresis.[63] They also actualize what Derrida calls the *citationalité,* the ability of language and signs to signify even if taken out of their original context or frame.[64] The displaced elements retain some of their properties because they are linked to specific contexts, but in their new environment they acquire supplementary meanings and properties, deautomizing readers' perceptions and making them aware of the semiotic properties of the displaced items. These literary explorations of and experiments with intertextuality are textual manifestations of a contemporary intellectual and artistic current encompassing philosophy, music, and painting; characterized by intertextuality, reframing, and the mingling of different semiotic systems. The works of Derrida, Cage, Xenakis, Jasper Johns, and Rauchenberg provide some of the most striking parallels.[65]

The narrators of *Mobile, Circus,* and *H,* these postmodern scribes, appear as semiotic pranksters, *bricoleurs* who recycle the past and create textual ready-mades in the manner of Duchamp. Their montages are the products of a multiple paternity pointing to well-known authors, to anonymous sources, and to themselves. Far from undergoing an anxiety of influence, a fear of the intrusion of a predecessor into their own imagination, these narrators co-opt the texts of others, integrating them into their own.

Readers of these texts participate in a complex experience. Involved in structures that foreground similarity and difference, signifieds and signifiers, mental and visual decodings, they are swept into a cultural anamnesis where they are caught between knowing and not knowing, between remembering and not remembering, between feeling that the works are too facile and feeling that they are innovative. Besides testing their memory and their knowledge, and deriving pleasure as well as annoyance, readers are made aware of several properties of language and communication. Reference is one of them. In these texts, readers decode meaning from a variety of fragmented notations, symbols, signs, quotes, portions of utterances, proper names, and nouns. And while they do not engage in a conscious comparative study of these routes of reference, they are reminded of how, by means of multiple symbol functions and systems, we create and comprehend the worlds we live in.[66]

The phenomenon that Michel Foucault calls "the principle of unevenness between discourses" is also very much present in the readers' experience. According to Foucault, some forms of discourse, texts, and documents are utilized for a while and shared, then disappear; others are quoted, used, and reused and have the power to signify in any period.[67] *Mobile, Circus,* and *H*, as intertextual constructs, exploit this principle of unevenness. Another phenomenon Foucault discusses that is relevant here is the fact that individuals do not react in the same way to all discourses: "It is as if discourse, far from being this transparent and neutral element in which sexuality is disarmed and politics is pacified, is one of the places where some of their most formidable powers exert themselves in a privileged way."[68] Pornographic slang describing intercourse or anatomy, and allusions or references to Hitler, Machiavelli, Marx, slavery, the plight of American Indians, or the destruction of the Cathars, are bound to be felt more provocative and more charged than neutral scientific discourse, which for the nonspecialist is not subject to emotional evaluation but accepted, believed, and trusted.

Mobile, Circus, and *H* are multidimensional montages that propose a mode of representation in which referentiality is splintered and heterogeneous. Readers who are willing to make the effort to enter into these texts, struggle with them, and perform with them will find that they are drawn into spaces that are springboards for the mind.

4

Les chemins et les travaux de
l'esprit que tente l'impossible
sont des sujets de méditations
inépuisables.
(The paths and the workings of
the mind that are tempted by the
impossible are inexhaustible
subjects of meditation.)
Maurice Blanchot

Reflexivities

Self-conscious narrators are familiar characters in such diverse works as *Don Quixote, Tom Jones, Tristram Shandy,* and *Jacques le Fataliste.* In these novels Cervantes, Fielding, Sterne, and Diderot invent narrators who take pleasure in elaborating lengthy texts, who are confident in their capacities as storytellers and writers, and who, by their interventions, attract attention to their presence. These narrators remind readers that what they are reading is an invented fiction, the result of a particular choice, and that other choices could have been made. Exuberant, full of humor, ironic, and assertive, the narrators underscore the immense freedom that allows them to invent anything they please.

In *L'Innommable* by Samuel Beckett, *Quelqu'un* by Robert Pinget, and *Fugue* by Roger Laporte, a new twist is introduced into the personality and the behavior of the self-conscious narrator. Doubt, boredom, torment, a feeling of the inadequacy of language, and a sense of the difficulty of writing plague the narrators of these texts. They grapple with writing, with language, with the possibility of creating representation, and even with their bodies and minds. They present themselves no longer as narrators who know, in the sense of the root of the word, *gno, gnarus,* but rather as *ignarus,* nonknowing. And instead of elaborating and constructing a narrative, they spend a considerable amount of time and energy undermining what they are in the process of writing.[1]

Anonymous individuals who manifest themselves as the voices of solitary beings, these narrators are not trying to recover the past, discover an identity, or tell a story. Their scriptive behavior has led critics to talk about a literature of exhaustion, of silence, reflecting deep pessimism and heralding, if not the end of literature as a whole, at least the end of the novel. Such evaluations, which seem to be warranted to a certain extent, do not account for what self-conscious or reflexive texts really are. They are appraisals that limit themselves to the examination of the deliberately abortive fiction these narrators create and to their negative comments. They take the invented narrator seriously, indeed literally, and never scrutinize the textual processes and patterns of which this narrator is a part.

By focusing on the types of activities performed by the self-conscious narrators invented by Beckett, Pinget, and Laporte, I propose a different analysis and interpretation. Crucial to my approach is a recognition of three overlapping, intersecting, and simultaneous roles that the narrators engage in: as creators of metafiction, as inventors of fiction, and as performers in the enunciation. First metafiction: each in his own way, these narrators reflect on the act of writing as they themselves are writing and integrate their reflections and comments into their texts. These reflections and comments can bear on their physical and mental state as they write, the language that they use, and the representation that they invent. At the same time, these narrators invent fiction not as narrative in the traditional sense but as portions of representation, where characters, settings, and actions can be imagined and visualized. Finally, in both their metafiction and their fiction, these narrators make themselves noticed by the ways they organize and utilize language, by their grammatical and stylistic manipulations, and by their intertextual effects. It is this role and activity of the narrators that I call the enunciation.[2]

These narrators, who claim to be in distress, to have difficulties, and to perform inadequately, have chosen to work with impotence. As Beckett once said to an interviewer: "I do not think that this possibility has been exploited before."[3] But to work with impotence does not mean to fail; rather, it proposes another alternative, one that paradoxically locates itself between failure and success while being neither. Hence the interest of this mode of representation.

A striking set of coincidences links Beckett, Pinget, Laporte, and the critic and novelist Maurice Blanchot, pointing to the critical perspective required to come to terms with *L'Innommable, Quelqu'un,* and *Fugue.* Intersections, overlappings, common attitudes and interests, and similarity of orientation relate these authors and critics within a constellation with intriguing ramifications. In his criticism and his own creative works, Blanchot privileges absence, neutrality, and indeterminacy. Kindred spirit with Beckett, he is one of the critics who praise *L'Innommable* for a momentum that leads nowhere.[4] Pinget is often associated with Beckett. Like Beckett in his novels, Pinget undermines what he writes and produces antinovels that remain inconclusive and are both ludicrous and tragic. Laporte is an admirer of Blanchot's novels and literary criticism and is attracted to the same writers Blanchot discusses: Char, Höderlin, Kafka, and Nietzsche.

Thus in Beckett, Pinget, and Laporte, intersecting with Blanchot, we are dealing with three minds that share the same intellectual, metaphysical, and epistemological orientation. They are fascinated by the dynamism of emptiness and negativity and by textual strategies that achieve dispersion from any goal and prevent any resolution or closure. In the following pages I examine the way these interests and preoccupations are concretized through the performance of their narcissistic, solipsistic, self-deprecating narrators, and discuss the possible significations and implications of textual strategies that valorize discredit, limitation, difficulty, and incompleteness.

L'Innommable: A Whirlpool of Words

Samuel Beckett's *L'Innommable* is the third novel of a trilogy that also contains *Molloy* and *Malone meurt.* Written in French, these three novels display a self-conscious narrator who enjoys discussing, commenting upon, even undermining what he writes. This narrator calls himself Molloy in the first novel, Malone in the second; he remains anonymous and nameless in the third novel.[5]

In *Molloy* and in *Malone meurt,* the narrator spends most of his time and energy writing a first person story about himself, inventing events, behaviors, and interactions with other characters. In *L'Innommable* he concentrates on reflections about writing, creating only a few fragments of fiction. He presents his enterprise as a journey through words:

> Il ne faut pas oublier, quelquefois je l'oublie, que tout est une question de voix. Ce qui se passe ce sont des mots. [p. 119]
>
> It must not be forgotten, sometimes I forget, that all is a question of voices. [p. 345][6]

> Moi qui suis en route, de paroles plein les voiles, je suis aussi cet impensable ancêtre dont on ne peut rien dire. [p. 134]
>
> I who am on my way, words bellying out my sails, am also that unthinkable ancestor of whom nothing can be said. [p. 352]

Let us embark on that journey and see how the narrator behaves, first in the metafiction, then in the fiction, and finally in the enunciation.

At the very onset of the text, the narrator warns: "Personnellement je n'ai pas l'intention de m'ennuyer" [p. 10] (Personally I do not intend to be bored [p. 292]), which implies that he can talk to amuse himself and that he does so out of his own desire and initiative. But at the same time he presents himself as someone compelled to talk by some mysterious power over which he has no control and which torments him:

> Il n'y a donc pas à avoir peur. Cependant j'ai peur, peur de ce que mes mots vont faire de moi, de ma cachette, encore une fois. [p. 31]
>
> So there is nothing to be afraid of. And yet I am afraid, afraid of what my words will do to me, to my refuge, yet again. [p. 303]

> Cette voix qui parle. . . . Elle sort de moi, elle me remplit, elle clame contre mes murs, elle n'est pas la mienne, je ne peux pas l'arrêter, je ne peux pas l'empêcher, de me déchirer, de me secouer, de m'assiéger. [p. 40]
>
> This voice that speaks. . . . It issues from me, it fills me, it clamours against my walls, it is not mine, I can't stop it, I can't prevent it, from tearing me, racking me, assailing me. [p. 307]

Repeatedly, the narrator refers to himself as someone obliged to write, using comparisons and qualifications that underscore the torment and the difficulties of his task. He talks about his "supplice tarabiscoté" [p. 55] (labyrinthine torment [p. 314]) and the "étrange peine, étrange faute" [p. 261] (strange pain, strange sin [p. 414]) that harass him. He also talks to himself about how to proceed, how to conduct his task. At the beginning of his journey the advice he gives himself is "salir puis nettoyer" [p. 25] (first dirty, then make clean [300]). In the middle of the text he reiterates the same idea in saying "L'essentiel est que je n'arrive nulle part" (the essential is never to arrive anywhere), which in the next sentence he makes more concrete: "L'essentiel est de gigoter jusqu'au bout de son catgut" [p. 105] (the essential is to go on squirming forever at the end of the line [p. 338]). Toward the end of the text the narrator formulates the same notion in the remark, "On annonce puis on renonce, c'est ainsi, ça fait continuer" [pp. 244–45] (you announce, then you renounce, so it is, that helps you on [p. 406]).

How is it possible, how should one behave in order to dirty then to clean, to wriggle or to squirm, or to denounce? The narrator is very resourceful in devising techniques that achieve the desired effects. He gives details about himself and about his characters, then cancels them systematically, explaining that he invented them, that he lied (see for instance pp. 34 and 54 in French, pp. 304 and 314 in English). He proposes topics he could develop but never does; instead he uses the future, the conditional, or the infinitive forms of verbs, this specific linguistic and stylistic feature replacing or announcing larger proposals that are never actualized but always remain potential, prospective. In addition the narrator contradicts himself constantly. On the one hand he points out that he does not know what he is doing: "A vrai dire, soyons au moins francs, il y a un bon moment déjà que je ne sais plus ce que je dis" [p. 73] (To tell the truth, let us be honest at least, it is some considerable time now I last knew what I was talking about [p. 323]). But on the other hand, he also notices with satisfaction: "Rien à faire, je suis sucrement bien informé" [p. 59] (No denying it, I'm confoundedly well informed [p. 316]); "Inutile de biaiser, je sais un tas de choses" [p. 60] (No good wriggling, I'm a mine of useless knowledge [p. 317]); "ça avance, ça avance" [p. 151] (we are getting on [p. 360]).

Toward the end of the text, reflecting on what and how he should write, the narrator advises himself to do precisely what he has been doing all along: "Qu'est-ce-que je vais pouvoir dire à présent, je vais me le demander, je vais me poser des questions, c'est un bon bouche-trou, non pas que je risque de me taire, alors pourquoi tant d'histoires, c'est ça des questions qu'on ne va pas dire . . . c'est ça, des aspirations. . . . Quoi encore, des jugements, des comparaisons, ça vaut mieux que de rire, tout aide" [pp. 234–35] (What am I going to say now, I'm going to ask myself, I'm going to ask questions, that's a good stopgap, not that I'm in any danger of stopping, then why all this fuss, that's right, questions . . . and then there are plans, right, aspirations. . . . What else, opinions, comparisons, anything rather than laughter, all helps [p. 401]). With his cancellations and negations, his never realized fictional projects, his contradictions, and his questions, the narrator goes nowhere; he merely spins and whirls words, thus creating constant and unresolved tensions between what he has created but then canceled, between what he plans and projects but never shapes.

Turning now to how the narrator talks about what he writes and to how he evaluates his inventions, we cannot but be struck by the quantity and the quality of these remarks. He punctuates his text with metaphors that refer to his writing:

Pour commencer. Quelques *pantins* [p. 9]

In the beginning. A few *puppets* [p. 292][7]

Alors on invente des *obscurités* [p. 13]

So one invents *obscurities* [p. 294]

Et voilà . . . que je glisse déjà . . . vers les secours de la *fable* [p. 43]

And I see myself slipping . . . towards the resorts of *fable* [p. 308]

J'ai le temps de la foutre en l'air cette *foire* [p. 73]

I've plenty of time to blow it all skyhigh, this *circus* [p. 323]

M'estime-t-on déjà suffisamment enduit de *balivernes* [p. 77]

Do they consider me so plastered with their *rubbish* [p. 325]

Ce *ramassis de conneries,* c'est bien d'eux que je le tiens [p. 99]

It is they who dictate this *torrent of balls* [p. 335]

Qu'en dire qui fasse cesser cette *rumeur de termite dans mon guignol* [pp. 106–07]

What to still this *gnawing of termites in my Punch and Judy box* [p. 339]

Deux trous. . . . Ou un seul . . . où les mots se bousculent comme des *fourmis, pressés, indifférents,* n'apportant rien, n'emportant rien, trop *faibles* pour creuser. [p. 139]

Two holes. . . . Or a single one . . . where the words swarm and jostle like *ants, hasty, indifferent,* bringing nothing, taking nothing away, too *light* to leave a mark. [p. 355]

Je suis en mots . . . je suis tous ces mots, tous ces étrangers, cette *poussière de verbe* [p. 204]

I'm in words . . . I'm all these words, all these strangers, this *dust of words* [p. 386]

Quand j'y pense au temps que j'ai perdu avec ces *paquets de sciure,* à commencer par Murphy [p. 213]

When I think of the time I have wasted with these *brand-dips,* beginning with Murphy [p. 390]

En voilà une histoire . . . est-ce le retour au *monde fabuleux* [p. 246]

There's a story for you . . . is it the return to the *world of fable* [p. 407]

Il faut essayer dans mes *vieilles histoires* venues je ne sais d'où, de trouver la sienne [p. 259]

The attempt must be made, in the *old stories* incomprehensibly mine, to find his [p. 413]

In these examples the metaphors and comparisons that the narrator invents all evoke dysphoric or negative elements. They connote imprecision, make believe, deception, and inferior forms of life. Some of them imply work, activity, creation, and process, but of a type considered unserious because it involves such popular entertainments as *foire* (circus) and *guignol* (Punch and Judy). And although the metaphors and comparisons imply mental activity, it is a flawed mental activity resulting in *balivernes* (rubbish), *conneries* (balls), fake or false creations or *histoires* (stories), refuse or *sciure* (sawdust, which Beckett translates "brand-dips"), or pests, *fourmis* (ants). At the same time the narrator talks positively about his writing and his situation; remarks like the following are also numerous and span the entire text:

Autant parler, tant qu'à faire. Quelle *liberté*. [p. 44]

One might as well speak and be done with it. What *liberty*! [p. 309]

Curieuse tâche que d'avoir à parler de soi. Etrange *espoir,* tourné vers le *silence* et la *paix*. [p. 48]

Strange task, which consists in speaking of oneself. Strange *hope,* turned toward *silence* and *peace*. [p. 311]

après je dirai n'importe quoi, tout ce qu'ils voudront, *avec joie,* pendant l'éternité, enfin, avec philosophie. [pp. 78–79]

then any old thing, no matter what, whatever they want, with a will, till time is done, at least with a *good grace*. [p. 326]

Evoquer dans les moments difficiles . . . l'image d'une grande bouche . . . *se vidant inlassablement* . . . des mots qui l'obstruent. [p. 212]

Evoke at painful junctures . . . the image of a vast . . . mouth . . . *extruding indefatigably* . . . the words that obstruct it. [p. 390]

Thus writing and speaking also generate freedom, hope, peace, and joy, and have a purging and relieving effect. The narrator even notices: "Oui, heureusement que je les ai, ces fantômes parlants" [p. 179] (Yes, I'm a lucky man to have them, these voluble shades [p. 374]). Here, then, is a narrator who discredits his creation while at the same time appreciating it and being soothed by it.[8] Given this schizophrenic attitude, what kind of fiction is he capable of inventing?

The fiction presented in *L'Innommable* is well known, and many critics have written about it; however, a brief summary may be useful. At the beginning of the text the narrator provides details about his appearance and setting. He describes himself as having a beard, tears falling like liquefied brain on his cheeks, red eyes with retinas that perhaps face each other, a round head like a ball, a body the consistency of mucilage. Wearing only leggings, he situates himself in a vast place lighted by feeble gray lights and specifies that this place is only twelve feet in diameter. Around him, coming from who knows where, Malone (the character he invented in *Malone Dies*), with little trace of his mortal liveliness, wearing a hat and holding his jaws, appears and disappears with the exactitude of a machine. In the immaculate silence a shout is heard, two oblong forms collide in front of him, and then someone comes toward him. Why all this happens, who these forms are, is not said.

Interspersed throughout the text are passages during which the narrator refers to groups of individuals he neither describes nor names, with the exception of one called Basile. He labels these individuals his tyrants, his tormentors. They are petty, they constantly watch over him and persecute him, and they force him to write. He feels that in the past it was they who taught him what he knows.

The narrator also invents a story about the return home of a character named Mahood. This individual is at the end of a trip around the world. He is progressing on one leg and crutches toward his house, a rotunda in which several members of his family live. Doting, death-fearing grandparents, his wife, his children, and the children who were born during his absence watch him, talk about him, and pray for him. When he finally enters the house, he finds them all dead, poisoned by a bad can of corned beef—he describes how he steps on their decomposed bodies with his crutches.

A second story is again about a character called Mahood, but it is not a continuation of the previous story. This time, Mahood has lost both legs. He is stuck in a jar, his head covered with pustules and blue flies. The jar, placed in front of a restaurant near a slaughterhouse, holds the menu, so that he hears the comments of the customers about the food served in the restaurant. His excrement is used in the restaurant owner's garden, and we are told that the salads are very tasty. To attract the attention of the owner, called Marguerite and then

Madeleine, Mahood bangs his head on the jar, throws saliva to her, and plays games with her; he hides his head, then suddenly raises it as if he were a jack-in-the-box. The owner places a frame in the jar in order to keep Mahood's head out of it, and now the immobilized Mahood catches flies with his mouth. He imagines that he manages to have an erection by thinking of a horse's behind.

For a very short time the narrator thinks of inventing another character whom he calls Worm, but except for a few details Worm never materializes into a full-fledged person. He remains a being "de règne inconnu" [p. 157] (kingdom unknown [p. 363]).

The last portion of fiction that the narrator invents resembles a short shaggy-dog story. Less than a page long, it is about a woman whose husband is supposedly killed during a war. She cries but soon remarries. The first husband is not dead and comes back, and she goes to the station to meet him. Meanwhile, her new husband hangs himself. This sad story, says the narrator ironically, was invented in order to experience what love, war, emotions, trains, and stations are all about.

Strange fiction indeed, these bits and pieces of representation that the narrator brings to life and then cancels by his metafictional comments, behaving very much like a textual jack-in-the-box. What is this all about? What does the narrator accomplish in performing the role of storyteller? At the outset of his verbal journey, he wonders whether he is going to create a "capharnaüm (a throng) and an "atmosphère de bazar" [pp. 9–10] (the crush and bustle of a bargain sale [p. 292]); later he calls his creation a *foire* [p. 73] (circus) [p. 323]). These terms connote exuberance, variety, compositeness, and teeming activity, and this is precisely the kind of text he writes. The various portions of representation, the bits of fiction that he invents in describing his own situation, the adventures of Mahood, the nonexistence of Worm, and the turmoils of the woman who loses her husband blend humor, horror, cruelty, derision, compassion, incongruity, and unexpectedness.

These old stories incomprehensibly his, as the narrator says [p. 259, French; p. 413, English], can be the result of dreams, hallucinations, fantasmas, or nightmarish visions à la Bosch or Dante. With its unrelated sequences, its strange situations, its repelling moments, and its varying moods and intensities, this fiction could constitute the scenario of a Surrealist film such as Dali and Bunuel's *Un Chien anda-lou* or Dali's *L'Age d'or*. German Expressionist painters could have created some of the gory scenes of maimed bodies, pus-covered heads, and rotting corpses.[9] The silent gray atmosphere perturbed by shouts, and the presence of hidden torturers definitely lend a Gothic atmosphere to the setting the narrator describes. At the same time these unrelated and disparate situations share a striking characteristic: the objects and the conditions of the characters tend to represent creatures in limbo — not yet in a particular or definite state, or between states, or after some previous state. The floating shapes that collide next to the narrator are an example of his unanchored, intermediary limbo. The image of the egg with which the narrator describes his head suggests life but only in its mere beginning; if taken as a bald head, it connotes old age and the proximity of death. Worm does not even reach the status of a living person. The jar in which Mahood rests can symbolize two possibilities: either the womb, and therefore gestation in process; or an urn, for Mahood is on the threshold of death. These various components of the fiction created by the narrator, then, hover between something and nothing. It is also significant that the narrator places himself in an empty room permeated by a gray atmosphere where Chagall- or Miro-like creatures float in space. He invents for himself a nonspatial, noncircumstantial, non-Euclidian environment. We are indeed in a very complex fiction that projects us into the realm of indeterminacy.

The performance of the narrator as a writer, the enunciation, is strange, puzzling, disorienting. While writing in a disorganized and erratic fashion, he makes his text a space of play and manipulation where he exhibits his virtuosity with words, his knowledge, and his erudition. *L'Innommable* is certainly considered by most readers a taxing, disturbing, and forbidding text because of its typographical presentation and its discursive heterogeneity, which requires constant readjustment, alertness, and concentration. The narrator says that words swarm and jostle like ants in his mouth. On the pages this teeming activity is reflected typographically. After a few pages with paragraphs and interruptions, the text becomes a dense flow of words. Written in free prose, it displays a hybrid verbal texture: in addition to declarative sentences the narrator uses many negative statements, asks questions, and utters exclamations, interjections, and insults.

Sentence length varies considerably. There are short utterances without verbs and well-formed, average-length sentences, but toward the end of the text the sentences tend to get longer; there is even a passage [pp. 200–211, French; pp. 385–89, English] where for several pages the words simply accumulate with no interruptions except commas. There is no logical continuity between sentences but, rather, nonsequiturs and disjunctions as the narrator moves in and out of his fiction and his metafiction, giving the impression that he is saying whatever comes to his mind at any time.

Several registers and varieties of French also contribute to the discursive variety of the text. The narrator switches from a familiar register to a pedantic or learned one, sprinkling his text with scatological or vulgar expressions. As he speaks he is particularly keen to foreground such phonic components of language as alliterations, assonances, and interior rhymes, and he frequently repeats the same words, so that the free prose that comes out of his mouth, dictated to him by some mysterious power, has features of poetry rendering it balanced, structured, and soothing. At times, however, the language becomes suddenly frantic, as in the following passage, which is so striking that it is almost always singled out by Beckett scholars:

> je suis tous ces mots, tous ces étrangers, cette poussière de verbe, sans fond où se poser, sans ciel où se dissiper, se rencontrant pour dire, se fuyant pour dire, que je les suis tous, ceux qui s'unissent, ceux qui se quittent, ceux qui s'ignorent, et pas autre chose, si, tout autre chose, que je suis tout autre chose, une chose muette, dans un endroit dur, vide, clos, sec, net, noir, où rien ne bouge, rien ne parle, et que j'écoute, et que j'entends, et que je cherche, comme une bête née en cage de bêtes nées en cage de bêtes nées en cage de bêtes nées en cage de bêtes nées en cage de bêtes nées et mortes en cage nées et mortes en cage de bêtes nées en cage mortes en cage nées et mortes nées et mortes en cage en cage nées et puis mortes nées et puis mortes, comme une bête dis-je, disent-ils, une telle bête, que je cherche, comme une telle bête, avec mes pauvres moyeus, une telle bête, n'ayant plus de son espèce, que la peur, la rage, non, la rage est terminée, que la peur. [pp. 204–05]

I'm all these words, all these strangers, this dust of words, with no ground for their settling, no sky for their dispersing, coming together to say, fleeing one another to say, that I am they, all of them, those that merge, those that part, those that never meet, and nothing else, yes, something else, that I'm something quite different, a quite different thing, a wordless thing in an empty place, a hard shut dry cold black place, where nothing stirs, nothing speaks, and that I listen, and that I seek, like a caged beast born of caged beasts born of caged beasts born of caged beasts born in a cage and dead in a cage born and then dead born in a cage and then dead in a cage, in a word like a beast, in one of their words, like such a beast, and that I seek, like such a beast, with my little strength, such a beast, with nothing of its species left but fear and fury, no, the fury is past, nothing but fear [pp. 386–87]

In this passage two features are particularly salient: the abrupt change of rhythms and the repetitions. After several short phrases a succession of crisp, one-syllable adjectives accelerates the tempo, then back to short phrases. During a stretch of five or six lines, five or six words are repeated and permuted, piled up as in a litany without semantic breaks or punctuation. Afterward there is a switch back to a more balanced rhythm of short phrases. This passage suggests pathological behavior, perhaps an obsession with particular words. It is a verbal skidding reminiscent of a broken record.

Another passage particularly attracts attention: it contains so many onomatopoeic and short words that the rhythm is broken, as if the narrator were panting or out of breath, extremely agitated and tormented, perhaps near hysteria. Or is the narrator simply playing with words and sounds, enjoying repeating them, permuting them, stringing them, trying them out outside storytelling, outside sensemaking?

C'est comme ça que ça finira, par des cris déchirants, des murmures intarticulés . . . par des gloussements, glouglou, aïes, ha, pah, je vais m'exercer, nyam, hou, plof, pss, rien que de l'émotion, pan, paf, les coups, na, toc, quoi encore, aah, ooh, ça c'est l'amour, assez, c'est fatiguant, hi, hi, ça c'est les côtes, de Démocrite, non de l'autre en fin de compte, c'est la fin, la fin du compte, c'est le silence [p. 248]

That's how it will end, in heart-rending cries, inarticulate murmurs, to be invented, as I go along, improvised, as I groan along, I'll laugh, that's how it will end, in a chuckle, chuck chuck, ow, ha, pa. I'll practise, nyum, hoo, plop, psss, nothing but emotion, bing bang, that's blows, ugh, pooh, what else, oooh, aaah, that's love, enough, it's tiring, hee, hee, that's the Abderite, no, the other, in the end, it's the end, the ending end, it's the silence [p. 408]

Here is an example in which while making fun of himself the narrator mingles scientific words and vulgar or popular ones in a pedantic and contorted sentence, attacking paternity, marriage, and the family:

Mais le bouquet a ça a été cette histoire de Mahood où je me suis représenté comme saisi par le fait d'être débarrassé à si bon compte d'un tas de consanguins, sans parler des deux cons tout court, celui maudit qui m'avait lâché dans le siècle et l'autre infundibuliforme, où j'avais essayé de me venger en me perpétuant. [pp. 72–73]

But the bouquet was this story of Mahood's in which I appear as upset at having been delivered so economically of a pack of blood relations, not to mention the two cunts into the bargain, the one for ever accursed that ejected me into this world and the other, infundibuliform, in which, pumping my likes, I tried to take my revenge. [p. 323]

In the following example the narrator again mingles his ghastly humor and his erudition with puns, word permutations, and sound repetitions:

Mais avant d'en brosser le portrait sur pied, il n'en a plus qu'un, mon prochain représentant en existence sera un cul de jatte, c'est décidé, la jatte sur la tête et le cul dans la poussière, à même Tellus aux mille mamelles, pour plus de douceur. [p. 256]

But before executing his portrait, full length on his surviving leg, let me note that my next vice-exister will be a billy in the bowl, that's final, with his bowl on his head and his arse in the dust, plump down on thousand-breasted Tellus, it'll be softer for him. [p. 315]

From such passages it is obvious that most of the time the narrator is not aiming so much to impart new information (that would be a way to develop and expand his fiction, which he does not want to do) as to attract attention to himself by performing lazzi-like pieces showing what he can do with words, indulging in sexual and scatological innuendos, being hilariously funny and at times embarrassingly vulgar.

One of the narrator's favorite behaviors consists in altering well-known expressions so that the original is still apparent: in "rien à faire, je suis sucrement bien informé" [p. 59] (no denying it, I'm confoundedly well informed [p. 316])—which in French derives from "rien à faire je suis sacrément bien informé"—he replaces the slightly blasphemous word *sacrément* by a neologism, as if he did not want to be overtly vulgar.[10] Of course this is all the more funny in that in most cases vulgar, scatological, and insulting words do not disturb him at all, and it is precisely such words he would choose.

The narrator is also prone to modify existing proverbs: "un moment de découragement à battre pendant qu'il est chaud" [p. 51] (a moment of discouragement, to strike while hot [p. 312]) derives from "Il faut battre le fer pendant qu'il est chaud" (One needs to strike the iron while it is hot). He also invents proverblike expressions: "La recherche du moyen de faire cesser les choses, taire sa voix, est ce qui permet au discours de se poursuivre" [p. 25] (The search for the means to put an end to things, an end to speech, is what enables the discourse to continue [p. 299]). This is a particularly clever move because in these examples the narrator makes paradoxical statements; he says that situations associated with difficulty, failure, and lack of creativity are positive and productive. And since he expresses these ideas in the marked form of the proverb, they are more likely to be noticed by his readers. By means of this technique, the importance of failure and impotence is foregrounded. But at the same time this "ignorant" narrator displays his awareness of particular forms of discourse, proverbs and clichés, and he draws attention to the fact that he can make up new expressions of this type. Therefore his knowledge of language and his inventiveness are also foregrounded.[11]

The striking set of metaphors that the narrator uses to talk about his own writing—verbal dust, circus, torment—contrasts with the metaphors employed in the classic topoi for writing, such as weaving or working on a loom. The new semantic possibilities that the narrator invents are one more instance of his creativity, further evidence that for him words are not weak or indifferent. Moreover, this narrator who claims to be ignorant is in fact very learned, as is apparent in his use of precise and specialized terms from such different disciplines as botany: "jungles rouges de rafflésie" [p. 62] (jungles red with rafflesia [p. 317]); chemistry: "les menstrues de Ptomaïne" [p. 63] (the period of Ptomaine [p. 318]); philosophy: "Peut-on être éphectique à son insu?" [p. 8] (Can one be ephectic otherwise than unawares? [p. 291]); and rhetoric: "D'où une certaine confusion dans les exordes" [p. 30] (whence a certain confusion in the exordia [p. 302]), and "J'ai oublié l'apodose" [p. 237] (I've forgotten my apodosis [p. 402]).

The narrator's intellectual sophistication is also apparent in his intertextual manipulations. Critics have pointed out that the opening sentences of the text—"Où maintenant? Quand maintenant? Qui maintenant? Sans me le demander. Dire je. Sans le penser. Appeler ça des questions, des hypothèses [p. 7] (Where now? Who now? When now? Unquestioning. I , say I, Unbelieving. Questions, hypotheses, call them that [p. 291])—might take both form and meaning from the passage that concludes Hume's skeptical survey of knowledge in his *Treatise of Human Nature.* They have also noted that the attitude which consists of invalidating what has been affirmed is inspired by the philosophy of Giordano Bruno, for whom any idea is reversible, and that when the narrator writes, "Il n'y a . . . qu'à être ce lent tourbillon sans bornes" [p. 235] (All that is needed is to . . . be this slow boundless whirlwind [p. 401]), he is referring to a concept stated by Descartes in his *Philosophical Principles.* Aspects of the Bible and of the *Divine Comedy* are also present in the text. [12]

Instead of cohesion, continuity, and unity, the narrator's verbal production is characterized by discontinuity, contrasts, diversity, and abrupt changes; it displays features symptomatic of works by such writers as Artaud, Céline, and Lautréamont, which have been identified by Julia Kristeva as bringing about a revolution in literary expression. Indeed, the narrator of *L'Innommable,* like the imaginary subjects of Artaud, Céline, and Lautréamont, does not repress his emotions or his unconscious drives. [13] Rather, through his various discursive manipulations he lets his body, his feelings, his anger, his joy, his depression, and his desire play, drift, and have free rein, concomitantly displaying a whole array of components and techniques that demonstrate knowledge, erudition, virtuosity, and complete control.

In his three roles—as inventor of fiction, as commentator on what he writes, and as manipulator of language and knowledge—the narrator of *L'Innommable* sets up a constellation of elements, techniques, and intertextual effects that contribute to the creation of oscillation and indeterminacy. He thus elaborates a busy, active, dynamic text that suspends and disjoints fiction, metafiction, and enunciation. As he says in a striking remark: "je ne suis ni d'un côté ni de l'autre, je suis au milieu, je suis la cloison, j'ai deux faces et pas d'épaisseur, c'est peut-être ça que je sens, je me sens qui vibre, je suis le tympan, d'un côté c'est le crâne, de l'autre le monde, je ne suis ni de l'un, ni de l'autre" [p. 196] (I'm neither one side nor the other, I'm in the middle, I'm the partition, I've two surfaces and no thickness, perhaps that's what I feel, myself vibrating, I'm the tympanum, on the one hand the mind, on the other the world, I don't belong to either [p. 383]).

Ruby Cohn writes very perceptively that with this narrator "Beckett succeeds in the paradoxical achievement of creating something which skirts nothing."[14] In retrospect, it appears that the title *L'Innommable* condenses everything the text is about. "Unnamable" means ghastly and disgusting, like the fiction invented by the narrator. "Unnamable" also means that which cannot be named or grasped: the identity of the narrator, his physical shape, and the atmosphere he lives in. Unnamable, too, is the performance of the narrator, who tells himself "il n'y a qu'à errer et à laisser errer, de mot en mot" [p. 235] (all that is needed is to wander and let wander [p. 401]).

Carried along by this momentum, the narrator wanders from word to word, through different moments of intensity, in a free space, mimicking schizophrenia or hysteria in his instability. He explodes, drags, skids, contrasts, affirms, negates, and exhibits himself in a dynamic and energetic proliferation of words, hating as well as enjoying his "supplice tarabiscoté" [p. 55] (his labyrinthine torment [p. 314]).

Quelqu'un: Prancing with Words

It seems to me that the interest of my work to date has been the search for a tone. It is a matter of form and this perhaps explains my belonging to what is known as the new novel. But it would be a mistake to think of me as partisan of a "regard" (look) school. If it is a matter of being objective, the ear also makes tyrannical demands. . . . I am not interested in all that can be said or signified, but in the way to say it . . . the narrative discourse will therefore consist of stories. If I say these stories do not interest me, it is that I know they could have been different ones . . . it could be that I find them [the stories] paramountly interesting or even spellbinding inasmuch as they illustrate in spite of me my entire emotional and intellectual life. [15]

These statements, partly serious, partly facetious, from his lecture aptly entitled "Pseudo-principes d'esthétique," form an excellent introduction to Robert Pinget's novelistic works, whose narrators invent a sad, moving, and funny fiction and delight in playing with storytelling, with words and with sounds. [16]

Quelqu'un[17] is about an anonymous narrator who presents himself as having lost a piece of paper and who, as he is looking for it, describes the people, the objects, and the activities in a boardinghouse somewhere in the small provincial French town where he lives. While he describes the different moments of this pseudo-quest, this banal setting, and these uneventful lives, he comments on his own writing and on writing in general.

In a set of metafictional interventions dispersed throughout the text, the narrator of *Quelqu'un* presents writing as a complex activity. On the one hand, he shows that he is free to choose among different possibilities for this creation; on the other hand, he says that he is at the mercy of his mood, his reactions, and his feelings. Near the beginning of the text, he remarks:

Je dois me tarabuster un peu, me secouer. Mon exposé y gagnera en clarté. Ce qui se conçoit bien. Et pour moi concevoir serait plutôt m'arrêter. . . . Trouver le mot juste, trouver exactement le mot, mais c'est divin. Je dois dire en passant que c'est souvent le mot caca qui est le plus précis. . . . Du reste ce principe de clarté est farfelu. Ce qui se conçoit bien ça ne s'énonce pas, ça se fait. . . . Le seul fait d'énoncer clairement ou pas, signifie qu'on est dans le . . . chose." [pp. 28–29]

I must badger myself a little bit, shake myself. My exposé will gain in clarity. What is clearly understood. And for me to understand would rather be to stop. . . . To find the right word, to find exactly the word, but it is divine. I must say in passing that often it is the word pooh which is the most precise. . . . Besides this principle of clarity is weird. What is clearly understood is not expressed, it gets done. . . . The very fact to express clearly or not, signifies that we are in the . . . mess.

Behind these words one recognizes Boileau's famous prescription concerning writing:

Avant donc que d'écrire apprenez à penser.
Selon que notre idée est plus ou moins obscure,
L'expression la suit, ou moins nette, ou plus pure.
Ce que l'on conçoit bien s'énonce clairement,
Et les mots pour le dire arrivent aisément.

Thus before writing learn to think.
Whether our idea is more or less obscure,
Expression follows it, either less precise, or more pure.
What is clearly understood can be clearly expressed,
And words to say it come easily.[18]

The narrator announces clearly at the beginning of his text that he is going to flout Boileau's prescription. This interplay is actually quite comical and desacralizing because Boileau's maxim is a golden rule, a vade mecum of French culture and education, according to which a text should be planned in advance, its thought-out order should be followed, and reason and logic should be its guiding principles. But this narrator repeatedly states that he follows no rule, that he can write without constraints, and that he can say anything he pleases:

Bref, pas d'inventaires. De temps en temps un objet oui d'accord, mais seulement pour le plaisir. Disons la détente, la récréation. [p. 23]

In brief, no inventories. From time to time an object yes all right, but only for pleasure. let us say relaxation, diversion.

J'écris comme ça, comme on parle, comme on transpire. [p. 45]

I write just like that, like we speak, like we perspire.

Je ne peux pas prévenir les surprises et les contradictions puis-
que je vais à la découverte. [p. 62]

I cannot anticipate surprises and contradictions since I am off in a spirit of discovery.

Quand je me fatiguerai, je ferai des descriptions de l'intérieur.
[p. 69]

When I will be tired, I will describe the inside.

However, if he has complete freedom regarding what he can write
about and how he can organize his material, he has to contend with
himself, because at moments he is bored or afraid:

Ca m'ennuie, ça m'ennuie. Pas de la mauvaise volonté du tout,
pas de la paresse. Une peur, une angoisse. [p. 3]

It bores me, it bores me. No unwillingness at all, no laziness. A fear,
an anguish.

Pourvu que je ne me dégôute pas trop vite de ce que je fais là.
Cet exposé. J'ai une peur bleue. Je prie le ciel. [p. 29]

Let's hope I do not get too quickly disgusted with what I am doing
here. This exposé. I am scared stiff. I pray to heaven.

Est-ce que c'est de l'amour? Je sais en tout cas que ça me fait
chier d'en parler. [p. 31]

It is love? Anyway I know that it bores the hell out of me to speak
about it.

At moments he feels that his enterprise is worthless, and he states
so repeatedly:

Ce qui est dit n'est jamais dit puisqu'on peut le dire autrement.
[p. 45]

What is said is never said since it is possible to say it otherwise.

Dans le fond plus je raconte notre vie plus je trouve inutile de
dire exactement ce qui se passe . . . de me torturer pour le dire
exactement, c'est tellement plat, tellement comme tout le
monde. [p. 211]

Really the more I recount our life, the more I find it useless to say
exactly what's happening . . . to torture myself to say it exactly, it is
so flat, so like everyone.

At one point, after a glib and vulgar play on words, the narrator,
remarking that it was involuntary, states that words have an autonomous power:

on les sort comme ça et un monde, un univers tout entier nous
est révélé, des gouffres, des enfers. . . . Mais je remarque que
c'est toujours les mots qui me révèlent ce genre de choses, toujours les associations involontaires, les accouplages ou les comparaisons, toujours ça. [p. 177]

we take them out like that and a world, a whole universe is revealed to
us, chasms, hells. . . . But I notice that it is always words which reveal to me this type of thing, always involuntary associations, couplings, or comparisons, always that.

Words come out unexpectedly, and suddenly a representation is
encoded that is frightening in its implications. When this happens,
the narrator is no longer in control; in fact, he is even led to the conclusion that "certaines choses . . . ne sont peut-être qu'une question
de mots" [pp. 177–78] (certain things . . . are perhaps only a question of words.) This is what the narrator demonstrates when he tells
what he calls the television story [pp. 218–21]. Once he and Fonfon,
a retarded boy living in the boardinghouse, remained alone during
the summer. They rented a television, and both enjoyed watching
adventure stories. But at the end of the summer the television had to
be returned, and Fonfon became very sad and depressed. The narrator
put an empty box in Fonfon's room and told him stories. Fonfon was
delighted and completely forgot the real television—the box and the
stories of the narrator provided him with the same excitement. By
means of this anecdote the narrator underscores both the power of
words, which, independent of any real situation, have the capacity to

create representation, and the importance of the storyteller, who by his inventions occupies and amuses his audience.

Like the narrator of *L'Innommable,* the narrator of *Quelqu'un* in his metafiction has an ambiguous attitude toward writing. Expressing himself in less violent or dysphoric terms, he also states that he is plagued by fear and boredom, that writing is worthless yet at the same time useful.

Pinget's narrators in general and the narrator of *Quelqu'un* in particular offer a rather entertaining fiction that also presents sad and shabby, even seedy, characters and situations. In fact, in many aspects Pinget's narrator produces almost readerly texts. In *Quelqu'un,* however, the narrator does not elaborate a well-built narrative, with a plot, a crisis, or a set of questions that are solved or remain problematic; rather, he juxtaposes scenes taking place at different moments in time in the kitchen, the dining room, the garden, and the small town; he succeeds in providing a description of a single day in the boardinghouse from morning to night, with many interruptions during which descriptions of moments from the past are introduced.

It appears that the narrator and his friend Gaston (with whom he directs the boardinghouse), the boarders, the house itself, and the garden have known better times. The kitchen and the dining room have a permanent smell of grease (*ça sent le graillon*), paint is chipping away, and plants in the garden are covered with dust. A feeling of decadence, of failure, and of poverty emanates from what the characters say and do. The narrator describes the routine, the pettiness, and the sadness of humble people for whom the smallest and most trivial event—spilling a glass of wine, buying a washing machine, being given tough meat by the butcher, visiting a niece, or making a new dress—is the subject of serious and endless discussion and consideration, as if it were a matter of life or death. Furthermore, the characters' financial situation is such that they have to deny themselves every pleasure and satisfaction:

> Le moindre petit désir de rien du tout est un luxe, on doit l'écraser. On passe son temps à écraser. Pas étonnant qu'on s'aplatisse, qu'on se tasse. Il n'y a qu'à voir la gueule de nos pensionnaires. Ils ont beau certains, avoir un gros ventre ou de gros seins, ils sont plats comme des limandes. . . . Tour ces désirs

écrasés, toutes ces aspirations tuées dans l'oeuf. Et l'espoir comme un petit trognon compact, genre chewing-gum. [p. 47]

The slightest small desire is a luxury, it must be squashed. We spend
our time squashing. Not surprising that we are getting flat, that we
are shrinking. Just look at the appearance of our boarders. Even
though some have a big belly or big breasts, they are flat like lemon
sole. . . . All these squashed desires, all these aspirations killed in the
egg. And hope like a compact little core, like chewing-gum.

The narrator places himself and his characters in situations where
conversations occur: various meals with their order and ritual from
hors d'oeuvres to coffee, afternoon and evening gatherings, encounters with the neighbors, and discussions with the servants. During
these conversations and other interactions, we hear the various characters gossip, exacerbate each other's susceptibilities, and talk about
their past and family tension. We also see them save appearances, involve themselves in petty fights, and exercise domination or pressure
when they deal with someone vulnerable and defenseless, like Fonfon.
As the narrator comments:

Quelle horreur la mistoufle, la vie en commun, les coeurs qui
s'étiolent, les rancunes qui mijotent. Elles n'éclateront jamais.
En petits postillons oui, en petites vacheries. [p. 126]

What a pity maliciousness, life in common, hearts which are simmer-
ing. They will never burst. Into little sputters yes, into little dirty
tricks.

And again, as in all of Pinget's novels, in *Quelqu'un* the narrator
invents characters whose behavior is unacceptable, who are marginal
for some reason, or who make remarks about other characters that imply illicitness, shame, or deviation: hence the character of the orphan,
half-cretin Fonfon. In fact the narrator, his colleague Gaston, and all
the boarders are outsiders, not really integrated into society. Rumor
has it that the boardinghouse cook's daughter is a prostitute, and the
narrator in a moment of frenzy imagines that Gaston has organized
orgies in the house next door. The narrator's fiction is rather grim.
The characters, the situations, the behaviors he invents are shabby,
dubious, unpleasant, and depressing.

At the same time, while spinning such a somber tale in his fiction and while discrediting and praising writing in his metafiction, the narrator is also hilarious because of his clownish scriptive behavior. He is incongruous, he blunders, he exaggerates, and his performance displays a virtuoso's repertoire. Thus the narrator, with the unexpected compulsion of a clown, suddenly feels like describing a piece of furniture, and off he goes:

> Un meuble pour récréation. Le buffet par exemple. C'est un buffet affreux. . . . Il est à deux corps, comme presque tous les buffets. Les panneaux sont sculptés. Sur ceux du haut, des têtes d'épagneuls dans un ovale. Sur ceux du bas, des trophées de chasse et des légumes. Des perdrix, des raves et des navets. Tout autour et le long des charnières il y a une torsade doublée de deux ou trois moulures en dents de scie ou d'autre chose, je ne l'ai pas sous les yeux. En haut au milieu du fronton, une espèce de parapluie et un frissottement de vagues jusqu'aux angles qui sont surmontés d'urnes funéraires ou de boîtes à puces, ce jeu qu'on jouait de mon temps. Et voilà. Dans les tiroirs entre les deux corps il y a à droite les couverts et à gauche les serviettes de nos convives. Ça pue ce n'est pas croyable. [pp. 33–40]

A piece of furniture for diversion. The dresser for instance. It is a hideous dresser. It has two parts, like almost all the dressers. The panels are sculpted. On those of the top, heads of spaniels in an oval. On those of the bottom, hunting trophies and vegetables. Partridges, rapes, and turnips. Around and along the hinges there is a cable molding lined with two or three jagged moldings, or something else, I do not have it under my eyes. On top in the middle of the center part a kind of umbrella and frizzy waves up to the angles which are surmounted by funeral urns or by tiddlywinks, that game we used to play in my younger days. That's it. In the drawers between the two parts there is on the right the cutlery and on the left the napkins of our guests. It is unbelievably stinky.

In this accumulation of many details, the dresser, a banal piece of furniture, becomes a weird and baroque object inhabited by a strange life. This description is also one of the many instances where the narrator uses the device of the inventory, a device he repeatedly tells himself to avoid and yet repeatedly employs. Perhaps the most clownish and ludicrous example of such listings is the passage in which the narrator thinks that the piece of paper he has lost is in the garbage can. Searching for it, he empties the can, enumerating systematically all the items he finds, delighting in mentioning gruesome details about rotten, soiled, or crumpled papers, cans, and rags. Fonfon is the pretext for scenes one might expect in films by Charlie Chaplin or the Marx Brothers—he always blunders. One of the most remarkable occurs at the dinner table: Fonfon keeps having trouble with whatever is in front of him; he pours too much water, his glass overflows, then he pulls the tablecloth, and so forth; the ensuing chain reaction affects the characters around the table and in the kitchen (p. 145). The narrator also chooses gaudy details having to do with clothes or a physical characteristic. Here is one of the boarders, Madame Apostolos, in a new dress:

> Elle apparaissait avec cette robe à grosses fleurs violettes sur fond émeraude. Elle en pince pour le violet. . . . Madame Erard . . . la faisait tourner pour la longueur de la robe. Et l'hippopotame tournait en se trouvant belle. Est-ce que ce n'est pas à vomir aussi? A pleurer en vomissant? [p. 92]

She would appear with this dress with big purple flowers on an emerald background. She is mad about purple. . . . Mrs. Erard . . . made her turn for the length of the dress. And the hippopotamus would turn fancying herself beautiful. Doesn't it make you throw up too? Cry in throwing up?

And here is a moment at the dinner table:

> Ils mangeaient leur fromage. Ça colle plus que le bifteck, je m'en rends compte avec Apostolos, son râtelier fait clac clac, pas clac clac, bien plus subtil, quand elle mange du fromage. Elle le repousse de la langue en avant pour attraper le fromage coincé et je pense qu'elle ramène aussi du bifteck. [p. 148]

They would eat their cheese. It sticks more than steak, I am aware of it with Apostolos, her dentures go clac, clac, not clac clac, much more subtle, when she eats cheese. She pushes forward with her tongue to catch the cheese which is stuck and I think that also brings back some steak.

To describe his characters, the narrator uses comical expression and comparisons: "Mademoiselle Reber, elle est Alsacienne, jusqu'au trognon, j'ai dit trognon" [p. 101] (Miss Reber, she is Alsatian to the core, I said core); "Reber a dit avec un sourir à fusiller à la merde ce n'est pas ce que je veux dire non, mais voyez-vous Monsieur Gaston" [p. 159] (Reber said with a smile which should be shot with shit it is not what I mean no, but you see Mr. Gaston).

Another technique that makes the narrator a clown involves his use of repetition, the machinelike behavior that Bergson describes as likely to provoke comedy. Not only does the narrator repeat the same details over and over, using the same distinctive words such as *la mouise* (hard times) and *la mistoufle* (maliciousness), but he also has his characters perform the same actions and repeat the same anecdotes. After a few pages, the reader knows that with a particular name or a particular situation a specific detail is always going to be mentioned. Thus Madame Apostolos always comes back from the bathroom (always called *les gogues*, a slang expression for bathroom) with a roll of tissue paper she has stolen. Gaston is associated with diarrhea. Every time Fonfon misbehaves, Madame Reber is ready to slap him (to give him *une mornifle*). The garden door, the scarecrow, and a weathervane are always mentioned in relation to the neighbor. When the conversation is about the meat at the dinner table, inevitably Madame Cointet brings up her trip with her husband to the Borromées islands in Italy. Madame Reber has only one topic of conversation, involving Alsace, storks, sauerkraut, and her nieces, which she always repeats. The tic or idiosyncracy the narrator attributes to himself is the habit of making memos or shopping lists: "Tell Gaston wine, light bulbs, Pernod."

The narrator also engages in a clownish performance in his discursive manipulations. He mingles slang and vulgar expressions with learned and sophisticated language, and constantly uses the prefix *re-*, which is common in French but here exaggerated to such a point that it becomes a mechanical feature of his style.

By means of his many verbal prancings, by attracting attention to himself as a joker, by seeming to sabotage his fiction with his metafictional comments, and by creating comic and tragic characters who are like caricatures in having one exaggerated defect, the narrator of *Quelqu'un* succeeds in performing a remarkable feat. He is a Balzacian narrator but one who makes fun of himself while describing the pathos, the absurdity, and the trivial quality of the boarders of a contemporary pension Vauquer—where, however, no Vautrin is going to be un-masked and nothing sordid is being plotted. He is also a narrator who draws attention to the act of storytelling. In not worrying about what is pertinent or necessary, in accumulating items as he pleases, and in asking whether one should write about feelings, objects, individuals, or metaphysics, he deconstructs the assumptions and conventions about what a narrative is or should be, and repeats what writers and readers know and have known: there are no fixed rules for telling stories.

The narrator also emerges as a sociologist-ethnographer. In his de-scriptions readers cannot fail to recognize familiar aspects of contem-porary French life, such as structured and repetitive existence and ev-eryday interactions and values of the French petite bourgeoisie. In fact, the narrator's details of what people eat (inexpensive meat, croquettes made with leftovers, fruit and vegetables of the season), what they wear (clothes from popular stores with bargains, one pair of new shoes a year), and their tastes (gaudy colors) are quite like the elements of sociologist Pierre Bourdieu's study of French life, documented in his book *La Distinction*. [19]

The presentation of spoken language in *Quelqu'un* mimics the natu-ralness, spontaneity, informality, and popular nature of conversation, gossip, and everyday interactions in the homes, neighborhood stores, local cafés, parks, and streets of contemporary France. In his "Pseudo-principes d'esthétique," Pinget explains that "spoken language, its noncodified syntax which molds the slight reflections of sensitivity, fascinates me," and he invents narrators who capture spoken language in their lexical choices and their syntactic constructions.

Quelqu'un's narrator uses such popular words and expressions as *en-quiquiner* (to irritate), *envoyer dinguer* (to push off), *allons-y mollo* (let's go easy), *je viens de me gourer* (I just made a boob). His characters express themselves in a very popular style: *il se souvenait bien, même qu'elle avait oublié sa valise* (he remembered well, she had forgotten her suitcase), *pas la peine de prendre du bleu qu'elle dit* (not necessary to buy blue cheese she said). The syntax of these examples is nonstandard, either because of the addition of superfluous words or phrases (*même que* in *même qu'elle avait oublié sa valise* or *qu'* in *qu'elle dit*) or because of the deletion of words (as in *pas la peine*). This seemingly careless and carefree narrator is quite aware of the social implications of different ways of speaking and com-municating. The following passage is truly a lesson in sociolinguistics:

Dire au voisin par exemple j'espère que notre pauvre petit ne vous importune pas. Dire importuner, ça fait cultivé. Qu'il ne me prenne pas pour n'importe qui, qu'il sente la distance. Ce con. . . . Le ton. Ce qu'il y a de plus difficile à attraper. Un faux ton peut vous amocher toute une vie. C'est effrayant quand on y pense. [p. 67]

Tell the neighbor for instance I hope that our poor little one does not trouble you. Say to importune. It sounds educated. So that he does not think I am just anybody, so that he feels the distance. That asshole. . . . The tone. It is what is the most difficult to catch. A wrong tone can mess up a whole life. It is frightening when you think about it.

Another striking aspect of the narrator's performance is his constant attention to the phonic components of language. This is achieved through the insistent and persistent repetition on the same page of the same name (Thérèse Newman, p. 157) or within the same sentence or paragraph of the same sound (*épouvantail, portail*). In addition, the narrator compulsively uses the names of his characters: Gaston, Marie, Madame Erard, Monsieur et Madame Cointet, Mademoiselle Reber, Madame Apostolos, and Fonfon. *Quelqu'un* is a mosaic of sounds in which Pinget shows concretely that he is a novelist who pays attention to and indeed highlights the aural and oral aspects of words.

Pinget states, again in his "Pseudo-principes d'esthétique," that his is a sort of automatic writing, an assertion implying lack of restraint and lack of control. But then he adds that he is completely conscious and that he screens what he writes. And even though he suggests that he does not understand his book very well, it is obvious that he has fully mastered his craft. Thus in *Quelqu'un* he invents a narrator who proposes conflicting but coexisting modalities. Indeed, *Quelqu'un* is both funny and sad, both playful and serious, both incongruous and logical, both repetitive and innovative. The narrator undermines and constructs, is bored and interested, exercises control and lets words take over. It is this movement of tension and these contradictions that push the text forward and give it momentum.

Fugue: The Adventures of Metaphors

Significantly, Roger Laporte's *Fugue,* published in 1970, is dedicated to Jacques and Marguerite Derrida. Like Laporte's previous works,

Fugue contains a set of meditations on and reflections about writing. Elegant, refined, and difficult, it is paradoxically exuberant and ascetic, static and dynamic, euphoric and dysphoric. As Laporte himself notices, the atmosphere of *Fugue* causes the reader to enter a very demanding world.[20]

Since Laporte believes that a writer's diary and notes are important to an understanding of his works, it seems appropriate to examine a selection of Laporte's comments from his *Carnets*, recorded about the time of the writing of *Fugue*.[21] In 1967 Laporte stated:

> I could not be just any writer, but a writer who, in one way or another, accommodates the "I," a solitary "I" of a solitude that shows concern for the problem of communication. [p. 249]

> I have not changed my mind: the work must have a single subject, a single theme: language, which is certainly narcissistic. . . . It should be that "the thing to say" = X be inseparable from language, understood not only as vocabulary, syntax but especially as rhythm. [p. 257]

> I have never accepted the classical opposition between saying and doing, even though it is a very ancient one since it is found in Heraclitus . . . to the contrary, I would like very much to do by saying, that my saying be a doing. [p. 258]

> To the degree that writing becomes in certain circumstances a receptive surface, it is this very act of writing that is suitable to emphasize. [p. 265]

These statements express the preoccupations and interests of the core of Laporte's enterprise: language, writing, reflections on language, and reflections on writing on the part of a self-conscious writer. They explain the essence of a strategy that is developed more fully in *Fugue*.[22]

Laporte invents an anonymous narrator who writes in the first person and who, in the space of nine numbered units that he calls sequences, presents his remarks and reflections about a set of interrelated topics centering on the subject of writing. Comments on the meaning of writing, on the status of the writer in general, and on the narrator's own feelings and attitudes about himself as a writer and on what he has written or is in the process of writing—all these make *Fugue* a reflexive text par excellence. Every word, every statement is an element participating in the exploration of the intellectual activity involved in writing at the very moment that the writing is taking place. This intense reflexive activity is not undertaken with a specific goal, as the narrator states very clearly: "Il n'appartient pas à l'aventure d'écrire, qui ne se dirige vers aucun but dernier, de s'achever d'elle même . . . mon parcours n'est donc pas guidé à distance par une fin ultime" [pp. 51–52] (It is not in the nature of the adventure of writing, which is not directed toward any final goal, to finish by itself . . . my journey is therefore not guided at a distance by some ultimate end).

The narrators of *L'Innommable* and *Quelqu'un* invent fragments of fiction, which they then comment upon, evaluate, and undermine by means of statements that are part of their metafiction. The narrator of *Fugue* behaves differently. His production is of a metafictional nature only. However, in order to discuss writing, he invents fictions; that is, instead of uttering abstract and general metafictional statements— such as "I do not like writing," "I am afraid of words," or "I do not feel like writing"—he expresses his feelings, ideas, and conceptions about writing by inventing metaphors. Beckett in *L'Innommable* also has his narrator behave in such a fashion, talking about his *supplice tarabiscoté,* his *foire,* and his *capharnaüm.* However, Laporte's narrator adds new dimensions and new possibilities to this technique. Instead of establishing an implicit rapport between an entity X and an entity Y, he presents X as Y modified by several factors. Here is an example in which the narrator discusses what it means to begin to write:

> Le commencement n'est pas tant une ligne à franchir qu'une période à traverser, un espace dans lequel il faut s'insinuer, espace qui n'est pas impénétrable, mais dont les pistes multiples se perdent ou s'enchevêtrent si bien qu'au lieu d'être rejeté au-dehors comme un intrus, on se retrouve avant le commencement et pourtant avec un passé derrière soi [pp. 16–17]

> The beginning is not so much a line to cross as a span of time to traverse, a space in which it is necessary to crawl, a space which is not impenetrable but where multiple trails become lost or so entangled that instead of being thrown out as an intruder, you find yourself again before the beginning yet with a past behind you.

In order to describe the pain he felt before beginning to write, he says:

> rien d'autre ne m'est arrivé que cette douleur, temps sans épaisseur qui précède le commencement; liséré vide qui borde le vide, très fine incision par laquelle l'écriture est touchée au coeur. [p. 17]

nothing else has happened to me besides this pain, time without thickness that precedes the beginning; empty edge which borders emptiness, very fine incision through which writing is touched to the heart.

The metaphors then lead to the invention of short narratives involving objects, characters, and actions where all the terms are pertinent because each additional element modifies the initial situation and makes it more complex, more concrete, and more refined. Fiction therefore is being created at the same time as metafiction, and Laporte through his narrator fulfills the wish he recorded in *Carnets*: to do while saying and make saying be a doing.

The content of *Fugue*'s mini-narratives is quite eclectic. A wide range of domains and activities, including various sciences, psychoanalysis, mythology, leisure and ludic activities, and crafts are referred to. In the following passages the narrator metaphorically discusses writing by inventing situations that refer successively to (1) gambling, (2) biology, (3) weaving, (4) a quest or search, and (5) banking.

> 1. Ecrire est une passion qui serait beaucoup moins vive, voire impossible, si l'ouvrage à écrire, et par conséquent l'écrivain lui-même, n'étaient misés à fonds perdus. [p. 22]

Writing is a passion that would be much less strong, if not impossible, were the work to be written and consequently the writer himself, not bet without backing.

> 2. J'oserai dire qu'un certain acte d'écrire est comparable à un mouvement amiboïde, est ce pseudopode par lequel le mobile vivant s'aventure vers l'inconnu. [p. 28]

I would go so far as to say that a certain act of writing is comparable to amoeboid motion, is this pseudopod by which the living mobile ventures toward the unknown.

3. Faut-il donc dire que l'acte d'écrire est analogue à un tissage où non seulement on ne saurait distinguer le tisserand de la navette, mais où celle-ci serait circonscrite, animée, voire tissée par les éléments actifs du tissu, véritables maîtres du jeu? Je le crois. [p. 48]

Should one say then that the act of writing is analogous to a weaving where not only could the weaver not be distinguished from the shuttle, but where the latter would be circumscribed, animated, even woven by the active components of the cloth, veritable masters of the game? I think so.

4. Ecrire est une chasse éperdue, une quête d'Isis, pour tenter de retrouver le fragment qui manque, une tentative désespérée pour rattraper ce qui fut perdu, pour recouvrer ce qui m'échappe et s'échappe. [p. 72]

Writing is a frantic hunt, a quest of Isis, to try to find again the missing fragment, a desperate attempt to regain what was lost, to recover what escapes me, and what escapes.

5. D'autres activités humaines demandent sans doute un investissement aussi grand que celui réclamé par l'écriture, mais à coup sûr ce dernier placement est le moins rentable de tous, car un immense travail se fait en pure perte. [p. 81]

Other human activities require without doubt as great an investment as that demanded by writing, but this is definitely the least profitable speculation, since an immense amount of work is done at a total loss.

Here are examples of mini-narratives that the narrator invents to discuss what a writer is. The writer is metaphorically described as (1) a pawn, (2) a puppet, (3) an archivist, (4) a tramp-wanderer, and (5) a weaver, hunter, and killer.

1. Je peux préciser que l'écrivain n'est pas tant un joueur qu'une pièce du jeu, pièce d'autant plus dangereusement exposée aux aléas de la partie qu'elle ne connaît par avance ni son rôle, ni ses pouvoirs, ni les règles de sa conduite. [p. 21]

I can specify that the writer is not so much a player as a piece in the game, a piece all the more dangerously exposed to the hazards of the game in that it knows neither its role, nor its powers, nor the rules of its behavior in advance.

2. Je n'érigerai point à la hauteur d'une lecture définitive cette figure apparue dans le texte, formée par le tissu, figure inattendue, dérisoire et quelque peu effrayante de cette marionnette à fils que l'on appelle communément l'auteur. [p. 49]

I shall not erect to the rank of a final reading this figure which appeared in the text, made up by the texture, unexpected, derisory and somewhat frightening of the string puppet, commonly called the author.

3. L'ouvrier en langage, loin d'être un créateur, travaille comme un singulier archiviste: il lit des documents qu'il a en partie rédigés lui-même, qu'il a jalousement conservés, non pas en raison de leur intérêt immédiat qui peut être nul, mais parce qu'ils sont susceptibles de former un autre texte [pp. 56–57]

The worker with language, far from being a creator, works like a peculiar archivist: he reads documents that he himself has partly drafted, that he has jealously guarded, not because of their immediate interest which may be null, but because they might well form another text

4. Sans domicile fixe, sans métier bien défini, l'anonyme, refoulé par l'ouvrage inconnu dans quelque no man's land, ne trouve point de repos: désoeuvré, pourtant il travaille, mais au sens où on le dit d'un navire, d'une maçonnerie, d'un étai [p. 61]

Without a fixed address, without a well-defined trade, the anonymous one, pushed back by the unknown book into some no man's land, cannot find rest: he is idle yet works, but in the sense in which this word is used for a ship, masonry, or a prop

5. Il rassemble en un réseau des éléments épars, il pratique le tissage, il joue donc le jeu de l'écriture; chasseur solitaire, homme de main du camp noir, il poursuit sans trêve ni pitié une proie invisible [p. 68]

He gathers scattered components into a network, he practices weaving, he is therefore playing the game of writing; solitary hunter, hired hand for the black camp, he relentlessly and pitilessly tracks down an invisible prey

In the passages where he assesses his own situation and his own writing, the narrator emphasizes that he cannot write what he wants— that his work progresses as if a virtual pseudopod were trying to take over parts of the text and the act of writing [p. 52]. At other times he describes himself as participating in a game in which he would be the only player, but in which his moves would be countered and his theories attacked by some impersonal opponent, a sort of unmanageable apparatus who despite this infringing behavior nevertheless permits the game to go on [p. 66]. Or he sees himself as being like a clockmaker who would try to repair a watch that has no hands and no dial [p. 69]. Or he feels that he has been expelled from his text, but at the same time the text is a net that keeps him prisoner [pp. 131–32].

For each of the topics he discusses—what is writing, what is a writer, what is the work that he is in the process of writing, what are his feelings as he writes—the narrator invents not one but several mini-narratives, resulting in the creation of an exuberant fictional-metafictional text. As in the musical form of the same name, in *Fugue* two principles or devices are put to work. On the one hand, there are repetitions and variations across the nine sequences, in which the same topics are discussed over and over. On the other hand, *Fugue* is animated by the forward movement of what the narrator calls "l'écriture et la contre-écriture" (writing and counterwriting). That is, once a fictional-metafictional statement has been elaborated, another one is invented that displaces the previous one. In fact, this constant displacement also occurs frequently within one statement or mini-narrative, as in example 5 cited above, where the metaphor of the weaver is displaced by that of the hunter which in turn is displaced by that of the hired killer. Consequently, the narrator, who is seemingly striving to capture the complexity of the experience of writing by exploring a multiplicity of facets and possibilities, is really constantly moving away from and avoiding a set of stable meanings.

The semantic network elaborated by the narrator is characterized by extreme diversity but also, because of the consistently negative connotations of the situations he chooses, by unity. Many of the activities chosen to represent writing—weaving, banking, using instruments and apparatuses, preserving documents, gambling, acting—imply knowledge, organization, and skill. But the behavior and the actions correlated with those activities show the participant, namely the narrator, as incapable of controlling the situation or without any possibility of control because there are flaws, failures, or disturbances or because parts are missing, broken, or torn. The references to tramps and nomads connote marginality, illegality, transiency; a pseudopod suggests an inferior form of life; puppets, harlequins, and mannequins suggest fabrication and make-believe.

In addition, the narrator inserts statements of doubt, admits his incapacities, and professes his ignorance: hence the frequent use of such expressions as "I am incapable of," "I know only," "I do not know," "I do not understand well," and "it might be." And he uses verbs in the future, the infinitive, and the conditional so that what is stated remains potential and prospective rather than actualized. In order to sap his verbal performance even more, he evaluates it in negative terms: "ce à quoi je tiens le plus me paraît à présent douteux ou du moins peu compréhensible" [p. 105] (that which I value the most seems to me doubtful at the present time or at least barely understandable); "une confusion sans nom . . . a gagné l'ouvrage tout entier" [p. 131] (a nameless confusion . . . has invaded the whole work). *Fugue* thus displays a constellation of components by which the narrator shows that his enterprise is a perilous quest fraught with dangers, problems, instability, and inadequacy.

However, although the narrator—like those of *Quelqu'un* and *L'Innommable*—does not offer explicit positive arguments to counter his negativity, he does provide many indications that writing, being a writer, and his own writing and his being a writer are in fact meaningful and important. Begun by chance, fortuitously, as the narrator says [p. 75], this enterprise is an adventure that pleases and fascinates him. For instance, *la contre-écriture*, which is a source of instability, provokes in him "un attrait violent pour l'inconnu" [p. 45] (a violent attraction for the unknown). He wonders "pourquoi cette aventure si risquée continue-t-elle à me tenir tellement à coeur [p. 75] (why does this adventure so fraught with danger continue to be so dear to my heart)? And he admits that a period during which he stopped writing was a "période aigre d'ennui ou d'agitation vaine, de souffrance sèche et surtout d'exclusion" [p. 107] (a bitter period of boredom or of vain agitation, of dry suffering and above all of exclusion).

At the beginning of the text, the narrator makes two statements that mingle positive and negative elements. He speaks of the literary enterprise as having the "caractère aléatoire de dangereuse merveille" [pp. 36–37] (aleatory character of dangerous wonder), and he compares the work that goes on within a writer's mind to *travail*—that is, to the warping, cracking, bending, and swelling that affect the hull of a ship, a wooden beam, or a concrete building, adding that for him who takes such a risk "un jour la chance peut sourire" [p. 61] (one day fortune might smile on him). These are signs, warnings, and promises announcing that something may happen, that there may be a favorable outcome to this perilous quest. And something does happen at the end of sequence 7 and of sequence 9, something one might call an illumination, or a revelation, or a rebirth, or a resurrection. These are temporary metaphors suggested by the text. My use of the terms is not a move aimed at coyly mimicking Laporte's narrator; it is the only way to approach the meaning that he wants to convey, for in *Fugue* no statement can be made that does not need correction or modification, especially in these particular sections of the text. The narrator describes intense feelings that he has experienced or that a writer might experience. At the end of sequence 7 he writes:

> une fois que j'eus découvert qu'en effet non seulement je travaillais en pure perte, mais que j'avais perdu même la possibilité de travailler, une fois donc que le vide se fut articulé sur le vide, je sus que tout s'était accompli, que, faute de pouvoir écrire, la chance m'avait été donnée de pouvoir dire: enfin rien n'est arrivé, rien d'autre ne m'est arrivé et ne m'arrivera jamais que ce rien devenu en secret une claire féerie réservée pour le matin de la résurrection. je suis seul à le savoir [pp. 101–02]

> once I had discovered that in effect not only was I working all for naught, but that I had lost even the possibility of working, once, then, emptiness had been articulated over emptiness, I knew that everything had been accomplished, that, although I could not write, I had been given the luck to say: finally nothing happened, nothing else has happened to me or will ever happen besides this nothing secretly become a clear enchantment reserved for the morning of the resurrection. I am the only one to know it

In this "revelation," what is impossible and paradoxical becomes possible, clear, and logical. Luck, enchantment, and resurrection are the result of emptiness and nothingness, but emptiness and nothingness are not signs of failure or misfortune. As the narrator sees it, nothing is everything. At the end of sequence 9, the final sequence of the text, he terminates his journey on the following note:

> Beaucoup est ainsi donné et surtout exigé, mais tout autre est l'énigmatique félicité apportée de loin en loin par la fête . . . ce "tu n'as pas encore commencé d'écrire", ce rien, loin de provoquer une frustration, donne bientôt un bonheur ignoré; par la faveur d'un temps prophétique qui à rebours annonce le futur antérieur, la main si jeune qu'elle n'a jamais tenu un style, est sur le point d'être touchée par la première lueur du soleil levant. [pp. 169–70]

> Thus much is given and above all demanded, but altogether different is the enigmatic felicity brought at distant intervals by the celebration . . . this "you have not yet begun to write," this nothing, far from provoking frustration, soon gives unknown happiness: owing to a prophetic time that backwards heralds the future perfect, the hand so young it has never held a stylus, is just about to be touched by the first light of the rising sun.

Two states are described in this passage, the result of not having written yet, of being faced with the white page. One connotes a euphoric condition par excellence, since it is a perfect state of "félicité" and "bonheur," which remains "énigmatique" and "ignoré" and therefore not banal, not common, because not completely known or accessible. The other state is a liminal one concretized also by two notions: that of dawn, between night and day, and that of a young hand that has never held a stylus, has not yet mastered the skills of an adolescent or an adult. Both these notions connote purity, virginity, and beginning. What the narrator discovers during his journey, then, is the revelation of the possibility or the promise of bliss and exaltation provoked by emptiness and nothingness.

The numbering of the sequences does not seem haphazard. The choice of nine sequences with important moments occurring at the end of sequences 7 and 9 makes the reader suspect or want to think of numeral symbolism. First, 7 and 9 reflect the positive and active qualities that are symbolically attached to uneven numbers.[23] In medieval philosophy the number 7 is associated with a set of positive circumstances; it signifies completeness and perfection. It also stands for the seven days of the week, the seven beatitudes, and the seven steps to wisdom. At the end of sequence 7, the narrator reaches an important moment in his journey: he realizes the value of nothingness. He has completed something after toiling and suffering during the seven sequences. Number 9 is considered to be a number close to perfection because of its nearness to the number 10. This closeness to perfection is what the narrator describes at the end of sequence 9. The enigmatic felicity is brought about by the fact that someone has not yet begun to write and that the young hand is about to be touched by the first glimpse of the rising sun.

It should be noted that the revelation of the power of nothingness, emptiness, and potentiality does not cancel out the difficulties of writing and of being a writer. The narrator finishes his journey by affirming that writing and the situation of the writer are such that joy and torment, strength and weakness, power and powerlessness are his lot:

> Il faut affirmer qu'en s'adonnant au jeu d'écrire, l'écrivain, même en tant qu'homme, accède à une intensité de joie, de tourment, d'effroi, de détresse, de liberté, de surprise, de verve [p. 168]

> It is necessary to affirm that in devoting himself to the game of writing, the writer, even as a man, reaches an intensity of joy, torment, fright, distress, freedom, surprise, verve

He also states that his task requires a combination of qualities that are directly opposed to one another: ambition and detachment, control and freedom, seriousness and lightness or even frivolity [p. 163].

This is what the narrator of *Fugue* has to say about writing in general. What about his own writing? The narrator elaborates a text that is a chain, a series of stages, steps, moments, within an overall productive effort. This chain, like a Cartesian meditation, does not establish an objective accumulation of results independent of the narrator who discusses them; rather, it both draws him inside the process of production and describes his efforts, his act of writing, and his writing. Consequently, the narrator establishes an interdependence between himself, the act of writing, and his writing, an interdependence that results in a centerless network of connected elements, recounting his mental, emotional, and physical journey through words.

Within the text of *Fugue* itself, the narrator states that writing requires both refined attention and a love of the most precise language. His text is a perfect demonstration of these general prescriptions. It is an elegant, logical, and perfectly balanced verbal construct where every sentence is tightly organized and every word carefully chosen. It avoids monotony and dryness by being poetical and emotive, scientific and argumentative, and by mingling declarative sentences, questions, and exclamations.

Fugue bristles with activity because of the sheer number of its metaphors. In his mini-narratives the narrator uses and modifies classic metaphors for writing—such as weaving or making an imprint with a stylus—and also invents new ones by exploiting various mythologies, alchemy, Indian philosophy, psychoanalysis, the performing arts, topology, technology, gambling, and such games as chess. His inventiveness is a constant invitation to coin new metaphors.

Aristotle writes that "good riddles do, in general, provide us with satisfactory metaphors: for metaphors imply riddles, and therefore a good riddle can furnish a good metaphor."[24] This proximity of riddle and metaphor is actualized in *Fugue,* in which one can consider the narrator to be a riddler in the process of experimenting with various metaphors in the creation of two-part statements describing writing, the writer, and the situation of the writer. The narrator never finds satisfactory solutions but keeps proposing new ones, so that his mind and the readers' minds as well are always alert, thinking, open to possibilities, and juggling elements in order to find solutions to the making of these riddles.[25]

The analogy with the riddler leads to an understanding of other aspects of the narrator's performance. Riddling is a form of speech play that enables children and adults to experiment with language and to explore facets and relationships of reality. Similarly, the narrator of *Fugue* is experimenting with his language, knowledge, and culture. In many societies riddles provide a ludic as well as a symbolic means of expressing and stressing metaphysical truths and realities. These often have to do with death, as in Caribbean societies in which riddling takes place during a wake, when family and friends mourn in the presence of the deceased.[26] Such practices illustrate the fact that life is a riddle, or a series of riddles, and that the ultimate riddle, death, cannot be solved. The narrator's production in *Fugue,* through its chains of metaphors, is capable of provoking uneasiness and reminding readers, overtly or covertly, that there are no final metaphors, that there is no answer other than the emptiness of death. Writing leads us to metaphor, metaphor to riddle, and riddle to death.

By means of his enigmatic metaphors and his metaphorical riddles, the narrator of *Fugue* experiences the power and the powerlessness of language and writing. His reflections have an ontological status because ultimately they ask what is language, how do we make sense, and what are the possibilities and limits of sense-making. On the one hand the narrator displays his creativity, and on the other he shows that it is impossible, that he is incapable of finding final metaphors defining what is writing and what is a writer, because, as he says, "il n'y a jamais correspondance terme à terme" [p. 97] (there is never a one-to-one correspondence).

It is of the utmost importance to realize that the narrator does not feel himself to be in a predicament. He specifies that no evil genius is preventing him from succeeding or is playing tricks on him, which was the case for the narrator of *L'Innommable.* "Ce qui compte c'est d'être en perpétuelle poursuite, en perpétuelle rupture" (what counts is to be in perpetual pursuit, in perpetual rupture), says Laporte quoting Blanchot, and this is the stance that he has his narrator adopt in *Fugue.*[27]

In his *Carnets* [pp. 288–89], Laporte explains: "Nothing resembles *Fugue* and *Fugue* resembles nothing, neither in literature, nor in music, etc., although for particular aspects, with regard to certain situations, it is possible to find harmonics: I think not only about certain works quoted above [*Destroyed Country* by Klee, *Man Who Walks II* by Giacometti], but also about certain works by Lardera, about Kowalski, and even more about *Memory* by Vieira da Silva."

Other harmonics also come to mind. There is the notion of convulsive beauty, coined by André Breton in *Nadja,* which he illustrates with a train in a station about to depart and by the fragment of a message received by a wireless operator but never completed and its sender never identified—situations that are neither dynamic nor static. In *Fugue*, the narrator's quest toward definitions of writing and of the status of the writer, definitions never satisfactorily formulated because of the game of writing and counterwriting, creates a text that is neither dynamic nor static but constantly pulsating, bristling with energy. Or, to state it from a more recent and quite compatible perspective, the movement created by the chain of metaphors in which one metaphor is constantly displaced by another makes *Fugue* a text that actualizes—stages, as it were—the notion of *différance* advocated by Derrida, for indeed each new metaphor introduces a difference and postpones a final meaning.

Another aspect of the narrator's performance, his use of nine sequences, suggests yet another perspective. *Fugue* is a mental and spiritual journey progressing through stages and leading to a mystical experience or to a revelation, as in *The Mind's Road to God* by Saint Bonaventure, presented in seven stages, and Descartes's six-stage *Meditations*. However, in *Fugue* there is no progression. Rather, there is a movement from metaphor to metaphor, each metaphor modifying the previous one without establishing an ascending or a descending chain. Furthermore, neither the presence of God nor the possibility of a certainty is posited, and no stability or resolution emerges from the deliberations and reflections of the narrator. Instead, he affirms, in a Mallarméan-like posture, the importance of nothingness and emptiness as an impetus that sets entities in motion, as a dynamic propeller that pushes them forward.[28]

Effects of Reflexivity

L'Innommable, Quelqu'un, and *Fugue* propose a type of representation that highlights and promotes the unfinished. By writing texts that read as though they were works in progress, including and indeed privileging backstage reflections and preoccupations, the narrators break with the tradition that readers should be provided with a completed text. Quite the contrary: in these texts the finished product reads as if it were an unfinished product. Of course, these texts are not really works in progress. They are fakes or imitations of works in progress, quite distinct from the unpublished drafts of novels that writers sometimes destroy, sometimes sell, or donate to libraries and other manuscript collections. They must also be distinguished from the oral and written statements, in letters and other documents and conversations, that writers often make about their creations. Rather, *L'Innommable, Quelqu'un,* and *Fugue* exploit the concepts of backstage scriptive behavior and works in progress, which are traditional behaviors in and of themselves, as resources in the creation of a finished, final product—just as Maurice Roche uses proofreader's notations as a resource in the creation of his finished product (see chapter 3). The result in each case is a text in which there is a constant oscillation and tension between the unfinished and the finished, between the real work in progress and the imitation work in progress.

The narrators of *L'Innommable, Quelqu'un,* and *Fugue,* as an important aspect of their creation of unfinished texts, are not assertive or affirmative. Instead, their discourse is elaborated by means of questions, negations, exclamations, and conditional and infinitive rather than indicative verbs, so that hypotheses, proposals, and approximations are favored. These narrators have opted to work with edges, borders, potentialities, and virtualities. For them, uncertainties, difficulties, and incompleteness do not have crippling consequences; on the contrary, they are positive elements that set the text in motion. These features and characteristics of the narrator's performance constitute reversals and questionings of logocentric practices, which imply closure, assertion, and stability. In addition, the narrators set up no polarities, or dichotomies; they are antidialecticians. They create contradictions but provide no mediation or synthesis, not even the possibility of achieving one.

The narrators of *L'Innommable, Quelqu'un,* and *Fugue,* who repeatedly proclaim their ignorance and lack of knowledge, are in fact skillful manipulators who reframe and thus reactualize works or intellectual attitudes of the past. By means of remarks in their metafiction, they overtly flout principles of order, logic, and continuity and as a result elaborate an implicit anti–*art poétique.* Beckett's narrator goes so far as to name the classic rhetorical principles and make fun of them. Pinget's narrator similarly mocks Boileau's famous distich. Laporte's narrator creates a network of topics, but instead of relating them in a logical, causal order, he juxtaposes them with the musical principle of the fugue. All three of these narrators, with their direct and at times arrogant interventions, playfully reframe the topos of affected modesty whereby a narrator excuses himself for his ignorance or his incompetence. And with the various techniques these narrators use to undermine and cast doubt on what they write, they elaborate a rhetoric of discredit. Marc Le Bot, in discussing Marcel Duchamp's artistic practices, notices that "all the activities seem to be situated under the sign of the unfinished, the temporary, the doubtful, the aleatory—in short, under the general sign of the failure of well-dominated artistic intentions. And doubtless their obsessive character is the product of a certain form of anguish."[29]

Similarly, as they state repeatedly, Beckett's, Pinget's, and Laporte's narrators endure anguish and torment, yet the unfinished, the doubtful, the seemingly negative are not to be considered as symptoms of failure or discouragement but rather as artistic springboards that keep the text in suspense, only seeming to be moving toward something to be realized, which will never be accomplished.

"The history of intruding narrators is full of sheer overflowing narrative exuberance, as if the story itself, good as it is, did not provide adequate scope for the author's genius," writes Wayne Booth.[30] The self-conscious narrators of *L'Innommable, Quelqu'un,* and *Fugue* display, in Booth's terms, "overflowing exuberance." Their "genius," however, is put into action not, as with the traditional intruding narrators of the type Booth has in mind, in order to devise strategies to explain or supplement what they write but to avoid writing a story and to overtly and resourcefully undermine what they write. By putting words and ideas into circulation, these fascinating individuals draw attention to themselves as narrators. Inserting themselves in a "neutral region when he, who in order to write has fallen into the absence of time, sinks henceforth having given himself to words,"[31] they experience a journey through different states, by means of language, during which the mind, the intellect, words, culture, hope, despair, joy, and boredom continuously interact. They demonstrate that writing is not an innocent act but an arduous task that involves a continuous fight with words and with oneself.

Self-assertive subjects, the narrators display the values of narcissism and of ludic exhibitionism, and point ironically to what they are not: romantic narrators inspired by a muse, or passive objects who do not speak themselves but are spoken to. They trust and mistrust language at the same time, observing themselves performing linguistically with virtuosity; manipulating the lexical, syntactic, and phonic properties of language. They also enjoy the confrontation they establish with those they are narrating to and with their readers, taunting them, testing their patience, and creating tensions. Their game, which involves excess and limitation, which is play in order to accomplish nothing, can be interpreted as having a metaphysical orientation. For indeed, like Sisyphus, these narrators are bound— but, bound by choice and with words, they are optimistic with regard to their fate. They actualize and enact the fundamental signifiers existing in the lives of all individuals:[32] the difficulty of being and of living, the torments of the uncertainties that disturb and at the same time stimulate individuals throughout their lives, the tensions between wanting to do and being able to do (*vouloir et pouvoir*), between activity and passivity, between creation and destruction.

5

**Postmodern
Feminist Fiction**

*A woman's writing is always
feminine; it cannot help being
feminine; the only difficulty
lies in defining what we mean
by feminine.*
Virginia Woolf

*It is up to the artist in
particular . . . to stress, to
place a maximal emphasis on all
that springs from the feminine
system of the world*
André Breton

This chapter is devoted to three
texts written by women about
women. It is deliberately placed
after the chapters dealing with
men's texts in order to achieve a
better understanding of the differences and similarities between
men's and women's writing. The three texts considered here are
Monique Wittig's *Les Guérillères*, Marguerite Duras's *L'Amour,* and
Hélène Cixous's *Souffles.* These three *écrivaines*, like the *écrivains* discussed in the preceding chapters, have all made theoretical statements
about writing.

Cixous in *La Jeune Née* enjoins women to write. Addressing herself
to them in a tone both intimate and galvanic, and using the familiar
pronoun *tu,* she states:

About femininity women have almost everything to write:
about their sexuality, that is about the infinite and mobile complexity of their eroticization, about the dazzling ignitions of
such a minute-immense region of their body, not about destiny,
but about the adventure of such a drive, trips, crossings, pro-

gressions, sudden and slow awakenings, discoveries of a zone formerly shy, now surging. . . . Write yourself: your body must be heard. Then the immense resources of the unconscious will spring out. Finally the inexhaustible feminine imaginary will deploy itself. Our naphtha, it is going to spread, without gold or black dollars, onto the world, of the free-floating securities which change the rules of the game.[1]

Duras in an interview explains:

I think "feminine literature" is an organic, translated writing . . . translated from blackness, from darkness. Women have been in darkness for centuries. They don't know themselves. Or only poorly. And when women write, they translate this darkness. Men don't translate. They begin from a theoretical platform that is already in place, already elaborated. The writing of women is really translated from the unknown, like a new way of communicating rather than an already formed language. But to achieve that, we have to turn away from plagiarism. There are many women who write as they think they should write—to imitate men and make a place for themselves in literature. Colette wrote like a little girl, a turbulent and terrible and delightful little girl. So she wrote "feminine literature" as men wanted it. That's not feminine literature in reality. It's feminine literature seen by men and recognized as such. It's the men who enjoy themselves when they read it. I think feminine literature is a violent, direct literature and that, to judge it, we must not—and this is the main point I want to make—start all over again, take off from a theoretical platform.[2]

And Wittig has her protagonists in *Les Guérillères* discuss and assess the situation of women in the following way:

The women say, unhappy one, men have expelled you from the world of signs. . . . They say, the language you speak is made up of signs that rightly speaking designate what men have appropriated. Whatever they have not laid hands on, whatever they have not pounced on like many-eyed birds of prey, does not appear in the language you speak.[3]

Given such declarations, what do these *écrivaines* have to say and how do they say it; how do they create representation and how do they organize it; what linguistic and discursive techniques do they elaborate?

There are texts of older women that I have recently read, which are texts going back to the very body of woman, very carnal, very sensual, texts of exploration. Texts of "hunger," indeed and of thirst: they bathe in lexicon, they devour words, they are like a kind of enormous verbal gourmandize. . . . You see suddenly an enormous bulimia of language or to the contrary a text of an alarming leanness. [4]

In a coincidental and indeed uncanny way, these remarks by Cixous, although not intended to describe the texts of Duras, Wittig, and Cixous herself, do so remarkably well. For *Les Guérillères* and *Souffles* are two types of text that exhibit exuberance and verbal greediness, while *L'Amour* is a lean and sober verbal construct. Certain crucial questions come to mind when we read and analyze these three texts, each offering dynamic and positive experiences in its own specific way. Are these texts different from those of the men I have analyzed in previous chapters? How should any difference be understood? What is feminine about these texts? How should we understand feminine? Are *Les Guérillères, L'Amour,* and *Souffles* feminist texts? In what ways? How do they insert themselves into the contemporary literary and cultural scene?

Les Guérillères: Systematic Reversals

Monique Wittig entered the French literary scene in 1964 with a great flourish, being awarded the prestigious Prix Médicis for her first book, *L'Opoponax*. A sensitive exploration of childhood in a style hovering between spoken and written French, it was hailed by critics as the vehicle for the invention of a new language. Since then Wittig has published several works: *Les Guérillères, Le Corps lesbien,* and *Brouillon pour un dictionnaire des amantes,* written in collaboration with Sande Zeig.

The title *Les Guérillères* is a portmanteau word, from *guérrières* (warriors) and *guérilla* (guerrilla). This might lead one to think that the text is essentially about warfare. There are indeed a few episodes describing actual battles, but it is in fact the peaceful activities the characters engage in, rather than their bellicose ones, that have the subversive implications and destructive effects of guerrilla and war.

Les Guérillères is about *petites filles* (little girls), adolescents or young women who live in an imprecisely located geographical and historical place and who are involved sometimes in pastoral activities, sometimes in highly technological and even futuristic ones; sometimes in violent actions and sometimes in hedonistic, poetical, and harmonious ones.[5] These little girls form a community with its own social organization and distinctive patterns of living, play, and ritual. Everything seems to be the result of a complex organization whereby every action is prepared and then performed according to a definite protocol. At no point, however, does the life in this community give one the feeling that a rigid system is imposed by some ruling authority; this is a collectivity where everything is decided upon in common and performed in common.

It is always as a group that the little girls participate in their various activities. They play games; they swim; they catch birds; and they perform such tasks as going to market, picking cherries, gathering leaves, and making ointments by pressing nuts and flowers. They engage in ceremonies and rituals. Their educational programs function mainly through oral communication: one of the little girls tells a story, another one relates a myth, and another interprets a picture for the entire community. They read books about women, which they call *féminaires* (feminaries), coining a neologism on the model of medieval bestiaries. In these feminaries they learn about women and womanhood. More specifically, they learn how the feminine body and its sexual organs have been talked about; how women have been treated, and what women have achieved. They talk about changing language and about making a new dictionary. In a kind of auto-da-fé ceremony they burn the feminaries because what these books say is outrageous, inacceptable, and above all passé. They pile up all the objects traditionally associated with women: sewing machines, typewriters, knitting materials, pots, pans, brushes, brooms, and washing machines. These objects, deemed prejudicial and harmful, are burned in a gigantic fire around which the little girls dance. They also declare wars and fight battles.

Les Guérillères is divided by means of typographical devices and content into three parts. In the first part, the little girls gain an awareness of their bodies and of society's attitude toward women. The second part, with the auto-da-fé and the wars against men, destroys the old order. The third part establishes a new order. "Elles disent qu'elles partent de zéro, que c'est un nouveau monde qui commence" [p. 121] (They say that they are starting from zero. They say that a new world is beginning [p. 85]). The little girls make peace with young men and cover them with flowers. They call for a halt to violence and for equality and harmony.

Because of its discursive, stylistic, semantic, and typographical characteristics, *Les Guérillères* is a highly structured and harmonious text containing just a few elements that create a slight imbalance in an uncanny fashion. Typographically, it is precisely constructed. Set between two poems, one at the beginning and one at the end, the text is broken up by several devices. Three times a circle appears on an otherwise blank page [pp. 2, 71, 138, French; pp. 7, 51, 96, English]. At intervals of five or six pages there is a centered block of women's names in capital letters, as in the following example [p. 119, French; p. 83, the English]:

VASA	FABIENNE	BELLISSUNU
NEBKA	MAUD	ARETE	MAAT
ATALANTE	DIOMEDE	URUK
OM	FRANCOISE	NAUSICAA
POUDOUHEPA		KOUWATALLA
ACATHOCLEE	BOZENA	NADA

The descriptions of the activities of the little girls are presented in short stanza-like sections, separated by blank space. An unnamed narrator whose gender is not recognizable and who never directly manifests any presence expresses himself/herself in the present tense, using third-person feminine pronouns (*elle, elles*) or names of women to the almost total exclusion of masculine counterparts.[6] This narrator repeatedly uses the same item of discourse—namely, speech acts of reporting—signaled by the phrase *elles disent* (they say), *L'une d'elles raconte* (one of them tells), or *elles rappellent* (they remind).

Another distinctive feature of *Les Guérillères* is its frequent enumeration of items belonging to specific semantic fields. The lists of women's names are instances of this device; other lists within the descriptions of activities create a feeling of abundance, exuberance, and exhaustiveness by the quantity of items juxtaposed without any punctuation. The following examples accumulate (1) spices, (2) varieties of cherries, (3) industries, and (4) imaginary tribes:

1. Ou bien on cherche, à tâtons en reniflant celle dont le parfum est honoré. L'amome l'anis le bétel la cannelle la cubède la menthe le réglisse le musc le gingembre le girofle la muscade le poivre le safran la sauge la vanille peuvent être honorées successivement. [pp. 9–10]

Or else they search gropingly, scenting the one whose perfume is to be honoured. Amomum aniseed betel cinnamon cubeb mint liquorice [*sic*] musk ginger clove nutmeg pepper saffron sage vanilla receive homage in turn. [p. 9]

2. Les paniers au pied des arbres peuvent être pleins de cerises à ras bord. Il y a des belles de Choisy des cerises anglaises des griottes des marascas des cerises de Montmorency des bigaudelles des guignes. Elles sont noires blanches rouges translucides. [p. 23]

The baskets at the foot of the trees are filled at times to overflowing. There are belles de Choisy English cherries morelles marascas Montmorency cherries bigaudelles white-hearts. They are black white red translucent. [p. 18]

3. Elles ont mis la main sur des usines d'aéronautique d'électronique de balistique d'informatique. Elles sont dans les fonderies les hauts fourneaux les chantiers navals les arsenaux les raffineries les distilleries. [p. 137]

They have taken possession of aeronautical electronic ballistic data-processing factories. They are in the foundries tall furnaces navy yards arsenals refineries distilleries. [p. 95]

4. Les Ophidiennes les Odonates les Oogones les Odoacres les Olynthiennes les Oolithes les Omphales celle d'Ormur celles d'Orphise les Oriennes ont passé à l'attaque, rassemblées. [p. 149]

The Ophidian women the Odonates the Oogones the Odoacres the Olynthians the Ooliths the Omphales the women of Ormur of Orphise the Oriennes have massed and gone over the attack. [p. 103]

Les Guérillères maintains a consistently elegant and refined style in which lexically there is a mingling of banal, colloquial, exotic, and scientific items. This device is exemplified in the listing of women's names, which combine such common European names as Marie, Renée, and Colette with others from various cultures that have an unfamiliar phonetic ring and morphological construction: Damhuraci, Poupouhépa, Kouwatally, Vivvarara, Bhatitarika. The many enumerations of items within the same semantic field are occasions for vocabulary displays. They constitute mini-poems inserted into the middle of narratives. The recurrence of lists inserted at regular intervals within narrative units provides cohesion to the text as a whole.

Cohesion is also created by the use of shape. Ricardou's, Robbe-Grillet's, and Simon's texts, discussed in chapter 2, each offers a type of representation in which repeated shapes foregrounded in different entities are factors of cohesion. In *Les Guérillères* one shape, the circle, is overwhelmingly prevalent, being indexed semantically and iconically in many entities and functioning as a unifying principle. In addition to being literally present on several pages, the circle is represented in objects (such as hoops and alveolar dwellings), movements (circular dances), and parts of the female anatomy, (vulva and breasts)—all entities that are described, alluded to, or utilized in the little girls' activities.

On the other hand, and against the backdrop of this cohesion, several devices in *Les Guérillères* create unbalance. Some affect the narrative organization of the text, some its discourse, and others its typography. No causal, temporal, or semantic links relate one section to another: they are simply juxtaposed, each being independent. Likewise, the events within each section are presented one after the other as independent entities; thus each section is a self-contained narrative with its own series of actions and behaviors.[7] Violent activities having to do with killing and torture conflict with and counterbalance idyllic and peaceful activities like picking cherries or making perfumes. There are also surrealist-futuristic scenes like the following:

Parfois elles tournent sur elles-mêmes comme des toupies, la
tête dans leurs bras. C'est dans ce mouvement qu'elles exhalent
un parfum d'arum de lys de verveine qui se répand d'un seul
coup dans l'espace autour d'elles. Le parfum est différent suivant
la vitesse de leurs rotations. Il se décompose en passant par des
tonalités diverses. . . . Cela sent les feuilles qui pourrissent
dans la terre, les cadavres d'oiseaux. Quand la nuit tombe, elles
quittent leurs fourrures pour se coucher. Elles les disposent en
formes de sacs, elles les suspendent aux branches des arbres et se
glissent à l'intérieur. Leur colonie est vue courant les arbres, à
perte de vue de grosses boules de fourrures. [p. 70]

Sometimes they spin on themselves like tops, heads in arms. It is during this movement that they exhale a perfume of arum lily verbena
which spreads instantly through the surrounding space. The perfume
differs according to the speed of their rotation. It disintegrates passing
through various tonalities. . . . It smells of leaves decaying in the
earth, the corpses of birds. When night falls they emerge from their
furs to go to bed. They arrange them in the shape of bags, they hang
them from the branches of trees and slip inside. Their colony is seen to
cover the trees, as far as eye can reach, with great fur bundles. [p. 50]

Slight syntactic manipulations also create unbalance. In the following example, adjectives are used inconsistently—sometimes
there are none or only one; at other times there are two:

On va au marché pour se procurer les provisions. . . . Il y a des
entassements d'oranges orange d'ananas ocres de mandarines de
noix de mangues vertes et roses de brugnons bleus de pêches
vertes et roses d'abricots jaune orange. [p. 13]

The women visit the market to obtain provisions. . . . There are piles
of orange oranges ochre pineapples mandarines walnut green and pink
mangoes blue nectarines green and pink peaches orange yellow apri-
cots. [p. 11]

Although grammatical gender is for the most part respected, at
times there are distortions, irregularities, and deviations. *Quelqu'un*
(someone) becomes *quelqu'une* (someone-feminine), which does not
exist in French. In a description of a landscape, instead of finding the

unmarked generic term *vaches* (cows), readers are surprised and amused by the mention of the presence only of *génisses* (heifers).

Typographically, once in a while and without any regularity, in the last of the three sections of the text, slashes interrupt the continuity of the mini-narratives:

> Quatre d'entre elles l'emportant en chantant, derrière mes paupières/le songe n'atteint pas mon esprit/que je dorme ou que je veille/il n'y a pas de repos. [p. 91]

> Four of the women carry her, singing, behind my eyelids/the dream has not reached my soul/whether I sleep or wake/there is no rest. [p. 64]

Raymond Jean, in trying to explain the odd quality of Wittig's writing in *Les Guérillères,* speaks of "sparseness and alacrity of language."[8] To these characteristics, with which I concur, it is necessary to add also the familiar and the unexpected; the normal and the uncanny; and the tightness, order, and regularity loosened by heterogeneity, disjunctions, and discontinuity.[9]

Atemporal, ahistorical, not describing recognizable geographical settings, *Les Guérillères* presents the progressive elaboration of a society where harmony is achieved thanks to the will, the intelligence, and the strength of its members. It is a utopia, but as a utopia it is double-edged: it not only creates an imaginary world but implicitly criticizes a specific historical situation. As Louis Marin notices in his study of utopias: "The function of representation thus constructed is to dissimulate and to present at the same time the historical and ideological contradiction."[10] What does *Les Guérillères* dissimulate and present?

The title is one of the clues to the text, and it points to what is going on strategically. *Les Guérillères* is a text that works on the model of guerrilla warfare; that is, instead of a large, massive deployment of force, it prefers small, sporadic, local operations frequently repeated. In its euphoric and triumphant series of tableaux, it orchestrates reversals and counterexamples that repeatedly attack and undermine behaviors and stereotypes about women in particular and about individuals' behavior and possibilities more generally.

The most obvious reversal concerns a literary convention. *Les*

Guérillères is almost exclusively about women. Instead of having male heroes or antiheroes with women as their companions, sex objects, wives, mothers, or lovers, life in this society functions by and with women. Men play a secondary role, and they are the victims: each new generation of young men is initiated according to the laws that the little girls have devised. However, *Les Guérillères* does not focus on a heroine or antiheroine; it is about no one woman in particular but about all women, who are summoned in its pages. The lists of female names that form onomastic poems group well-known mythological or literary heroines, goddesses, criminals, and victims with the names of anonymous women who exist somewhere in many different countries. Women are not "chassées du monde des signes" [p. 162] (expelled from the world of signs [p. 112]); they are the dominant signs. And it is no longer phallic but feminine symbols that tend to dominate, massively inscribed by means of the circles and circlelike shapes.

In this society all stereotypes about woman's passivity, weakness, sensitivity, and lack of organization are countered. The little girls are cruel and insensitive. They organize and participate in a set of activities requiring energy and planning. As far as their sexuality is concerned, they make fun of theories claiming that to experience pleasure a woman requires vaginal penetration; they reject the Freudian theory of penis envy; and they refuse to be objects of exchange. [11] They are involved in what are or have been considered strictly masculine activities. They play games considered typical of small boys: they urinate together, show their sexual parts to each other, and catch birds. They hunt and play the trumpet. They are interested in strategy and tactics, in open battles and in guerrilla activities. Men watch cockfights; these little girls watch catfights. And, like King Louis IX, the familiar Saint Louis of French historical textbooks, they administer justice under a large oak tree.

Breaking with the stereotype that women are more sophisticated about color than men and use a range of more subtle colors in their attire, the little girls of *Les Guérillères* choose only the bright colors, blue, red, and orange. As distinct from texts in which women are portrayed in masochistic situations or being tortured by sadistic men (such as the notorious *Histoire d'O*), in *Les Guérillères* the women perform the tortures. Pride in and insistence on masculinity and the male genital organ are replaced by pride in and insistence on femininity and the female genital organ: the little girls make fun of the male organ.

Many behaviors no longer or not yet commonly accepted in our contemporary authoritarian, patriarchal, Judeo-Christian society are practiced in this female community. In fact, what is presented as licit and perfectly natural for *Les Guérillères* is precisely what our society condemns in the name of reason or morality. The social organization of the little girls' community is that of a collectivity where no one is in power, where hierarchy is nonexistent, and where learning is practiced not through individual reading and writing but through oral exchange. Indeed everything is devised so that there are constant face-to-face interactions and constant participation by all members of the community. Body wholeness and hedonism are valued by the young girls, who "appréhendent leur corps dans sa totalité" [p. 80] (perceive their bodies in their entirety [p. 57]), massage each other, and make ointments for their bodies. Excess is fully tolerated, and in certain rituals alcohol and drugs are consumed to the point of unconsciousness.

In many of their activities the little girls do not follow Cartesian conventions. They perform chants without a single logical sentence, and one of them begins her story with the playful nonsense "plume, plume, l'escargot, petit haricot" [p. 55].[12] They cultivate disorder; they honor not individuals who conform but those who rebel. They rewrite fairy tales and biblical stories: thus the Caucasian Eve becomes a black Eve, who is told to eat the apple because it will enable her to gain knowledge and power. Furthermore, in this version there is not one snake but many; symbolically, life, nature, and sexuality are celebrated and not repressed.[13]

Finally, it is most striking that the lives of these little girls are governed by multiplicity rather than unity, questioning rather than acceptance, and initiative rather than passivity. They reject the dichotomy between intellectual activities and manual occupations by engaging in both. Through their ubiquitous existence they implicitly emphasize and denounce the monotony of most Western individuals' lives.

Michel Foucault, in his preface to *Les Mots et les choses,* writes: "Utopias console; it is because even though they do not have a real place, they however blossom in a marvelous and smooth space; they open up cities with large avenues, well planted gardens, easy countries, even if their access is chimerical."[14] This is what *Les Guérillères* proposes, an idyllic way of life that seeks to overturn all the excesses, the mistakes, the biases of the past. In it there is a constant underlying desire for harmony and balance, which manifests itself through the recurrence of circles and circlelike shapes. As is well known, the figure of the circle is a mandala which represents individuals' impulses toward wholeness and harmony. It symbolizes protection, fecundity, and perfection.

In reading *Les Guérillères*, one cannot help feeling that it displays a deceptive simplicity, that under its surface lies a powerful layer of documents and texts that have participated in its elaboration. As the most obvious manifestation of this underlying layer, the text dares to break with a typical Eurocentric content by naming characters who belong to Mexican, Indian, and Chinese literatures and mythologies, and by telling portions of legends or stories from various cultures. What are the documents which create these intriguing effects of intertextuality? The answer is provided at the end, where a postface explains that *Les Guérillères* is the meeting place of specific texts. The list of some thirty texts that follows includes Aristophanes' *Lysistrata*, Beauvoir's *The Second Sex*, Clausewitz's *About War*, Confucius' *Shi-Jing*, the *Dictionary of Sexology*, the book of *Genesis*, Homer's *Iliad*, Lacan's *Ecrits*, Mao Zedong's *Problems of War and Strategy*, Marcuse's *Eros and Civilization*, Pascal's *Pensées*, Sahagun's *General History of New Spain*, and Sappho's poetry.[15]

Les Guérillères is thus the result both of invention and of the compilation and intertextual grafting of an impressive set of other texts. It constitutes a complex interconnection of literary, historical, and political domains pointing to the past and the present, the Occident, the Orient, Latin America, sexology, military strategy, fairytales, psychoanalysis, and philosophy—in other words, a sophisticated kaleidoscope of literary, cultural, and historical experiences, all at work under and within the surface of its words.[16]

Les Guérillères, because of its content, belongs to the utopic genre: that is, to a Western architext. It also constitutes a textual manifestation of other Western cultural components. The freedom, initiative, and joy of the little girls is a topos, that of woman-in-charge, found in

the medieval carnival customs and festivities described by the historian Natalie Davis in "Women on Top."[17] And the focus on women's
anatomy and on the genital organs in particular is the concern of contemporary women artists, of whom the most obvious representative is
the painter Judy Chicago.[18]

At the same time, although a written text, *Les Guérillères* contains
features that connect it to the oral literature, especially the oral poetry, of preliterate and nonliterate societies in many parts of the world.
The incantatory use of sounds, the repetition of forms, the listing of
lexical items and names, the direct quotation of actual speaking
voices, and the poetic lines all contribute to the sense that this text is
an oral epic, a mythic poem.[19]

The content of *Les Guérillères* also links it to non-Western societies.
The type of life described in this imaginary ethnography is reminiscent of a myth still chanted today by the Waurà women of central
Brazil's Xingu River, which recounts how women followed an arma-
dillo to a distant place, constructed homes and weapons, and started a
new life independent of men.[20] Variations on this myth are frequently
told by South American tropical forest tribes. Thus *Les Guérillères* is
also tied with a South American mythical architext.[21] Furthermore,
several descriptions of the little girls' practices are more than textual
or literary inventions; they are verbal renderings of behaviors and customs still in existence in many indigenous communities, again in
South America, where drinking is practiced to the point of losing consciousness; where individuals paint their bodies with dyes made from
local plants; and where teaching and governing are performed
through oral communication, with the participation of the whole
community.[22]

Indeed, *Les Guérillères* is more than a text of revolt against male
hegemony or a work of propaganda in favor of lesbianism. It is poetical, political, sophisticated writing at its best, combining wit, erudition, violence, simplicity, and roguishness.[23]

L'Amour: Choreographing the Said and the Unsaid

Novelist, playwright, film director, Marguerite Duras has been writing since the 1940s.[24] Her early works, such as *Un Barrage contre le
Pacifique,* tend to be detailed and descriptive novels, but her tech-

niques gradually evolved more and more toward spare simplicity, and her most recent texts are striking for their poignant and elegant starkness. *L'Amour* belongs to this last phase in Duras's writing style. Its title suggests fulfillment, pleasure, and happiness in its generic absoluteness. But in *Les Parleuses,* where she discusses her works with Xavière Gauthier, Duras explains that she chose this title in reaction to its usual use and that *L'Amour* is not a love story.[25] What is it, then?

L'Amour[26] presents the fortuitous meeting of three characters who remain unnamed. A man called the traveler has just arrived on a beach, where he comes across a woman seated against a wall. This woman is described as "posée sur le chemin" [p. 10] (set down on the path). In the distance the traveler sees a man who walks with a regular pace. "Trois, ils sont trois dans la lumière obscure, le réseau de lenteur" [p. 9] (Three, they are three in the dark light, the network of slowness). This statement — because of its placement at the opening of the text, the number 3 repeated twice, the oxymoron "dark light," and the hieratic slowness — appears like a bad omen of the sort announced by a diviner reading the future, like the pronouncement of a messenger in Greek tragedy that a fatal conjunction is taking place. And indeed something happens.

The meeting of the three characters causes an eruption of the past into the present. In Proustian fashion, seeing a person or a place casts the characters back to their pasts, and scenes and situations return to consciousness. They recognize one another as having been involved in a traumatizing incident that took place in a nearby resort called S. Thala. This event, never described, is like a stone thrown into the water, provoking a series of waves: its repercussions began at the moment of its occurrence and continue into the present, and it is some of those repercussions that *L'Amour* presents.

L'histoire. Elle commence. Elle a commencé avant la marche au bord de la mer, le cri, le geste, le mouvement de la mer, le mouvement de la lumière. Mais elle devient maintenant visible. C'est sur le sable que déjà elle s'implante, sur la mer. [p. 13]

The story. It begins. It began before the walk along the sea, the shout, the gesture, the movement of the sea, the movement of the light. But it now becomes visible. It is on the sand that it already becomes implanted, on the sea.

On the beach the traveler, the woman seated, and the man walking with a regular pace form a triangle:

Quelque part sur la place, à droite de celui qui regarde, un mouvement lumineux. . . .

A gauche, une femme aux yeux fermés. Assise.

L'homme qui marche ne regarde pas, rien, rien d'autre que le sable devant lui. . . .

Le triangle se ferme avec la femme aux yeux fermés. . . .

Du fait de l'homme qui marche, constamment, avec une lenteur égale, le triangle se déforme, se reforme, sans se briser jamais. [p. 8]

Somewhere on the beach, to the right of the one who is looking, a luminous movement. . . .

To the left, a woman with her eyes closed. Seated.

The man who is walking does not look, nothing, nothing else but the sand in front of him. . . .

The triangle is closed with the woman whose eyes are closed. . . .

Because of the man who is walking, constantly, with an unvarying slowness, the triangle is deformed, reformed without ever breaking.

From that moment on, the traveler, the woman, and the man are linked in this triangular relationship, which is formed in different places and at different times. The woman is a centripetal force attracting both the traveler and the man walking. The traveler is drawn to the woman. He visits her on the island where she sleeps, and he says to the man: "J'ai du mal à rentrer à l'hôtel, j'ai du mal à m'éloigner d'elle" (I find it hard to go back to the hotel, I find it hard to get away from her), to which the man answers: "Je comprends . . . moi-même je ne peux pas" [p. 47] (I understand . . . myself I cannot either). This man is described as being always with the woman, taking care of her, walking with her on the beach, and sleeping next to her on the island.

Within this triangular relationship a striking interplay and contrast of forces establish themselves. The woman is described as absent, prostrated, often sleeping, and nauseated because she is pregnant. She is called *une force arrêtée* (a stopped force); that is, she is powerful in her absence. The man and the traveler, and other characters related to her indirectly, are described as living disruptive experiences that are exteriorized in violent physical reactions. The traveler, upon seeing the woman for the first time prostrated on the beach, walks away; then a shout is heard.

> Et puis il y a un cri:
> l'homme qui regardait ferme les yeux à son tour sous le coup d'une tentative qui l'emporte, le soulève, soulève son visage vers le ciel, son visage se révulse et il crie. [p. 12]

> And then there is a shout:
> the man who was looking closes his eyes in turn under the blow of an attempt which carries him, raises him, raises his face toward the sky, his face contorts and he shouts.

> De nouveau on entend son pas, on le voit, il revient de la direction de la digue. Son pas est lent. Son regard est égaré. [p. 13]

> Again his step is heard, he is seen, he comes back in the direction of the jetty. His step is slow. His look is lost.

As he approaches the traveler, the man who walks on the beach looks at him with a "regard bleu . . . d'une fixité engloutissante" [p. 17] (a blue look . . . with an engulfing fixity), and he cannot speak—his emotion is such that he loses his voice. When the three characters meet in a bar and hear a piece of music, they cannot refrain from crying. One day the woman meets the traveler in the hotel courtyard. She tells him that she knows him and that she remembers this place. We are told that in the traveler "le désarroi grandit tout à coup" [p. 57] (helplessness increases suddenly). Later the three of them are in an empty ballroom. The man walks onto the dance floor, sings, and dances:

> Le corps s'emporte, se souvient, il danse sous la dictée de la musique, il dévore, il brûle, il est fou de bonheur, il danse, il brûle, une brûlure traverse la nuit de S. Thala. [pp. 70–71]

The body gets carried away, remembers, it dances under the dictation of music, it devours, it burns, it is crazy with happiness, it dances, it burns, a burn traverses the night of S. Thala.

The traveler visits a woman, who is not named, in her house in S. Thala. This woman recognizes the traveler and remembers the events of the past, but again readers are not told what these are. She has an intense experience, as is evident in the descriptions of her reactions to seeing the traveler arrive on her terrace:

> Le regard le quitte d'un seul coup. Le visage se ferme, les yeux, une douleur irrésistible semble traverser le corps. [p. 77]

The look leaves him abruptly. The face closes, the eyes, an irresistible pain seems to traverse the body.

The traveler's wife and her children come to S. Thala. Upon learning that the traveler will never come back to them, they react with different emotions. The children stare at their father with their mouths half open "sur l'avidité sans bornes de la connaissance" [p. 97] (with the limitless avidity of knowledge). The woman "a poussé un cri sourd de suffocation" [p. 98] (uttered a dull shout of suffocation). At one point the traveler goes to see the ballroom of the casino in S. Thala. He asks the guard for information, and it is noted that this guard "doit voir la violence des yeux du voyageur" [p. 127] (must see the violence of the traveler's eyes). Once he has seen the ballroom, the traveler feels so much emotion that he "jette sa tête dans ses bras repliés. Des sanglots éclatent de lui" [p. 131] (throws his head in his folded arms. Sobs burst from him).

In these passages what is captured are states in which the body is suddenly affected. Facial expressions, gestures, and physical reactions such as shouting or crying are described. The characters, on seeing a person, hearing a piece of music, or returning to a place they used to know, undergo a sort of inner catastrophe that alters their normal state and behavior; during this experience they are completely centered on their body and on their emotions.

L'Amour, then, is about the upheaval and sufferings provoked by the sudden return or departure of someone, by the surging of painful memories, and by the sudden irruption of traumatizing moments from the past. It is a particularly disturbing and moving text, which speaks to us about the physical and physiological manifestations of sorrow and pain and about the intricate interactions between the mind and the body. The landscape surrounding the characters is flat and static. The beach is empty, and one hears the regular ebb and flow of the sea. But in this peaceful setting there are phenomena that disrupt the calm: shrieking seagulls, shrill sirens, blinding sunlight, a violent storm. The congruence between the agitations of the characters and the disruptions of the landscape reinforces the poignancy of the text.

A complex mood emanates from the representation proposed by *L'Amour*; it combines impersonality, hieratic solemnity, contrasts, and violence. This special mood derives from the plight of the characters and from the tensions and torments they represent, but it also springs form Duras's powerful and idosyncratic narrative techniques. A series of scenes are simply juxtaposed in a loose temporality. Now it is day, then it is night. The next day the characters meet, then they are separated, then they meet again. No links of causality are established. One encounter follows another just as one day follows another. Smoothly, slowly, time flows, and encounters occur inevitably.

The text offers a stark, stylized representation by providing a minimal number of details. Many scenes are described as taking place on a beach, or on an island, in horizontal and deserted landscapes, "pays de sable et de vent" (land of sand and of wind), edged by the sea and the sky and by very few vertical elements, such as the hotel on the beach, the wall against which the woman is seated, or the town of S. Thala in the distance. Against the geometry of this landscape, there is the triangle formed by the man, the woman, and the traveler. The bodies, clothes, and faces of these three characters are not described with precision. They are three-dimensional figures that vary their position: the man is walking while the traveler is standing next to the seated woman, or the woman is lying down and the two men are seated next to her.

Sparseness also occurs in the chromatic domain. Two colors only, blue and white, are mentioned in the text; two others, green and brown, can be inferred from the elements of the landscape. The striking blue eyes of the man are often described. White is the color of the seagulls, of the dress that the woman wears one day and of her bag, of S. Thala's skyline, and of the blinding light. In addition, readers can imagine the blue and green colors of the sea and the light brown color of the sand.

Duras has chosen discursive strategies that reinforce the starkness of this representation in *L'Amour*. Its components, its place and characters, are indexed by generic nouns: the man, the woman, the traveler, the sky, the beach, the sea, and the hotel. These nouns are almost never modified by adjectives, so that they are reduced to their basic, intrinsic, semantic primes. Similarly, verbs are almost never modified by adverbs or adverbial phrases, so that only the abstract idea of an action is expressed. With regard to verbal / social interaction, it is significant that in spite of their past and present relationship, the characters use the polite, impersonal, and formal pronoun *vous* when addressing each other, rather than the intimate, personal, and informal *tu*. *Vous* is unmarked and uncommitted with regard to information about relationships. Like the generic nouns referring to persons, it functions to keep personal relations at a distance, playing off against the intense emotions between characters. Further, it confers a neutral tone, a solemnity and a universality that prevent the text from being a banal, sad love story.

Typography also plays a role in the creation of the sparse and stark mood of *L'Amour*. The text is punctuated by blank spaces, pauses during which nothing happens. Paragraphs consist of one nominal sentence or of very few short sentences; short cryptic dialogues or quoted speeches are always placed toward the left side of the page. As a consequence, readers enter a controlled, uniform, yet diversified space where action takes place laconically by means of absence rather than presence.

A neutral and objective style is maintained throughout the text, but skillful variations in narrative techniques prevent monotony. At first, events are described as they take place, as if the narrator were witnessing each movement, gesture, and facial expression in slow motion—reporting it in the active voice and its result in the passive voice.

> Le triangle se défait, se résorbe. Il vient de se défaire: en effet, l'homme passe, on le voit, on l'entend.
> On entend: le pas s'espace. L'homme doit regarder la femme aux yeux fermés
> posée sur son chemin.
> Oui, le pas s'arrête. Il la regarde . . .
> La femme est regardée. [p. 10]

The triangle is undone, disappears. It just became undone: in fact, the man passes by, he is seen, he is heard.
It is heard: the footstep is less frequent. The man must be looking at the woman with closed eyes set down on his path.
Yes. The footstep stops. He is looking at her. . . .
The woman is looked at.

The narrator, like a camera operator, presents various scenes, changing angles, distances, and speeds so that contrasts are set up to reflect the changing states of the characters. A wide-angle description opening the text captures the span of the landscape and the sky, with the characters standing out against this background. Between sky and sea, three individuals are in the hands of cosmic destiny.

> La mer, le ciel, occupent l'espace. Au loin, la mer est déjà oxydée par la lumiére obscure, de même que le ciel.
> Trois, ils sont trois dans la lumière obscure, le réseau de lenteur. [p. 9]

The sea, the sky, occupy the space. In the distance, the sea is already oxidized by the dark light, as is the sky.
Three, they are three in the dark light, the network of slowness.

In the following example the camera first follows the movement of the man approaching, next stops in front of the traveler. Then, without transition, a close-up brings a sharp focus on one part of the body: on the eyes, and on the quality of the look.

Il arrive. Il s'arrête face à celui, qui se tient contre le mur, le
voyageur. Ses yeux sont bleus, d'une transparence frappante.
L'absence de son regard est absolue. [p. 16]

He is coming. He stops in front of the one who is standing against the
wall, the traveler. His eyes are blue, of a striking transparency. The
absence in his look is absolute.

After this scene the man and the traveler exchange a few words. Then
the man gets closer to the traveler, and this time it is said that "le
regard bleu est d'une fixité engloutissante" [p. 17] (the blue look is an
engulfing fixity).

At times the narrator's camera, by means of repetition and the
accumulation of short units, captures the agitation that suddenly
takes hold of the characters. Here the actions of the traveler's wife are
described:

Elle arrive, elle les bouscule avec force. Le petit garçon tombe.
Elle le ramasse, le fait tenir debout, le pousse, prend la petite
fille, la bouscule aussi, la pousse, pousse devant elle, n'arrive pas
à rassembler, pousse, fait avancer, hurle, hurle avec les sirènes.
[p. 100]

She arrives, she jostles them with strength. The little boy falls. She
picks him up, makes him stand up, pushes him, takes the little girl,
jostles her too, pushes her, pushes in front of her, does not succeed in
bringing together, pushes, makes go forward, screams, screams with
the sirens.

L'Amour with its stylized representation, its lexical simplicity, and its
narrative laconism is a fluid, incantatory prose poem interrupted by
sudden moments of febrility and violence.

To this point, my rendering of the representation of *L'Amour* has
focused on what it says and how it says it. However, another aspect of
this text gives it a special and peculiar character. The man, the
woman, and the traveler are caught in a web of circumstances that
link the present and the past, memory and consciousness, but this
web is never completely untangled; the circumstances leading to the
present situation are only partially specified. Instead of providing
answers, the text raises questions; instead of explaining facts, it sets
up situations that might be interpreted symbolically. As a conse-

quence there is a constant tension between the said, the unsaid, and the suggested; between what appears as factual and what seems symbolic. The woman tells the traveler that she was married, had children, and then became ill; her children were taken away from her and her husband died. This is the triangle of the past, which disintegrated. But why did this happen? Why did the woman become ill? Why does she tell him that the police know her? Is she the woman the police are looking for? Why does she have black hands one morning? Why did the traveler decide to come back to S. Thala and kill himself? In what capacity was the man who says he is mad involved in the event of S. Thala? The text is filled with narrative ellipses that are impossible to complete. Yet despite the degree to which the unsaid pervades the text, the conjunction of a certain number of elements suggests supplementary levels of meaning. Although the precise nature of the event that took place in S. Thala is never specified, this event represents an extremely sensitive and delicate period in the life of the woman, the man, and the traveler, who repeatedly refer to it during their encounters.

Several details of the description of the visit of the traveler and the woman to the casino of S. Thala are suggestive and elliptical rather than fully explicit. After walking in the sun, the woman is tired and lies on the beach:

> Il n'est plus là. Elle est seule allongée sur le sable au soleil, pourrissante, chien mort de l'idée, sa main est restée enterrée près de son sac blanc." [p. 125]

> He is no longer here. She is alone stretched out on the sand in the sun, rotting, dead dog of the idea, her hand remained buried near her white bag.

The image of the dead dog has appeared several times before in the text. At the beginning a dog is seen walking on the beach; after the storm its dead body is found lying on the sand. The metaphor of the dead dog used to symbolize the woman sleeping on the sand suggests elliptically that the woman is also the victim of a storm that destroyed her. It is very significant that she does not enter the casino; she falls asleep while the traveler goes in and relives a moment of the past which is so disturbing that it makes him cry. Upon his return, he tells the woman that once the two of them had come to the same beach in search of coolness. She does not answer. By not entering the casino, by not answering, she prevents the crucial, traumatizing moment of her past from invading the present, preferring instead forgetfulness.

For this outing to S. Thala, the woman wears a white dress and carries a white bag, as if she were a bride going to her own wedding. At night, while she and the traveler are sitting together on the beach, they hear the noises of a couple making love next to them. This scene is a blank wedding: the woman is with the traveler and wears the wedding dress, but love is consummated by others.

The relationship between the man and the woman is intriguing. We do not know why he walks on the beach, why he lives on the island with the woman, or why he is insane. However, through his behavior he shows that he has ties with the woman, that he is attached to her. He always comes back to her; he walks back with her to the island; he is the one who dresses her in white for the trip to S. Thala with the traveler. While she never expresses any feeling toward this man, the woman seems equally attached to him. She is always concerned with his whereabouts. She seems to have found a routine and a balance with him, which is exteriorized by the fact that she walks with the same rhythm as he does and sleeps on the island in his company. Without ever explicitly saying so, all these details suggest that the two help and comfort each other.

Casually and unexpectedly, the text says that since the arrival of the traveler there are many fires in S. Thala, and that on the night when the traveler and the woman go back to the casino and the beach of S. Thala, the man starts a huge fire in the heart of the town. Again a suggestive, elliptical symbolism is at work. If we think of setting fires as a symbolic manifestation of sexual torment and jealousy, then the man has been pushed to act as he does by the arrival of the traveler.

S. Thala is a place by the sea where the characters have chosen to withdraw from normal life, to live as outsiders. The symbolic meaning of the sea adds another supplementary level to the text, for the sea represents peace, comfort, and the return to the womb. And this is the state to which the characters aspire.[27]

Gilles Deleuze writes, "The novel has never ceased to define itself by the adventure of lost characters who do not know their names any longer, what they are looking for, nor what they do, amnesiac, ataxic, catatonic."[28] This remark applies to Duras's novels in general and to *L'Amour* in particular. It should not be taken in a negative sense, because Duras invents characters for whom amnesia and madness are positive values.

Duras is fascinated by the insane, by criminals, and by prostitutes.[29] All these individuals are outsiders. They are rejected by society, which treats them as dangerous, abnormal, and transgressing. Duras herself experienced outsiderhood: in various conversations and interviews she explains how in Indochina, where she was born, she always felt different, apart from the other French people, an outsider among them because of her social class and her family's poverty.[30] She remembers that when she was about eleven years old she heard of an accident that made a strong impression on her. Rumor had it that the wife of a high-ranking French official provoked the suicide of a young man in love with her. And she specifies, "C'est cette femme qui m'a amenée à pénétrer dans le double sens des choses. . . . Elle m'a amenée à l'écrit peut-être" (It is this woman who led me to penetrate into the double meaning of things. . . . She perhaps lead me to writing).[31] This woman, who resembles Anne-Marie Stretter of *Le Vice-consul,* was an outsider too: "Elle donnait le sentiment de ne pas être du tout dans la société coloniale . . . elle sortait seule, elle n'avait pas d'amies; elle recevait, il y avait des réceptions officielles; elle avait des amants mais elle n'avait pas d'amies femmes" (She gave the feeling of not being at all in colonial society . . . she would go out alone, she did not have friends; she would entertain, there were official receptions; she had lovers but did not have female friends).[32]

This fascination for outsiders and these personal experiences did not remain merely a trait or an idiosyncrasy of Duras's personality. For her the power of the outsider was such that it brought forth emotion demanding expression. Outsiderhood, a dynamic force permeating her works, is a breakthrough, not a breakdown.

The woman of *L'Amour* is an outsider. But she goes a step further into outsiderhood than Duras's previous characters. Anne-Marie Stretter of *Le Vice-consul* and Lol of *Le Ravissement de Lol V. Stein* are women who set themselves outside the mainstream of society by leading a life that oscillates between two opposites. Anne-Marie is the irreproachable wife of the French ambassador to India and a good mother; at the same time she is a prostitute. Lol is a good housewife who likes order and raises her children well, but she also wanders the streets aimlessly and absentmindedly, not having completely recovered from her mental illness. The woman of *L'Amour* lives completely outside the norms and boundaries of society and morality. As the man tells the traveler: "Elle a habité partout, ici ou ailleurs. Un hôpital, un hôtel, des champs, des parcs, des routes" [p. 53] (She has lived everywhere, here or somewhere else. A hospital, a hotel, fields, parks, roads). Now like a tramp she lives on an island, in an abandoned building. Her goal is to have nothing and to be nothing. With the traveler she avoids involvement, protecting herself by means of forgetfulness. She is indeed "une force arrêtée, déplacée vers l'absence" [p. 10] (a stopped force, displaced toward absence).

How does *L'Amour* relate to other forms of contemporary expression? With regard to content, it contains one thematic component that makes it akin to other texts written by women. Duras's text has harmonics with George Eliot's *Mill on the Floss* and Madame de LaFayette's *La Princesse de Clèves*. For indeed the woman of *L'Amour* is a counterpart of Maggie Tulliver and of Madame de Clèves, both of whom after unsuccessful love experiences come to the realization that they must refuse involvement and that they prefer withdrawal from society. Refusal and withdrawal are strategies that the woman of *L'Amour*, Maggie Tulliver, and Madame de Clèves adopt in order to protect themselves and to avoid further suffering.[33]

One aspect of *L'Amour*, the choice of and the characteristics attributed to settings and landscapes, is perhaps an expression of feminine sensibility that can be observed in the works of Virginia Woolf as well. According to Claudine Hermann, women writers tend to privilege descriptions of settings and landscapes characterized by emptiness and a lack of hierarchy and by vast expanses of land and sea.[34] In *L'Amour* the space where the characters are situated, "pays de sable et de vent" (land of sand and of wind), is striking for its vacuity. Now the characters are on the empty beach, now on a deserted island, now in an empty hotel falling into ruins—spaces that do not imply any activity, any domination, any control.

In addition to reflecting women's aesthetic tendencies, *L'Amour* belongs to an artistic mode governed by the principle that less is more. Duras believes that describing only part of a human being or situation is more effective than complete description. The art historian E. H. Gombrich quotes a Chinese formula that applies perfectly to Duras's achievement in *L'Amour*: "Ideas present, brush may be spared performance."[35] And his colleague Henri Maldiney echoes this same idea: "Art too always proceeds by suppression; and all things equal or otherwise similar, the more it is great, the more it suppresses. Indeed where in a work of art does the strange power of the simple come from?"[36] Duras's aesthetic depends on laconism in reference, spareness in content, and stylization of landscapes; it leaves many elements unsaid, so that the said is as powerful as the unsaid, the unsaid as powerful as the said.

Harmonics with other contemporary artistic creations come to mind as well. Like Edvard Munch's famous painting *The Cry*, *L'Amour* opens with a shouting figure standing against the empty sky, sea, and sand. In a ballet choreographed by Merce Cunningham with a music / noise / text montage by John Cage, as in *L'Amour*, the suffering of individuals would be expressed in their bodily postures and facial expressions against the background of a stark landscape, suggestive in its absence. Lighting would alternate from bright and blinding to subdued and dusky, and silence would be interrupted by sirens, shouts, sounds of the sea and of a storm, steps on the sand, hysterical shouts, and noises of a couple making love.

L'Amour: ironic title, indeed, for a text characterized by its starkness, which affects not only the landscape but the life that the characters have decided to lead. Ironic title, also, for a text which, with an implacable fatality, brings together three individuals in this sensitive place called S. Thala and makes some of them endure physical and mental suffering, while others remain absent and uninvolved.

Souffles: Mental and Physical Exhilaration

Hélène Cixous is a compulsive, prolific writer. She is the author of an impressive number of works, including a book on James Joyce; one on Lewis Carroll; one dealing with Freud, Hoffman, Kleist, Poe, and Joyce; several novels; a play; and an opera libretto. An active feminist, she writes theoretical essays that underscore, attack, and make fun of various forms of phallocentrism that have permeated Western society and culture.

Cixous's creative works display an interesting heterogeneity and exuberance. Representation is elaborated by portions of narrative that are partly invented and partly autobiographical; for instance, she refers to episodes from her childhood in Algeria. There are also descriptions of dreams and hallucinatory states. In an interview Cixous explains, "Most of the time what I inscribe is of the nature of fantasy, of the unconscious, of the dream."[37] These portions of narrative form units not correlated by causality or logic. At times they are linked by a fortuitous pun or other word play, but more often they are autonomous units, simply juxtaposed. The referentiality encoded in these portions of representation is multilevel. Numerous direct references or allusions to various literary and psychoanalytical figures and texts add dimensions and effects of meaning. An omnipresent play with words multiplies these allusions and references. Cixous's style—poetical, harmonious, and lyrical, shifting abruptly into vulgarity and obscenity and becoming violent and disjointed—also contributes to the heterogeneity of her creative works.

An examination of *Souffles* will enable me to analyze Cixous's scriptive techniques. About this particular text she explains that it is as erotic as possible and that it poses the following questions: what is eroticism, and how and where does it touch and affect us?[38] How does Cixous write about eroticism in *Souffles,* and what does this text accomplish?

Souffles[39] is about the mental and physical experiences of an anonymous female narrator who is never situated or described and who, sometimes in first person and sometimes in third, recounts experiences that take place or took place. In fact, it is unclear whether these experiences are imagined, lived, or dreamed; they seem to be visions—hallucinations during which the character has intense feelings of bliss and exaltation of a sensual and erotic nature. During these moments the narrator is free from the control of reason; she is outside the boundaries of normal life in which pragmatic, material activities are carried out. Her body and her mind are open to conscious physical sensations; she freely expresses unconscious, uncontrolled, and spontaneous drives.

The text begins with the description of an experience during which a voice takes hold of the narrator and provokes erotic physical reactions:

Là! c'est la voix qui m'ouvre les yeux, sa lumière m'ouvre la bouche, me fait crier. Et j'en nais. [p. 9]

Here! It is the voice which opens my eyes, its light opens my mouth, makes me shout. And I am born from it.

Son corps me fait parler: il y a un lien entre mon souffle et son éclat. Un bond! Devant moi! En coup de vent. Surprise! La beauté m'arrache, un cri, oui! Il y a un lien entre cette sorte d'astre et l'irruption de mon âme! Ainsi se répand-elle dans l'air qu'il fait bouger, et du mélange de ses rayons et de mon haleine naît un champ composé de sang d'astre et de halètement. Sa beauté me frappe. Fait jaillir. Me fait couler. Elle séduit mes forces. Douceur. [p. 10]

Its body makes me speak: there is a link between my breath and its brilliance. A leap! In front of me! In a whirlwind. Surprise! Beauty wrings from me, a shout, yes! There is a link between this kind of star and the eruption of my soul! Thus it spreads in the air that it makes move, and from the mixture of its beams and my breath is born a field made of star's blood and panting. Its beauty strikes me. Makes me spurt. Makes me flow. It seduces my forces. Sweetness.

A little further on, the narrator recounts a dream in which she climbs a tree. The trunk is described as being alive, an entity with which she is having intercourse and which provokes a climax. Then suddenly she is projected into space, into an atmosphere that is celestial, milky, and soothing yet dynamic and alive with movement, and in which her body is in a state of rapture.

A vive allure l'arbre cingle. Nous tournoyons, un sursaut, l'arbre rue, je lâche tout, quelle terreur! C'est moi, moi seule la gorge nouée sans proférer un son m'en vais valser là-haut dans un champ frétillant de bancs d'étoiles, elles filent et virent à coups de queues humides en silence autour de moi qui ne puis, abîmée de volupté, lever le petit doigt. Tournoyade, le dais céleste répand ses fleuves de lait, je succombe, je roule long-temps, longtemps insensible dans les vagues de ma propre chair qui déferle sur la terre. Survolée. [pp. 21–22].

At top speed the tree lashes. We whirl, a jump, the tree kicks, I drop everything, what terror! It is me, me alone my throat knotted without uttering a sound go waltz up above in a quivering field of beds of stars, silently with bursts of their wet tails, they dash past me and turn around me who cannot, overwhelmed by voluptuous pleasure, raise my little finger. Whirl, the celestial canopy spreads its milky rivers, I succumb, I roll a long long time numb in the waves of my own flesh unfurling over the earth. Flown over.

There are also dreamlike descriptions of weird, unexplained trips. The narrator is pursued by the sea, which keeps rising. She takes refuge in a castle where, as in a Gothic novel, a strange, almost magical atmosphere reigns:

> Il émane de cet espace une apaisante pression — un air épais contraint les corps à des allures cérémonieuses. Je bouge entre des tissus de cet air ameublant, qui m'oblige à des gestes sculptés. [pp. 79–80]

> A calming pressure emanates from this space — a thick air compels the bodies to adopt ceremonious bearings. I move between cloths of this furnishing air, which forces me to sculptured gestures.

It is not only during flights outside reality that the narrator experiences such moments of elation and rapture; real and banal events and situations have also provoked such effects. She recalls states of heightened sensation or perturbation that took place during her childhood. The communion she did not receive because she was Jewish, "étrangère" (a foreigner) as she says, aroused burning, pain, jealousy, and torment in her, feelings exacerbated by the whiteness of the clothes of the other children she watched walking in the streets of the neighborhood. Stealing a small piece of costume jewelry in a tobacco store and being caught in the act are moments which are glorified. In the preparation for the act of stealing, her whole body is transformed:

> L'intention du vol transformait immédiatement la densité de ma chair, affinait mes sens et me félinisait, m'ailait. Je devenais chimérique: en vérité, c'est pour cette métamorphose que je volais. Dans l'ignorance des affinités qui font les préliminaires du vol l'équivalent des préparatifs amoureux, je n'en avais pas

moins découvert par expérience les étranges connexions sensuelles. [p. 165]

The intention of stealing immediately transformed the density of my flesh, sharpened my senses and made me feline, gave me wings. I became chimerical: the truth is that it was for this metamorphosis that I would steal. In the ignorance of the affinities that make the preliminaries of stealing the equivalent of lovemaking preparations, I have nonetheless discovered through experience the strange sensual connections.

Then the actual stealing is presented as bringing about intense physical pleasure:

Il fut dans mon sang, je brûlais, je sus que dans le sang peut éclater un feu qui coule sans mal et allume chaque nerf jusqu'au plus humble, la chair est alors intérieurement étincelante de milliers de flammes qui ne se confondent pas, mais séparément produisent un suave embrasement — c'est la fête, le corps se découvre incalculablement riche en voluptés: des millions de régions, zones, puits, âmes, sillons, têtes, contrées, se font simultanément reconnaître et nous comblent de bontés. [p. 172]

It entered my blood, I was burning, I knew that in the flood a fire can burst which flows without pain and lights each nerve up to the most humble, the flesh is then internally sparkling with thousands of flames which do not mingle, but separately produce a sweet blazing. It is a celebration, the body finds itself incalculably rich in voluptuous pleasures: millions of regions, zones, wells, souls, furrows, heads, lands, make themselves recognized simultaneously and fill us with kindness.

Completing the whole adventure, the effects and the feeling experienced after being caught — being made ashamed publicly by being slapped on the buttocks — are described in minute detail, including the changes in body temperature, the shivering, the fear, the excitement and pleasure, in a masterful prose that attains epic qualities.

In these visions, dreams, and personal experiences, the narrator's body is never passive: it reacts powerfully to joy, pain, anger, or shame. Extremely sensitive and versatile, it is capable of a diverse range of reactions that yield pleasure and elation. The interactions between the narrator and her different sexual partners immediately attract attention. The dichotomy passive/active, in which masculinity is correlated with activity and femininity with passivity, is completely nonexistent in the experiences of the narrator; rather, two modes coexist, the active and the passive, so that no one individual dominates or takes advantage of another. The narrator acts and initiates actions, but she also answers to solicitations and interacts in a relationship where both partners are equal and enjoy each other. By inventing such characters and situations, Cixous concretizes her notion of bisexuality, which she advocates in her essay "Le Sexe ou la tête?" (sex or head) and which she defines in the following terms:

> Somewhere, feminine sexuality is always bisexual. Bisexual does not mean, as many people understand it, that she makes love with a man on one hand and with a woman on the other; it does not mean that she has two partners, even if it can mean that occasionally. Bisexuality at the level of the unconscious is the possibility of prolonging oneself toward the other, being in a rapport with the other in such a way that I pass in the other without destroying the other; that I go and look for the other there where heshe is without trying to take everything to myself.[40]

The constant presence and intermingling of masculine and feminine elements are distinctive and meaningful features of *Souffles*. In one of the dreams where there is a castle, the inner courtyard is labeled a female sexual organ and the pagoda erected in the middle is a penis. In one vision unicorns appear, combining masculine and feminine attributes. The narrator at one point sees creatures that are half masculine and half feminine. Whereas most literary texts tend to privilege phallic symbols, and whereas Wittig in *Les Guérillères* counters this tendency by using only the circle symbolizing female sexual parts, Cixous's narrator in *Souffles* opts for a compromise which perhaps represents more accurately what exists in reality or what should exist: a constant interaction of feminine and masculine elements.

In her exploration of the nature of eroticism, then, Cixous presents it as a complete experience affecting the whole body and implying activity, equality, and reciprocity in both partners. How does she write about bliss, about sexual activity, sexual satisfaction, about such moments as those that the narrator of *Souffles* describes as disrupting yet pleasurable and exhilarating? In the passages quoted and many others, movement and vitality constantly affect all parts of the body, of the mind, and of nature. Human and natural elements interact and interpenetrate not in symbiotic or parasitic relations but in sensual ones. Transformations are common. What is inanimate becomes animate. While these interactions and transmutations are taking place, Euclidean coordinates and the laws of gravity are nonexistent. The images and situations described connote verticality and ascending movement. Violence exists at times, but it is not sadistic; chemical, physical alterations yield positive, pleasurable sensations. There are numerous references to sap, milk, sperm, and feminine secretion, and to stars, flowers, and life. Eroticism and sensuality indeed give rise to a fantastic alchemy: they make the narrator who experiences them enter a world *fabuleux* (fabulous) and *chimérique* (chimerical), as she calls it, a euphoric world where everything exudes vitality, dynamism, and pleasure.

Vitality, dynamism, gusto are also terms that characterize the performance of the narrator of *Souffles*. She is a self-conscious narrator who discusses her text and the process of writing as she writes; she constantly draws attention to herself as a writer by means of her virtuosity, her linguistic manipulations, and her knowledge, which is expressed through her explicit references and allusions. Contrary to the convention that the text is the product of the stylus, the narrator specifies that her text is the product of her womb. It is a child, and a child who is not led but who leads her: "Il me mène par le bout du nez" [p. 138] (It leads me by the tip of the nose). And to evaluate her text she says that it is "contre fait, sans corps sans membres, mais tout lévres et tout sourire" [p. 138] (misshaped, without body without limbs, but all lips and all smile).

The narrator inscribes images, visions, and scenes as they come to her mind without motivating or explaining their appearance. She says: "Passons-nous de causes" [p. 114] (Let us do without causes). Thus *Souffles* is a text in which the unexpected becomes a structuring device, in which cohesion is achieved by the fact that all the experiences the narrator describes share a common feature: they all take her outside reality into intense and exhilarating states. In order to describe these states, the narrator utilizes syntactic devices that translate emotions and feelings into discourse. An emotive syntax is created by many questions, exclamations, interjections, sudden accumulations of words, abrupt changes of sentence lengths, tempos and rhythms that constantly animate and disrupt the surface of the text. While inscribing this splintered and unpredictable representation, the narrator displays a fascination with and a pleasure in words. She makes words coalesce and yield several meanings. For instance the name *Jenais* is to be read aloud as *Genet,* the name of the playwright and novelist, and at the same time as *je nais,* "I am born." In the bilingual portmanteau word *Flytemnestre,* the narrator condenses into one word the name of the queen who killed her husband, the consequent invasion of flies in the city of Thebes, and the verb *flyte* which means to mock by name-calling. In one of her dreams, after having mentioned Jenais, a Nô monastery, and Novalis, the narrator comments: "Je pressens que l'art du Nô et l'art de mes romantiques allemands ne vont plus tarder à s'adjoindre pour produire un théâtre hybride, l'Orient et l'Occident s'échangeant en noces poétiques" [p. 80] (I feel that the art of Nô and the art of my German Romantics will not be long in uniting to produce a hybrid theater, East and West exchanging poetic vows.) A hybrid theater is certainly what the narrator creates by her constant flirting with name-dropping and her concomitant display of erudition and knowledge: Blake, Genet, Freud, Clytemnestra, Delilah, Electra, Poe and Lacan and the famous "Purloined Letter," Rilke, Haroun-al Raschid. Such references to literary, mythological, and psychoanalytic figures are not neutral but are semantically charged and overdetermined.

The narrator also adapts well-known utterances to her own text and context. "Encore un effort mon corps allons, porte-moi" [p. 217] (One more effort my body come on, carry me) recalls Marx's famous exhortation to the working class. "Écrire, ne pas écrire. Angoisse" [p. 217] (To write, or not to write. Anguish) is modeled on the beginning of Hamlet's soliloquy. *Souffles* is thus a web of allusions, references, and modified quotations that index a host of meanings. In addition, the narrator's verbal texture mingles flowing passages of sensuous lyricism, didactic essays, pornographic slang, and prose poems with dislocated syntax—with the consequence that rhythms, tones, syntax, registers, and styles constantly shift. This exploitation of the plasticity of words, of the connotations of certain names or utterances, and of the possibilities of discourse is yet another manifestation of vitality and exuberance, repeating and reinforcing the vitality and exuberance encoded in the descriptions of the narrator's experiences.

The narrator of *Souffles* explains that the aim of her enterprise is "faire bouger, déraciner" [p. 166] (to unsettle, to uproot). In what ways does she succeed in unsettling, in uprooting? One stereotype has it that women are passive beings, quite often victims of men's whims and desires. The narrator undermines this stereotype by citing names of women who have manifested themselves not as victims but as victimizers. She mentions women who dared to revolt and have their husbands killed, like Clytemnestra; or who pushed men to action, like Electra begging Orestes to vindicate her mother's crime; or who defeated men by cunning, like Delilah.

Cixous's descriptions of the narrator's feelings, actions, and reactions emphasize the fact that a woman is not a dull passive being but an individual whose body is extremely sensitive, and the eroticism is centered not on sexual parts only but on the whole body, which is an accumulation of erogenous zones. *Souffles,* like *Les Guérillères,* thus counters the ideas of Freud and Lacan, who call woman the black continent and believe that a woman does not know herself and cannot talk about her sexuality and her physical pleasure. In her essay "Le Sexe ou la tête?" Cixous remarks:

> As for Grampa Lacan, he takes up [Freud's] formula: "What does woman want?" saying "Of her sexual pleasure a woman can say nothing." Now that is very interesting: it is all there: A woman cannot, does not have the ability; let us not even mention the power to speak: that is precisely what she has been stripped of forever. No talk about sexual pleasure = no sexual pleasure, no will: power, will, speech, pleasure, none of that is for woman.[41]

In *Souffles* the narrator verbalizes her feelings and describes the sensations of a body acutely alive and finely tuned for pleasure.

Souffles unsettles because it offers a series of behaviors counter to those considered appropriate in Western society. While according to the Western norms women should refrain from vulgarity, the narrator describes how she achieves major satisfaction by using vulgar language. And while in Western society stealing is strictly forbidden, the narrator intensely enjoys stealing. She remembers that when she stole the costume jewelry, she was reading the Bible, giving the famous passage of Genesis her own interpretation:

> À l'époque de la fessée, redoublant son effet je lus la Genèse à ma façon; je me représentai le tentateur comme un grand nègre-serpent tout en tête et en queue ornée de diamants. Je le trouvai d'une rassurante beauté, en contraste avec les membres en sucre des autres personnalités. Quant à Eve, que je trouvais niaise . . . je la pressais de manger le fruit . . . je m'indignai du tour de passe-passe qui transformait un fruit fondant en instrument d'une vaste opération d'asservissement à la mort. [pp. 180–81]

> At the time of the spanking, increasing its effect I read Genesis my way; I pictured the tempter as a big negro-snake, all head and tail, bedecked with diamonds. I found his beauty reassuring, as opposed to the treacly limbs of the other characters. As for Eve, whom I thought a simpleton . . . I urged her to eat the fruit . . . I was indignant at the cheap trick that transformed a luscious fruit into the instrument of a vast plot of subservience to death.

This rereading recalls that of the little girls in *Les Guérillères,* who also transformed this famous passage of the Bible in which woman is forced into an inferior position, into the role of the victim. The little girls, too, insist that the snake motif symbolizes sexuality and vitality. The narrator of *Souffles,* here also a young girl, adds a new dimension: she makes the snake a hybrid creature which mingles a black man and a serpent, thus flouting the whites' fear of blackness and of black sexuality. And in reading the myth to the letter, with seeming innocence she points out the amount of disbelief, blindness, and credulity that has been necessary for the acceptance of the vast enterprise of domination implied in this biblical myth. The allusions to Genet are another example of an incitement to be different, to reject power. For Genet, the thief, the homosexual, the transgressor, who dares write about his experiences, who takes the side of the blacks and of the oppressed, represents a direct attack against all that society considers normal and licit.

"Culturally speaking," writes Cixous, "women have cried a lot, but once the tears have stopped, instead of tears what we will have in abundance is laughter. It's an outburst, an outpouring, a certain humor you would never expect to find in women, and yet it is surely their greatest strength because it is humor that sees farther into man than he has ever seen into himself before."[42] Cixous's narrator in *Souffles* displays a sense of humor that is neither aggressive nor bitter. She makes fun of "Uncle" Freud, taking the patriarch of psychoanalysis down from his pedestal and demoting him, as it were, to the role of a familiar kinsman. Clytemnestra, the doomed and tragic character of Greek drama, is lowered to the vulgar rank of mother-whore by the portmanteau word *mèrepute*. Novalis, the German Romantic, tormented by love and madness, becomes the banal Mr. Novalis. The episode of the theft of the piece of costume jewelry takes place in a tobacco store, a banal, down-to-earth place where the narrator says she found no less than the secret of eternity. She is pleased that it happened in such a place, since the visionary poet William Blake was visited by angels in his kitchen, a no more decorous place than the tobacco store. The rapprochement of a tobacco store and of a kitchen with great moments of revelation is ironically humorous, as is the narrator's comparison of herself to Blake.

Souffles, then, proposes a representation that celebrates the body, sensuality, and mental and physical states outside the control of consciousness and reason. It does not violently attack or reject masculinity, nor does it privilege femininity. Rather it valorizes reciprocity. It celebrates rebellion and nonconformism and is a hymn to freedom and vitality, aimed not at conquering another but at enhancing one's own capacities and possibilities in conjunction with others.

Souffles can be placed within a network of other texts. Because its representation encodes dreams, visions, and other flights outside reality, it belongs to an architextual complex that includes Rimbaud's *Illuminations*. His poem "Aube" (Dawn) comes to mind. This poem describes a walk at dawn during which the protagonist participates in the awakening of nature. He causes darkness to go away, and pearls of dew look at him; he talks to flowers, smiles at waterfalls, and takes dawn wrapped in her veils in his arms and embraces her body. In

Souffles this coupling is reversed; nature is masculine and the protagonist is feminine. The visions of the protagonist of Nerval's *Aurelia,* with their movement, their activities, their mythological syncretism, their intertextual allusions, and their emotive syntax, are also reminiscent of those of *Souffles.* And visions and exhilarations found in the writings of female mystics are strikingly akin to those of Cixous's female narrator. For example, Hildegarde de Bingen (1099– 1179) writes:

> Je vis une grande machine ronde et ombragée comme un oeuf dont le sommet est étroit, le milieu large et l'extrémité resserrée; et tout l'extérieur de cette machine était entouré de feu; et au-delà était une peau sombre. Or, dans ce feu était un globe de feu brillant d'une si grande dimension que la machine en était entièrement investie; ce globe avait au-dessus de lui trois étincelles disposées à empêcher le globe de tomber. Ce globe s'éleva quelque temps en l'air et beaucoup de feux vinrent s'y joindre.

> I saw a great machine round and shaded like an egg whose top is narrow, middle large and end compressed; and all the exterior of this machine was surrounded by fire; and beyond there was a dark skin. Now in this fire was a globe of bright fire of such a great dimension that the machine was entirely invested with it; this globe had above it three sparks arranged to keep the globe from falling. This globe rose for a while in the air and many fires came to join it.

> Je vis ensuite une splendeur d'une grande et très sereine étendue, éclatant d'une multitude d'yeux, tournée vers quatre angles comme aux quatre coins du monde qui, annonçant le secret du suprême Créateur, me fut manifestée sous la plus grande réserve. Et dans cette lumière m'apparut une autre splendeur semblable à l'aurore, qui tenait aussi de la clarté couleur de pourpre.

> Next I saw a splendor of vast and serene expanse, bursting with a multitude of eyes, turned toward four angles as toward the four corners of the earth which, announcing the secret of the supreme creator, was made manifest to me with the greatest reserve. And in this night appeared another splendor like the dawn, which also had a brightness of crimson hue.

In Jean Vuarnet's *Extases féminines,* from which I quoted the fore-
going passages,[43] there are many other similar examples of women
who express themselves with a poetical intensity about their over-
abundant intimacy, about those moments close to delirium during
which they were transported toward God. Such verbal delirium, such
fantastic images, and such sexuality are also present in *Souffles,*
although they are not directed toward God.

Harmonics can be found as well. Play and manipulation with
words, which produce excess and multiply meaning, are Joycean
practices that Cixous consciously emulates. Placing herself, too, in
the wake of the *Wake,* she is in the company of Roche and Sollers; she
also manipulates words like Derrida and Lacan, being aware of the
value of play with language and culture. The emphasis on erogeneity,
on the fact that woman is not passive, and on the fact that she knows
what pleasure is involves notions that are very much part of contemporary feminist rhetoric and strategies aimed at countering the patriarchal, phallocentric conventions which would have women naive
and passive and centering their pleasure on the vagina. The best-
known examples of such work in France are Luce Irigaray's *Speculum de
l'autre femme* and *Ce Sexe qui n'en est pas un.*[44] It should also be kept in
mind that the insistence on physical pleasure, on *jouissance,* is not an
obsession among feminists; it is also a trait of contemporary Western
society. In recent years, shame about the body and the fear of sin
fostered by the Judeo-Christian religion have dwindled. All individuals, men and women, have expressed their right to experience pleasure. *Souffles,* with its definitely hedonist slant, places itself in this
ambiance.

Multileveled, multifaceted, full of hustle and bustle, bursting
with joy and vitality, written in praise of healthy eroticism, *Souffles* is
an important text of our postmodern era.

Writing and Sexual Difference

Some women writers and critics argue that texts written by women
have specific characteristics which make them different from texts
written by men. Xavière Gauthier explains why, in the published version of *Les Parleuses* (her interviews and discussions with Marguerite

Duras), nothing has been deleted or corrected, why the text has not been edited or polished:

> We both are women. It is not impossible that if full and well-seated words from time immemorial have been utilized, lined up, piled up by men, the feminine could appear as this slightly wild grass. . . . It is perhaps one of the reasons why these discussions run the risk of appearing to nostalgics of beet fields (or of the ordered battlefield) like an inextricable tangle of liana and ivy, an entanglement of climbing or subterranean plants.[45]

Gauthier advocates and therefore valorizes disorder and looseness instead of order and tightness, which she calls men's modes of writing. Claudine Herrmann suggests that women's writing exhibits an interest in and a search for incoherence; that it has less tendency to subordinate and coordinate elements, to order them hierarchically.[46]

Cixous herself speaks of the femininity of the text, which manifests itself in its immediate flux: "nonsens, chantson, sangson" (nonsense, chantsound, bloodsound).[47] But my examination of texts written by women and by men reveals that the differences between them are not so clear-cut and categorical as these theorists in their feminist enthusiasm would want them to be. Like the men's works I have analyzed, the texts of Cixous, Duras, and Wittig are open texts characterized by fragmentation and discontinuity. Abandoning plot and causality; dislocating narrative organization; disrupting syntax; exploiting word play and intertextuality; displaying lexical, narrative, and typographical manipulations; favoring repetition, looseness, and lack of hierarchy—these texts clearly belong to the same postmodern epistemology as those of Beckett, Butor, Laporte, Pinget, Ricardou, Robbe-Grillet, Roche, Simon, and Sollers.

Also within the line of reasoning insisting that there are sharp differences in the ways men and women writers inscribe representation, Annis Pratt—commenting on American and British fiction from the last two centuries—arrives at the following conclusions:

> Women's fiction manifests alienation from normal concepts of time and space precisely because the presentation of time by persons on the margins of day-to-day life inevitably deviates from the ordinary chronology and because those excluded from

the agora are likely to perceive normal settings from phobic perspectives. Since women are alienated from time and space, their plots take on cyclical, rather than linear, form and their houses and landscapes have surreal properties.[48]

While there may be such tendencies in the texts Pratt describes, they cannot be taken as clear markings, as absolute distinguishing features differentiating men's and women's writing. The texts of Cixous, Duras, and Wittig, too, deviate from chronology, manipulate it, and contain surreal and uncanny landscapes; but such characteristics cannot reflect their biography or their alienation. Otherwise, the conclusion that imposes itself is that since the works of the male writers I have examined also manipulate temporality and chronology, their authors are also marginal and alienated individuals. In contemporary French texts, male and female writers alike avoid linearity and chronology—not because of discrimination and exploitation, not because of particular details in their personal or psychological histories, but because they are avant-garde explorers of the possibilities and limits of representation.

Is it a question of content, then, that makes texts written by women different from texts written by men? In order to come to terms with this issue, I find it helpful to suspend disbelief for a moment and borrow from Freud certain distinctions, now recognized as inadequate conventional dichotomies, which are nevertheless useful as working hypotheses. In his essay, "The Relation of Poetry to Daydreaming," Freud argues that creativity is the result of unsatisfied wishes that vary according to the sex of the creator: "Either they are ambitious wishes, serving to exalt the person creating them, or they are erotic. In young women erotic wishes dominate the fantasies almost exclusively . . . in young men egoistic and ambitious wishes assert themselves plainly enough alongside their erotic desires."[49] What about the texts that have been my focus here? Those written by women may well be shaped by erotic desires, but erotic daydreamings are certainly blatant also in Ricardou's, Robbe-Grillet's, and Simon's morphological, erotic, voyeuristic writing; in Roche's word play, where sexual innuendo is constantly lurking; and in Sollers's *"fiches de baisage"* (screwing ledger), as his narrator expresses it.

Some texts have been labeled "feminine" or "masculine": Lisa

Appignanesi notes that a feminine imagination informs the works of Henry James, Robert Musil, and Marcel Proust, and that the writing of George Eliot and George Sand is said to have a strong masculine side. Appignanesi's idea of femininity and masculinity in the creative imagination corresponds to Freud's characterization of woman as passive, emotional, and uninvolved in everyday life, and of man as active, rational, and participatory. She defines feminine art as "distinctly separate, wholly alienated from common daily reality; art which may see life from a depersonalized position as a static object to be described, not as a complex process in which the artist is a participant; art which gives evidence of that social irresponsibility which is akin to Freud's description of the feminine as lacking conscience and a higher moral sense."[50] Are Cixous, Duras, and Wittig writing feminine works in this sense? And what about the men's works discussed here? According to the Freudian definition, *Les Guérillères* is definitely masculine; it presents female characters aware of their marginal situation and energetically involved in changing it. Rationality, involvement, and action aimed at having an influence on one's surroundings are the animating principles of the text. *L'Amour* defies classification; it is neither feminine nor masculine in the sense discussed here. It is neutral, because its characters have opted for outsiderhood and anomie; they refuse involvement with anything in order to protect themselves. *Souffles* is both masculine and feminine: masculine because it contains awareness of and takes a stand on a widely discussed and debated contemporary issue—the domination by the patriarchal society—but also feminine because it describes interiority and irrational feelings; it contains states outside reality and movements toward the hedonistic enjoyment of one's own body.

What about the men's texts—how do they align in relation to this feminine/masculine dichotomy? One would have to say that Ricardou's *L'Observatoire de Cannes*, Robbe-Grillet's *La Maison de rendez-vous*, and Simon's *Triptyque* are feminine texts: they are written by narrators who are completely involved in their apolitical, asociological, self-centered representation. Beckett's *L'Innommable*, Pinget's *Quelqu'un*, and Laporte's *Fugue* are also feminine in that they portray narrators turning inward on themselves in solipsistic examination of themselves as writers in the very moment of writing and as part of what they write. Butor's *Mobile*, Roche's *Circus*, and Soller's *H* could be characterized as displaying masculine traits because they implicitly present political and sociological issues through their montage of discourse.

My remarks here are not intended to pit women and men against each other or to say that feminine writing is better than masculine writing or vice versa. The morphological writings of Ricardou, Robbe-Grillet, and Simon and the solipsistic stance of Beckett's, Pinget's and Laporte's narrators are not instances of passivity; rather they are intellectual explorations of representation and reflections on the act of writing. And what these comparisons show is that in contemporary French writing, the active and the passive, introspectivity, sensitivity, goal orientation, involvement, and outwardness are independent of the gender of the writer.

That women tend to be more politically oriented and to write masculine texts is understandable, given the intellectual climate of our time. By writing about absence, difference, their bodies, eroticism, and sexuality, Wittig, Duras, and Cixous legitimize them; through their discourse they propose alternatives to male-oriented representation and expression. As Lyotard points out, scientists legitimize their research and their discoveries by writing narratives about them.[51] Women achieve a similar effect by writing about such topics as sexuality, vitality, independence, awareness of themselves as women; they confer legitimacy upon these topics and upon themselves. The message of these writers is not directed toward women alone; it is addressed to individuals in general, teaching them to deconstruct their ways of thinking and of being—that is, teaching them to question what they have always accepted, to examine the underpinnings and the assumptions they live by. These women are not highstrung, excited, or biased, as might be suggested; they are lucid, learned, and concerned. However, if pragmatic readers expect to find characters they can identify with, they may be disappointed. For these writers at the cutting edge of feminism, each in her own way, propose characters who escape from reality—either because they live in a utopia as in *Les Guérillères,* because they live in a semimystic mental and physical high as in *Souffles,* or because they are immobile and prostrated individuals as in *L'Amour.*

Let us examine another statement that purports to distinguish women's writing from men's. Jean Larnac, in his *Histoire de la littéra-ture féminine,* writes that "in the center of every feminine novel, one discovers the author."[52] Is biography a source of inspiration only for women? It is a fact that certain female writers have used aspects of their lives in their texts. Duras discusses how she was influenced by scenes from her childhood in Indochina, and she explains that these elements are part of a sort of primeval scene that she keeps writing about. Cixous in both her theoretical and her creative works quite often refers to herself as someone born in Algeria and therefore consid-ered a *pied noir,* as someone coming from a Jewish family and speaking German with her mother—all this contributing to make her feel eccentric and not completely French, explaining her awareness of oppression and her sensitivity to difference.

However, women's fiction is not necessarily more autobiographical than men's fiction. Pinget's sketches of provincial life, Simon's de-scriptions of village life, Ricardou's Cannes, and Robbe-Grillet's Hong Kong are certainly in some ways derived from their personal experiences. Sollers in *Vision à New York,* an interview with David Hayman, talks about his childhood and his upbringing and provides details that are also found in *H.* That Beckett studied Dante and phil-osophy at Trinity College certainly accounts for his references to the *Divine Comedy,* to Descartes, and to Bruno. Similarly, it would be erroneous to say that only women inscribe their unconscious and their drives; as Kristeva has shown, texts from the end of the nineteenth century to the present day have continually freed themselves from the constraints of syntax, causality, and reason and let the unconscious surface—or, as she puts it, we witness an irruption of the semiotic and a disruption of the symbolic.[53]

Another question is that of influences. Is it possible to say that men writers are indebted to past or contemporary novelists or philosophers and that women writers are not, or vice versa? Again, concrete exam-ples show that there is no difference. Cixous is influenced by Joyce, Freud, and Lacan. Wittig acknowledges her debt to Robbe-Grillet, Pinget, and the films of Godard. Roche points to Rabelais and Joyce; Sollers to Joyce, Lacan, and Derrida; Laporte to Blanchot and Der-rida. This creates an interesting constellation and intersection indeed, again pointing to the same postmodern set of characteristics: fragmentation, manipulation, play, openness. Even the refusal to emulate anyone, the adamant desire to keep one's own independence, is not specific to one gender: Duras and Beckett share this very attitude.

Thus, experimentation in representation and in language, eroticism, femininity, masculinity, the presence of autobiographical details, and influences from other writers are components that cut across sexual differences. Can we conclude, then, that there are no differences between the ways men write and the ways women write? Despite similarities, it is undeniable that women bring a distinct perspective to the panorama of contemporary French writing. I am not claiming here that only women can write as Cixous, Duras, and Wittig do or that only women can write about certain topics. I am pointing out that women have written about certain topics and men have not. While some men's texts, like *Mobile, H,* and *Circus,* flirt with social and political issues, they are not committed; they do not overtly denounce evil and exploitation. Other men's texts, like those I have included in the chapters on serial constructs and reflexivities, do not even refer to social or political problems. The women's texts adopt much more clear and precise stances. Cixous and Wittig aim directly at subverting phallocentric stereotypes, and Duras takes a stance by writing about outsiderhood, by refusing any involvement that she considers a political move. Cixous, Duras, and Wittig—like Ricardou, Robbe-Grillet, Roche, Simon, and Sollers—write about the body, eroticism, and sexuality. But unlike those men, who adopt an ambiguous attitude at best or who treat woman's body as an object, these women deliberately attack such phallocentric and patriarchal attitudes and propose a more healthy and harmonious sexuality.

Certain archetypes in the texts of Cixous, Duras, and Wittig are distinctive features that do not exist in men's writings. The affirmation of woman's strength, her possibility of rebelling and becoming independent, and the enjoyment of her body, which manifest themselves in *Souffles* and *Les Guérillères,* can be identified as belonging to the Demeter/Kore archetypal system, Demeter representing feminine power and determination because she dared prevent Pluto from attempting to rape her daughter. The cult of Isis and Dionysus, permitted to women throughout Greek and Roman history, provided them with an outlet for celebrating their eroticism, pride, and joy. *Souffles* and *Les Guérillères* are also reminiscent of such rituals. The woman of *L'Amour* is like Daphne, who transforms herself into a laurel to escape the amorous enterprises of Apollo. Absence, withdrawing into herself, is for the woman a way to protect herself by having nothing to do with the rest of the world. The presence of these archetypal patterns and of ritual behavior in the writings of Cixous, Duras, and Wittig link the texts to systems of the ancient past; they rediscover existing knowledge and practices; and they relate our technological, monotheist society to agrarian and polytheist ones.[54]

A remark by Virginia Woolf is often quoted: "It is fatal to speak consciously as a woman." Cixous, Duras, and Wittig demonstrate that this is no longer true.

6

Effects of Representation in Contemporary French Fiction

Il faut opter pour l'affirmation joyeuse d'un monde chaotique, intensif et fragmentaire et par contre coup pour une écriture fragmentaire.
(It is necessary to opt for the joyful affirmation of a chaotic, intensive, and fragmentary world as a consequence for a fragmentary writing.)
Maurice Blanchot

Il compito della litteratura é di tenere il linguaggio in esercizio.
(The task of literature is to keep exercising language.)
Umberto Eco

After this exploration of twelve texts, it is appropriate to assess what I have done. First I will reflect on my critical approach, then discuss the properties of representation in postmodern texts, and finally show how these texts fit their specific cultural setting and the epistemology of our time.

Given the polyvalent nature of the texts I have chosen, it is productive to enter into them by means of several perspectives. My practice of thick description allows just that. My starting point is always an examination of the textual properties of the works, a process which requires linguistic and stylistic tools. As I grasp the specificity of the discourse of each text, insights and concepts developed within different disciplines become relevant. They open up new ways of assessing effects of meaning in the representation of these texts. In sum, in this book, critical approaches dialog and intersect with concrete specific textual material. I have not tried to pit modes of criticism against one another; my aim is to show how these postmodern texts function, not to test the validity of approaches. Yet what clearly emerges is the fact that post-structuralist concepts are indispensable in coming to terms with these texts.

Unique to my approach is the fact that I do not limit myself to intertextual interplay among literary texts. I relate contemporary French fiction to other artistic productions such as music and painting, to other ways of rendering experience in the world such as mathematics and philosophy, and to non-Western artistic practices such as the oral performances of South American Indians. These isomorphisms and harmonics offer another slant on these texts and increase our understanding of them. They illustrate with more familiar entities, or on the contrary, more esoteric forms of expression how these postmodern texts signify, and how the writer's work takes place in a vast field of artistic and cultural practices.

My analysis of the various texts makes it possible to delimit a certain number of diagnostic features that are specific to French postmodern fiction. I have identified four modes of representation with three variations within them. The repetitiveness of serial constructs contrasts with the heterogeneity of the multimedia montages. Both modes, displaying absent-present narrators, in turn contrast with the reflexive texts, which focus on the performance of their narrators. And the feminist texts are three variations on women played in a postmodern key. Contemporary French fiction displays a remarkable diversity.

The study of these texts makes readers realize concretely that the techniques used to render experience and to create fictive worlds have changed. These changes are apparent in the structuring of representation, in the characteristics of the narrators, and in the language used.

The modes of structuring representation displayed in these texts bring about a mutation of literary space. Serial constructs, multidimensional montage, reflexivities, and feminist fiction constitute different ways of decentering representation. Of the texts analyzed in these different categories, none is structured by an axis with ramifications; in each of them continuity, orientation toward a goal, and causal or logical connections are dispensed with. The concept of *rhizome,* borrowed from Gilles Deleuze and Félix Guattari, accurately describes these kinds of textual organization.[1] In rhizomatic structures the patterning is that of a mesh, where any item can be connected to any other, thus preventing hierarchies, closure, stability, and univocity. Yet no matter how disjointed, how heterogeneous these texts are, one or several components always create cohesion: semantic fields; various kinds of repetition; constant reflexive, self-conscious comments of a narrator; or typographical organization. The presence of order within disorder constantly manifests itself.

Roland Barthes theorizes in *S/Z* that in the writerly text, representation is theatricalized.[2] A consequence of this theatricalization is, according to Barthes, an alteration of the convention of the pictorial code that has traditionally underlined literary mimesis. Barthes means that writerly texts are spaces in which several components work together to create a polyphonic and polymorphic representation offering aural as well as visual and mental experiences. I have shown how this theatricalization is actualized in various texts by means of manipulations affecting both language and typography.

Repeatedly I have pointed out the importance of aurality and orality as constituents of representation. The foregrounding of phonic and rhythmic components is a significant feature of contemporary French fiction. These components are concretized by various techniques and devices. Phonic effects are created by the recurrence of sounds, words, or groups of words. This principle is at work in the uncanny texts I call "serial constructs," in the harmonious and dissonant text of *Les Guérillères,* and in the clownish prancings of *Quelqu'un.* The use of unfamiliar names, such as those of Indian tribes in the onomastic montage of *Mobile* and the exotic women's names of *Les Guérillères*; the accumulation of names in poemlike structures in both of these texts; and the banality and simplicity of the generic nouns used repeatedly in *L'Amour,* creating an incantatory effect, are all discursive techniques and lexical choices that draw attention to the sounds of language. Rhythms and rhythmic variations are taken advantage of in several texts. Displaying this technique are *H* with its uninterrupted but disjointed flow of words, *L'Amour* with its hieratic looseness, *L'Innommable* with its hysterical whirlpool of words, and *Souffles* with its wild and urgent vitality.

Repetition is a salient feature in several texts I have discussed; in fact, each of them explores the resources and possibilities of repetition. Repetition is a factor that alters traditional mimetic practices: instead of being organized by means of dissimilarity and difference, representation is elaborated by similarity and sameness. Repetition in its most common form, the recurrence of a particular item, is used frequently. I have mentioned that repeated sounds create phonic effects, but repetition is also a structuring device in *L'Observatoire de Cannes, La Maison de rendez-vous, Triptyque,* and *Les Guérillères,* which inscribe the same shape insistently. In addition to the semantic and the phonic, there are also typographical repetitions. The stanza-like units and onomastic poems of *Les Guérillères,* the sequences of *Fugue,* and the different typographies in *Mobile* are such structuring devices.

Repetition with variation is also used as a means of presenting facets of a situation. This effect is achieved when the same notion is encoded with different signifiers: the various metaphors invented by the narrator of *Fugue* in order to discuss interrelated topics—what is writing and what is the writer—are examples. Repetition can also be set up when different semantic items appear in the same discourse unit, as in *Mobile* with its presentation of the different states of the United States by means of the names of cities, mountains, rivers, ethnic groups, and animals and plants. Semantic fields provide another way of creating repetition with variation, since around one idea or one concept are grouped many others, thus presenting a net-work of related features and aspects. *Circus* and *H* are examples where typography, iconic components, and semantics are utilized to index repeatedly a certain number of topics such as death, love, childhood, drugs, writing, science, and culture.

These are intratextual repetitions that structure the texts with sameness and difference. What about intertextual effects? Are they not also instances of this sort of repetition, since an utterance, a sign, or a symbol from another text is repeated—either as is or with mod-ifications—and made to function in the text in which it is inserted? Many of the texts I have discussed exhibit intertextual repetitions, which take several forms. There are direct and exact quotations of documents from the past in *Mobile,* and reproduction—therefore quotation—of Giordano Bruno's diagram *Figurae Intellectus* in *H.* Often the borrowed sign or unit of discourse is repeated in the new text with alterations which nevertheless let the original appear: *H* modifies literary and political utterances; *Circus* tampers with signs and snatches of recognizable texts, and transcreates from the visual to the verbal. A special case of intertextual repetition appears in *Les Guérillères,* into which modified units of discourse and allusions coming from an impressive list of texts are grafted. Isomorphisms deliberately thought of by the writer are also instances of repetition at work in the texts. Robbe-Grillet recycles the popular detective and pornographic novel in *La Maison de rendez-vous,* and Wittig in *Les Guérillères* invents a utopia. Several of Rabelais's and Joyce's writing techniques are consciously repeated by Roche and Sollers. Two of Bruno's philosophic principles — affirmation can become negation, and multiplicity does not prevent unity — are used respectively by Beckett and Sollers to organize *L'Innommable* and *H.* Derrida's notions of *écriture* and of *différance* are concretized in Laporte's *Fugue.*

The various forms of repetition structuring the representation of these texts phonically, semantically, and typographically, establishing links with present and past writers, philosophers, or artists, produce an uncanny textual and intertextual interplay between sameness and difference.

The status and the behavior of the narrators of the various texts introduce a new perspective in the encoding of representation. The narrators remain in the minds of readers as uncanny absentees who are very much present. They give the unsettling feeling that behind what they name, describe, or discuss, insanity is lurking. Another effect produced by these unanchored narrators — who never specify how they see, feel, or think, where they come from, or why they write the way they do — is that the representations they encode are akin to or perhaps are fantasmatic productions. Discussing this psychic phenomenon, Catherine Clément writes: "Scenario, staging, sequence of images, fantasma is at the limit of representation and of its production; at the limit of structured subjectivity and of the anterior and future time which determine it."[3] It is precisely a playing with limits that is the central enterprise of these narrators. Strong subjectivities, they express themselves without indicating that they are involved. Never defined, never precisely located, there is just a *he* or a *she.*

Despite this imprecision, each text manages to make sense, as does a hypothetical sentence used as an example in linguistic analysis, in which the pronouns *I, he,* or *she* are utilized without having to be specified. But anonymity does not indicate a lack of subjectivity. In fact, these anonymous narrators are strong personalities, strong subjectivities, utilizing writing as a field for play and each exhibiting a passion for language.[4] Never neutral, these manipulators of forms of discourse, of lexical items, of sounds, and of texts manifest their presence by their eccentric behavior. Some of them, like the narrators of *H, L'Innommable, Les Guérillères,* and *Souffles,* are animated by a linguistic exuberance. Others, in the texts grouped under serial construct, reveal an obsession with morphological details that borders on the pathological. The narrator of *Circus* enjoys crafting his parodies and tampering with signs and symbols, and the narrator of *Mobile* remains objectively distant, while the narrator of *L'Amour* is mysteriously present-absent behind the poetical and hieratic incantations of the text. Whatever their behavior it is always marked by excess, either in exuberance or in sparseness.

The consequence of these practices is that the texts discussed here do not present language as a static system, as limited and limiting, or as inadequate or arbitrary. Quite the contrary, they celebrate language in taking advantage of its potentialities and versatility. As Wittgenstein points out, there are countless ways to combine and use words, and "this multiplicity is not something fixed, given once for all, but new types of language, new language games, as we may say, come into existence."[5] In this perspective each of the texts analyzed here constitutes a new language game, an idiosyncratic use of language. Each text is a discrete linguistic and discursive organization invented out of the infinite permutations of language. Each author is an inventor who combines the possibilities inherent in language.

Some comparisons and generalities are in order. With regard to sentence and paragraph structures, these texts display great disparity. Between *H,* which is a continuous sentence with no paragraphs, and *Mobile* and *Circus,* which at times offer pages with but a sprinkling of single words, there is *L'Amour* with its short sentences, semisentences, and many breaks and spaces; *L'Innommable* with its frenzied whirlpool of words; *Fugue* with its elegant, balanced grammatical sentences and its difficult syntax; and *Les Guérillères* with its same-length prose units interrupted by onomastic poems.

In matters of style there is again great diversity. The objective, matter-of-fact, standard prose of *L'Observatoire de Cannes, La Maison de rendez-vous,* and *Triptyque* contrasts with the clownish incongruities and disjunctions brought about by the juxtaposition of slang, vulgar, and formal registers in *H* or *Circus* and the hieratic simplicity of *L'Amour.*

Signification, too, is encoded by a variety of means. *Circus* integrates signs and symbols taken out of their normal context. *Mobile* and *Les Guérillères* display names and nouns placed loosely and freely, without the anchoring of the sentence mold. *H* and *Mobile* juxtapose unrelated portions of utterances and units of discourse. Generally speaking, a shift of priorities is taking place in the discourse of these texts, since the referential function of language is no longer dominant, and phonic, graphic, and diacritical components are promoted. It is also interesting to notice that the discourse in these texts tends to avoid adjectives; consequently, they do not encode qualities, which is the function of adjectives. This particular aspect is significant because of its implications. As Robert Blanché notes: "Judging by the vocabulary in which it is expressed, thinking about qualities is first entirely based on the opposition of opposites."[6] The tendency not to use adjectives, therefore not to express semantic polarities and not to express any judgment, is a characteristic that contributes to the undecidability of several of the texts.

The characteristics of the discourse of these texts alters the texture of literary expression by broadening the ways in which meaning can be expressed. Another important consequence is a blurring of distinctions between genres, or the constitution of a new genre that cuts across several older ones. With repetitions, phonic foregroundings, and typographical organizations of various kinds, prose and poetry coexist in several texts, which therefore hover on the margin between novels and poems. The presence of repetition, parataxis, acausality, and achrony connects these contemporary French texts with the oral performance that existed and still exists in preliterate and nonliterate societies.[7] Puns, word play, and sound play of different kinds are ludic elements that link these texts with the language of preschool children exercising and developing their own linguistic abilities. In texts with heterogeneous textures mingling several types of registers with various typographical arrangements, the blurring occurs between literary language and nonliterary language, or between high art and the mass media culture of advertising and newspaper writing. It appears, then, that these texts take advantage of techniques and devices that exist in different forms and genres, and that they can be located along a continuum that includes high art, popular culture, children's folklore, and non-Western verbal performance.

What are some of the effects of the discursive properties I have discussed? These properties are in fact very meaningful because they deconstruct patterns and conventions recognized as norms—such as hierarchy, the superiority of high culture, normative syntax, cohesion, and direction toward a recognizable goal. Furthermore, they displace the boundaries of what is possible, licit, and readable in a text.

Why should these texts be read? Are they byzantine linguistic games, formal and intellectual constructs? Are they self-indulgent exercises, exhibitionist productions dissociated from reality, history, and political commitment? Such opinions would be biased byproducts of superficial, casual readings conditioned by the reader's critical orientations and reading practices, and an epistemology belonging to an earlier period. The body with its physical and emotional reality as well as different aspects of psychic and perceptual life are very much present in this fiction. Within the surrealist *elucubrations* (wild imaginings) of the narrator of *L'Innommable,* the prancings of the narrator of *Quelqu'un,* and the quasi-mystic quest toward the unattainable ultimate metaphor of the narrator of *Fugue,* readers are made aware of the torment, boredom, discouragement, and joy of individuals striving with themselves and grappling with their craft. Suffering is everywhere in the pages of *L'Amour.* Death is ever present in *Circus.* Love and sexuality are two of the semantic fields of *H.* Woman's body and sexuality are the preoccupations of *Souffles* and *Les Guérillères.* The many instances of word play at one level are manifestations of unconscious drives. And the construction and creation of reality through visual perception are what serial constructs are all about.

It is obvious that there is no overt political message in the texts I have studied. Here and there in *H,* Sollers flirts with political discourse, but he never really takes a stand on anything; in *La Maison de rendez-vous* Robbe-Grillet also flirts with an antisexist and antiracist stand, but instead of denouncing anything, he manipulates shapes and anchorings of experience. Butor and Roche allude to racism against blacks and Indians, but only in passing. Wittig and Cixous are indeed *engagées*: they both directly address such women's issues as phallocentrism. But the political importance and relevance of these texts emerge not from their subject matter alone but from the fact that they favor undecidability, indeterminacy, and openness; that is, they embrace modes that encourage freedom and alertness rather than passivity, domination, and acceptance. The choice of intertextual relationships is in many cases an implicit political move: Giordano Bruno, Rabelais, Joyce, Freud, and Derrida each in his own way brought about changes in textual, psychoanalytical, and philosophical matters that subverted accepted patterns and behaviors.

While not a sociological study, this book demonstrates the diverse ways in which contemporary authors draw on, exploit, and reflect contemporary cultural realities in France. Kristeva points out that "following upon the phenomenological and existentialist shock of the postwar period, the sixties witnessed a theoretical ebullience that could roughly be summarized as leading to the discovery of the determinative role of language in all human sciences."[8] She refers further to "a desire for language," "a passion for ventures with meaning and its material," which are the forces underlying her earlier theoretical work. Without intending to minimize her stance, we can say that this passion for ventures with meaning was an attitude that affected not only Kristeva but other critics as well, such as Barthes, Cixous, Deleuze, Derrida, Foucault, Lacan, Lévi-Strauss, and Sollers. It is in this effervescent atmosphere that the writers I discuss here have been writing — exploring the possibilities and resources of language and modes of representation with a dionysiac enthusiasm.

Concomitant with language experimentation and exploration in this particular historical moment (1960s to late 1970s) of French intellectual life is a desire to challenge, to question, and to deconstruct logocentric, patriarchal, and other authoritarian attitudes. These texts participate in this effervescence. In this perspective the use of puns, portmanteau words, slang, neologisms, and syntactical and typographical manipulations is a strategy devised by the writers to express theoretical ideas and to subvert the authority of logocentric discourse.[9] The presence of explicit references to texts from other disciplines — such as anthropology and psychoanalysis in *H, Les Guérillères,* and *Souffles* — perhaps manifests an unconscious desire for legitimation, but it also reflects a contemporary cultural situation in which boundaries between disciplines have loosened and an interdisciplinary awareness has cross-fertilized literature.[10]

In a 1981 interview, the contemporary composer Iannis Xenakis insists on the importance of the aleatory and the noncausal, on mobility and the necessity of relearning a mental nomadism—ideas found in quantum mechanics, he specifies.[11] These modes are the ones the texts studied here propose. By their lack of temporality, past, present, or future—a framework replaced by mere process and relationships—and by being decentered, these texts inscribe a reality that is isomorphic with the reality of the universe from the point of view of quantum mechanics. According to its findings—whatever we may experience mentally or emotionally—time does not pass, nor does there exist a past, a present, or a future, and there is no center of the universe that we can discern even with the largest telescopes.[12]

François Lyotard defines the epistemological components of Postmodernism as follows: "By being interested in undecidability, in limits of control and precision, in quanta, in conflicts with incomplete information, in 'fracta,' in catastrophes, in pragmatic paradoxes, postmodern science theorizes its own evolution as discontinuous, catastrophic, nonrectifiable, paradoxical. . . . It produces not known entities but unknown ones."[13] The Nobel Prize-winning physicist Ilya Prigogine echoes these remarks: "We may say our interest is shifting from substance to relations. . . . Today . . . the ideas of nonlinearity, instability and fluctation diffuse into a wide field of scientific and even social thinking . . . now most people believe in an internal history dominated by fluctuations and multiple solutions."[14] Undecidability, nonlinearity, the shift from substance to relations (in my terms, an emphasis on process rather than ultimate meaning), multiple solutions (in my terms, openness, polyvalence, polysemy) are precisely some of the concepts that have emerged from my studies of these texts. *L'Observatoire de Cannes*, *La Maison de rendez-vous*, *Triptyque*, *Mobile*, *H*, *Circus*, *L'Innommable*, *Quelqu'un*, *Fugue*, *Les Guérillères*, *L'Amour*, and *Souffles* emerge from, relate to, and contribute to the epistemology of our time. Close to our daily experience, these texts mimic the fragmentation and the multiplicity of experience that individuals are confronted by and must cope with in a technological, mass media society. Borrowing from Umberto Eco, we can say that these texts function as epistemological metaphors because the ways in which their representation is structured reflect those of the science and the culture of our time.[15]

Finally, we must ask the question, how should these texts be read? Readers must not approach this fiction with a mental set that makes them expect a story with actions, characters, and suspense; they must not look for cues that would orient them. Rather, they must enter the textual turbulence knowing they are going to have a multifaceted experience. In a discussion of the poetics of indeterminacy in the poetry of Beckett, Cage, Pound, and Rimbaud, Marjorie Perloff remarks that their texts do not mean in conventional ways.[16] This remark is pertinent to the works I have analyzed here. Readers of postmodern poems and of postmodern fiction must not look for a specific meaning and must not demand certainty; they must be aware that they are entering domains or fields of signs that are polyvalent. Furthermore, readers must be aware that such modes of expression are meant to initiate performance rather than formulate meaning, that they are emergent structures which necessitate collaboration. Readers must also be prepared to experience contradictory feelings because of the tension between continuity and discontinuity, between innovation and repetition. At the same time they must realize that the new perspectives and new possibilities opening up in the familiar domain of words and signs can renew their habits for understanding, listening, and seeing. Lyotard writes: "Postmodern knowledge refines our sensitivity to differences."[17] So do these texts.

What do we expect from a work of art? The answer certainly varies from reader to reader, but let us consider the following statement by Gilbert Lascaut: "One of the most important functions of art is to render manifest the complexity of our desires in front of works. We feel at the same time the desire for simplicity and that for intricacies, and we look at the same time for an easy access and a difficult path."[18] Each of the texts discussed here allows readers to play out such contradictory attitudes, for they are at the same time both simple and intricate, both easy and difficult to read. More generally they play out basic components of human experience, where difficulty and easiness, simplicity and complexity constantly interact.

Notes

Chapter One

1. Jean Ricardou, *Problèmes du nouveau roman* (Paris: Seuil, 1967), 31. Unless otherwise indicated, all translations are mine. When a published translation exists, I have generally used it; both French and English versions are then cited in the notes.

2. For an interesting discussion of titles of novels, see Leo H. Hoek, "Description d'un archonte," in *Nouveau Roman: Hier, aujourd'hui I* (Paris: UGE, 1972): 289–326.

3. Postmodernism has been and continues to be widely discussed. Some representative studies are Ihab Hassan, "Culture, Indeterminacy and Immanence: Margins of the (Postmodern) Age," *Humanities in Society* (Winter 1978): 51–85; Jean-François Lyotard, *La Condition postmoderne* (Paris: Minuit, 1979); Marjorie Perloff, *The Poetics of Indeterminacy* (Princeton, N.J.: Princeton University Press, 1981); Hal Foster ed., *The Anti-Aesthetic: Essays in Postmodern Culture* (Port Townsend, Wash.: Bay Press, 1983).

4. Roland Barthes, *S/Z* (Paris: Seuil, 1970), 11; *S/Z,* trans. Richard Miller (New York: Hill & Wang, 1974), 5.

5. Lyotard, *La Condition postmoderne,* 7.

6. Michel Butor, *Répertoire I* (Paris: Gallimard, 1960), 8.

7. For specific studies on connotations, see Roland Barthes, "Rhétorique de l'image," *Communication* 4 (1967): 40–51; and *S/Z.*

8. See, for instance, Julia Kristeva, *Le Texte du roman* (Paris: Seuil, 1970); Michael Riffaterre, *La Production du texte* (Paris: Seuil, 1979); Gérard

Genette, *Introduction à l'architexte* (Paris: Seuil, 1979), and *Palimpsestes* (Paris: Seuil, 1982).

9. I borrow the last term from Jacques Derrida, *La Dissémination* (Paris: Seuil, 1972), 395–98. He uses it to describe how Sollers in *Nombres* incorporates material from other texts. Sollers presents this material by means of his own personal style, so that he essentially reinscribes, or grafts, concepts and ideas into his own prose.

10. Boris Uspenski, "Structural Isomorphism in Verbal and Visual Art," *Poetics* 5 (1972): 5–39; passages quoted from pp. 20 and 26.

11. Imbrie Buffum, *Studies in the Baroque from Montaigne to Rotrou* (New Haven, Conn.: Yale University Press, 1957); Mario Praz, *Mnemosyne: The Parallel between Literature and the Visual Arts* (Princeton, N.J.: Princeton University Press, 1970), 54–77.

12. Roger Laporte, *Carnets* (Paris: Hachette, 1979), 288–89.

13. For a discussion of literary texts as staggered systems of meaning, see Michael Holquist and Walter Reed, "Six Theses on the Novel and Some Metaphors," *New Literary History* 11 (1979–80): 413–23.

14. Emile Benveniste, *Problèmes de linguistique générale* (Paris: Gallimard, 1966); Louis Hjelmslev, *Prolegomena to a Theory of Language*, rev. trans. (Madison: University of Wisconsin Press, 1961); Roman Jakobson, "Linguistics and Poetics," *Style in Language*, ed. Thomas Sebeok (Cambridge, Mass.: MIT Press, 1964): 350–77, J. L. Austin, *How to Do Things with Words* (New York: Oxford University Press, 1965); John Searle, *Speech Acts* (Cambridge: Cambridge University Press, 1969); Erving Goffman, *Frame Analysis* (New York: Harper & Row, 1974); Ludwig Wittgenstein, *Philosophical Investigations* (New York: Macmillan, 1968); Jacques Derrida, "La Différance," *Théorie d'ensemble* (Paris: Seuil, 1968): 41–66, and "Structure, Sign, and Play in the Discourse of the Human Sciences," in *The Languages of Criticism and the Sciences of Man: The Structuralist Controversy*, ed. Richard Macksey and Eugenio Donato (Baltimore, Md.: Johns Hopkins University Press, 1970); Gilles Deleuze and Félix Guattari, *L'Anti-Oedipe* (Paris: Minuit, 1972); and Gilles Deleuze, *Milles Plateaux* (Paris: Minuit, 1980).

15. Clifford Geertz, "Thick Description: Toward an Interpretative Theory of Culture," *The Interpretation of Cultures* (New York: Basic Books, 1973): 3–32.

16. I borrow this term from Barthes, *S/Z*, (p. 9 in Richard Miller's English translation).

Chapter Two

1. Roland Barthes, *Essais critiques* (Paris: Seuil, 1964), 63; *Critical Essays*, trans. Richard Howard (Evanston, Ill.: Northwestern University Press, 1972), 51.

2. Jean Ricardou, *L'Observatoire de Cannes* (Paris: Minuit, 1965). Page numbers in the text refer to this edition.

3. Jean Ricardou, *Révolutions minuscules* (Paris: Gallimard, 1971).

4. Ricardou, *Problèmes du nouveau roman,* 73–74.

5. Alain Robbe-Grillet, *La Jalousie* (Paris: Minuit, 1957); *Projet pour une révolution à New York* (Paris: Minuit, 1970).

6. Alain Robbe-Grillet, *La Maison de rendez-vous* (Paris: Minuit, 1965). Page numbers given for quotations in French refer to this edition; the English passages and page numbers are from Richard Howard's translation (New York: Grove, 1966).

7. Claude Simon, *Triptyque* (Paris: Minuit, 1933), and the English translation by Helen R. Lane (New York: Viking, 1976). Page numbers in the text refer to these editions.

8. Focusing on the fact that *Triptyque* is both fragmented and cohesive, Ricardou, in his *Nouveaux Problèmes du roman* (Paris: Seuil, 1978), 232–43, characterizes its representation as organized by a *dispositif osiriaque* (an osiriac mechanism), whereby what is cut up (Osiris's body) is brought back together and reassembled (by Isis). Seriality performs this same process.

9. Illicit love is a topic present in all of Simon's works. For a discussion, see *Sub-Stance* 8 (1974), which also contains Claud DuVerlie's very interesting interview with Simon in which he explains his ideas about writing.

10. Helen Lane has translated the word *nacelle* once as "chassis" and once as "buggy." From the point of view of my analysis, these translations do not respect the original, in two senses. First, they lose the repetition of the word *nacelle*; second, neither English word connotes the roundness and curviness that Simon definitely intended to suggest.

11. Claude Simon, "Claude Simon à la question," *Claude Simon: Colloque de Cerisy,* ed. Jean Ricardou (Paris: UGE, 1975), 425.

12. Claude Simon, "La Fiction mot à mot," in *Nouveau Roman: Hier, aujourd'hui II* (Paris: UGE, 1972): 80.

13. René Thom, *Structural Stability and Morphogenesis* (Reading, Mass: W. A. Benjamin, 1975), 7–10.

14. Georges Raillard, "Le Rythme des choses," *Critique* 414 (November 1981): 1169. I borrow the phrase paronamasia of things from this article.

15. Claude Simon, *Orion aveugle* (Paris: Skira, 1970), 10.

16. Roman Jakobson, "Linguistics and Poetics," *Style in Language,* ed. Thomas Sebeok (Cambridge, Mass.: MIT Press, 1964): 350–77.

17. For a discussion of oral literature in a preliterate society, see Dina and Joel Sherzer, "Literature in San Blas: Discovering the Kuna *Ikala,*" *Semiotica* 6 (1972): 182–99.

18. D'Arcy Thompson, *On Growth and Form* (Cambridge, Mass.: Cambridge University Press, 1961), 72–73.

19. Benjamin Whorf, *Language, Thought and Reality* (Cambridge, Mass.: MIT Press, 1956). For a study updating the ideas of Whorf and relating them to literary language, see Paul Friedrich, "Poetic Language and the Imagination: A Reformulation of the Sapir Hypothesis," *Language, Context, and*

the Imagination (Stanford, Calif.: Stanford University Press, 1979), 441–512.

20. Pierre Francastel, *Peinture et société* (Paris: Gallimard, 1965), 195.

21. For a study of the device of *mise en abyme* in contemporary novels, see Lucien Dällenback, *Le Récit spéculaire* (Paris: Seuil, 1977).

22. Derrida, *La Dissémination,* 324.

23. As Freud taught us in *Beyond the Pleasure Principle* (New York: Norton, 1961).

24. *La Maison de rendez-vous* is listed in the *Dictionnaire des oeuvres érotiques* (Paris: Mercure de France, 1971), 297–98.

25. In *La Maison de rendez-vous*, 85, Laureen's pose compared to Manneret's *Maia* conjures up a series of Western paintings representing naked women on display: Goya's *The Naked Maja,* Ingres's *Large Odalisque,* Manet's *Olympia,* and Titian's *Venus of Urbino.* I am indebted to Carolyn Nizzi Warmbold's unpublished paper, "The Manneret Connection," for pointing out this series of paintings.

26. DuVerlie interview with Claude Simon, 17–18.

27. See Robbe-Grillet's remarks in *Nouveau Roman: Hier, aujourd'hui II,* 141.

28. See, e.g., the drawing by Saul Steinberg in E. H. Gombrich, *Art and Illusion* (Princeton, N.J.: Princeton University Press, 1972), 238–39, in which a single horizontal line is made to play different roles (sea, clothesline, desert horizon, railroad tracks, table top, ceiling); Warhol's series of the Mona Lisa and Jackie Kennedy in Gillo Dorflès, *Kitsche* (New York: Bell, 1968), 296–97; and Jacques Derrida's presentation of Adami, "Valerio Adami: Le Voyage du dessin," *Derrière le miroir 214* (Paris: Editions Maeght, 1975), a later version of which appears in *La Vérité en peinture* (Paris: Flammarion, 1978), 167–209.

Chapter Three

1. I borrow the expression from René Payant, who uses it to discuss heterogeneity in the works of Jasper Johns; see "Collage at large: Le Texte déchaîné," *Rhétoriques sémiotiques (Revue d'Esthétique 1–2)* (Paris: UGE, 1979), 254.

2. Quoted by Barthes in "Drame, poème, roman," *Théorie d'ensemble* (Paris: Seuil, 1968).

3. For a detailed study of Proust's narrative techniques, see Gérard Genette, *Figures III* (Paris: Seuil, 1972).

4. Since the introduction of the term *intertextuality* by Julia Kristeva, who was influenced by Mikhail Bakhtin, the process has been widely studied. See Julia Kristeva, "Le Mot, le dialogue, et le roman," *Semiotiké* (Paris: Seuil, 1969): 143–73; Laurent Jenny, "La Stratégie de la forme," *Poétique 27* (1976): 257–81; *La Parodie (Cahiers du 20 ème siècle 6)* (Paris: Klincksieck,

1976); *Collages (Revue d'Esthétique 3–4)* (Paris: UGE, 1978); *Rhétoriques sémiotiques (Revue d'Esthétique 1–2)* (Paris: UGE, 1979); Genette, *Palimpsestes.*

5. For an excellent discussion, see Jean-Jacques Thomas, "Lecture/Montage/Espace," *Stanford French Review* (Spring 1982): 87–100.

6. These recurrences are *isotopies* that organize the text. For an analysis using this concept, see François Rastier, "Systématique des isotopies," in *Essais de sémiotique poétique,* ed. A. J. Greimas (Paris: Larousse, 1972): 80–106.

7. For a comprehensive study of textual cohesion see M. A. K. Halliday and Ruqaiya Hasan, *Cohesion in English* (Londn: Longman, 1976).

8. Jacques Derrida, *Marges de la philosophie* (Paris: Minuit, 1972), 381.

9. Michel Butor, *Mobile* (Paris: Gallimard, 1962), and the English translation by Richard Howard (New York: Simon & Schuster, 1963). Page numbers in the text refer to these editions.

10. Quoted by Jean Roudaut, *Michel Butor ou le livre futur* (Paris: Gallimard, 1966), 153.

11. Alan Gardiner, *The Theory of Proper Names,* 2d ed. (Oxford: Oxford University Press, 1957).

12. For a fascinating study of this topic, see Jack Goody, *The Domestication of the Savage Mind* (Cambridge: Cambridge University Press, 1977).

13. Barthes, *Essais critiques,* 179; *Critical Essays,* trans. Richard Howard, 176.

14. John Searle, "Proper Names" *Mind* 67, no. 266 (1958): 166–73.

15. Leo Spitzer, "Quelques Aspects de la technique des romans de Michel Butor" *Etudes de style* (Paris: Gallimard, 1970): 482–531.

16. As distinct from John Dos Passos's earlier and experimental *USA,* which contained a story; it was a modern but not postmodern text.

17. Michel Butor, *Repertoire II* (Paris: Minuit, 1964), 96.

18. Marcel Proust, *A la recherche du temps perdu: Noms de pays* (Paris: Gallimard, 1954), 387–88.

19. Geoffrey H. Hartman, *Saving the Text* (Baltimore, Md.: Johns Hopkins University Press: 1981), 127.

20. Jean-Paul Sartre, *La Nausée* (Paris: Gallimard, 1938), 52–53; *Nausea,* trans. Robert Baldick (Harmondsworth, Eng.: Penguin, 1969), 53.

21. In an interview with Paolo Caruso, "Michel Butor" *Aut Aut* 68 (March 1962): 168.

22. For a discussion of the discourse of tourist guides, see Roland Barthes, "Le Guide bleu," *Mythologies* (Paris: Seuil, 1957), 121–24; *Mythologies,* trans. Annette Lavers (New York: Hill & Wang, 1975), 74–77; Dean Mac-Cannel, *The Tourist* (New York: Schocken Books, 1976).

23. In an interview with Eva Corredor, "Théorie de la fiction et fiction théorique," *French Review,* 54, no. 4 (March 1981): 540.

24. Maurice Roche, *Circus* (Paris: Seuil, 1972); page numbers refer to this edition. I have chosen to render the semantic content as well as the rhythm of

Roche's prose whenever possible. When there are play and manipulation with sounds not accounted for in the English version, I will draw specific attention to them.

25. In this example, notice the repetitive sound in *roupies* and *roupettes*.

26. Expression used by Claudel and quoted by Michel Butor, who in two essays of *Répertoire II* (Paris: Minuit, 1964)—"Sur la page," 100–103, and "Le Livre comme objet," 104–23, praising Mallarmé and Rabelais among others—calls for a creative use of the resources of typography, which he himself practices in *Mobile* and his subsequent works. Roche, of course, is particularly creative in his use of space.

27. In an interview with Patrice Fardeau, "Manif," *France nouvelle* 1690 (April 1978): 44.

28. The repetition and permutation of *r*'s, *d*'s, *t*'s, *a*'s, and *i*'s, which confer a definite rhythm to the French text, are unfortunately lost in translation.

29. Such parodies are common in children's play, including parodies of the Lord's Prayer: "Lead us not into Penn Station"; "Give us each day our jellied bread." See Mary Sanches and Barbara Kirshenblatt-Gimblett, "Children's Traditional Speech Play and Child Language," *Speech Play,* ed. Barbara Kirshenblatt-Gimblett (Philadelphia: University of Pennsylvania Press, 1976), 65–110.

30. *Brique* is a pun here which has the meaning of brick, and also of money; in slang *une brique* means 10,000 francs. My translation cannot render the play on OR or on *a* and *o* in *repas / drague, repos / drogue.*

31. See George Vaillant, *The Aztecs of Mexico* (New York: Doubleday, 1944), 332. During their sacrificial ceremonies the Aztecs would hang the skulls of victims on racks.

32. For a fascinating analysis of the *vanitas,* see Bernard Lamblin, "Vanitas: La symbolique de l'objet," *Pour l'objet (Revue d'Esthétique 3–4)* (Paris: UGE, 1979), 197–232.

33. "Entretien avec Anne Fabre-Luce," *La Quinzaine Littéraire,* 139 (1972): 3–4.

34. *French Review,* 54, no. 4 (March 1981): 548.

35. Jacques Henric, "Deux Entretiens avec Maurice Roche," *Maurice Roche par les autres* (Paris: L'Athanor, 1978), 108. The following journals also contain useful studies on Roche: *Change* 5 (1972): 72; *Encres vives* 74 (Spring 1973); *TriQuarterly* 38 (Winter 1977); *Textuerre* 13–14 (October 1978).

36. Philippe Sollers, *L'Ecriture et l'expérience des limites* (Paris: Seuil, 1968).

37. *Magazine littéraire* 65 (1972) contains a presentation of Sollers's career and selections from reviews of his first novels, as well as his commentaries on these novels and his conception of the novel in general.

38. Stephen Heath in *The Nouveau Roman* (Philadelphia: Temple University Press, 1972) discusses *Drame* and *Nombres*. See also Barthes's analysis of *Drame* in "Drame, poème, roman," 25–40; Derrida's analysis of *Nombres* in *La Dissémiantion,* 319–99; and Kristeva's in *Semiotiké,* 290–371.

39. Philippe Sollers, *H* (Paris: Seuil, 1973). Page numbers in the text refer to this edition.

40. From an interview with Jean-Louis de Rambures, *Le Monde,* November 29, 1974, p. 24.

41. In an interview with David Hayman, *Iowa Review* 5, no. 4 (1974): 101.

42. As in *Circus,* my translations render the semantic level of the text, and many of its phonic aspects are not accounted for. For instance, in the French version there is the repetition of *j* in *jeu joie juif jouissance,* and of the group of letters *oyau* in *noyau boyau aloyau.*

43. This juxtaposition of an author's biographical name and pseudonym is of particular interest to Sollers. He analyzes its implications in the case of Lautréamont, who signs *Les Chants de Maldoror* with his invented name, Conte de Lautréamont, but *Poésies* with his biographical name, Isidore Ducasse: see Sollers, *L'Ecriture et l'expérience,* 139–90.

44. David Hayman, "Some Writers in the Wake of the *Wake,*" *Tri-Quarterly* 38 (Winter 1977): 22.

45. Rambures interview, 24.

46. Here is Rimbaud's "H" in French and in English, the latter quoted from Enid Rhodes Peschel's translation of *The Illuminations* (New York: Oxford University Press, 1973):

Toutes les monstruosités violent les gestes atroces d'Hortense. Sa soliture est la mécanique érotique; sa lassitude, la dynamique amoureuse. Sous la surveillance d'une enfance, elle a été, à des époques nombreuses, l'ardente hygiène des races. Sa porte est ouverte à la misère. Là, la moralité des êtres actuels se décorpore en sa passion ou en son action. —O terrible frisson des amours novices sur le sol sanglant et par l'hydrogène clarteux! trouvez Hortense.

All the monstrosities violate the atrocious behavior patterns of Hortense. Her solitude is erotic mechanics; her lassitude, amorous dynamics. Under the supervision of childhood, she has been in numerous epochs, the ardent hygiene of races. Her door is open to misery. There, the morality of actual beings is disembodied in her passion or in her action. —O terrible thrill of new loves on the bloodstained soil and through the transparent hydrogen! find Hortense.

47. For a presentation of Bruno's philosophy, see Frances Yates, *Giordano Bruno and the Hermetic Tradition* (Chicago: University of Chicago Press, 1964); for a discussion of diagrams and memory wheels, see Yates, *The Art of Memory* (Chicago: University of Chicago Press, 1966).

48. Philippe Sollers, Logiques (Paris: Seuil, 1969), 105.

49. Examples of these various speech acts include insults: *bande de cons* [p. 10] (pack of assholes), *ta gueule vieux schnock* [p. 182] (shut up old schnook); commands: *tiens toi droit* [p. 57] (sit up straight), *va te laver* [p. 95] (go get

washed); exclamations: *qu'est-ce qu'ils peuvent être chiants* [p. 27] (what pains in the ass); declarative statements: *je prendrais bien un sandwich et un demi* [p. 60] (I could have a sandwich and a beer), *tu vois ça m'rapelle les tournesols de van gogh* [p. 154] (you see it reminds me of Van Gogh's sunflowers); nursery talk: *une bouchée pour papa une bouchée pour maman* [p. 61] (one for daddy one for mommy); anonymous broadcasts: *voici notre bulletin d'information* [p. 134] (and now the news), *au quatrième top il sera exactement* [p. 107] (at the tone the time will be), *immediate boarding* [p. 175]. For tellings or retellings of jokes and personal experiences see, e.g., pp. 53 and 177.

50. The purpose of these examples is to illustrate the various types of phonic play. I have not translated them because the effects would be lost in English.

51. This last example is in fact made up of Arabic words, but for most French readers these are just strange sounds, unlike Kif-Kif, razzia, or casbah, which are widely used in contemporary France.

52. Rambures interview.

53. Roland Barthes, *La Plaisir du texte* (Paris: Seuil, 1973), 104.

54. For a discussion concerning the role of speech play in the different phases of language acquisition, see Sanches and Kirshenblatt-Gimblett, "Children's Traditional Speech Play."

55. Rambures interview.

56. Sollers, *L'écriture et l'expérience,* 16.

57. I quote the English translation from Julia Kristeva, *Desire in Language,* ed. Leon S. Roudiez (New York: Columbia University Press, 1980), 181; the original appeared in Kristeva's *Polylogue* (Paris: Seuil, 1980), 195–96.

58. Gregory Bateson, *Steps to an Ecology of Mind* (New York: Ballantine, 1972), 113. Several works by the American composer Philip Glass also achieve this sustained fluidity and progress within a limited range of variations.

59. Roland Barthes, *Sollers écrivain* (Paris: Seuil, 1979), 56.

60. Richard Ellman, *James Joyce* (New York: Oxford University Press, 1965), 558.

61. See, e.g., the introduction of Anthony Burgess to *A Shorter Finnegans Wake* (New York: Viking, 1968), xviii; Aldo Tagliaferri, *Beckett et la surdétermination littéraire* (Paris: Payot, 1977), 35–46; and commentaries on Gadda by Philippe di Meo, *La Quinzaine Littéraire* 366 (March 1–15, 1982): 22–23.

62. Kristeva, *Semiotiké,* 298–99.

63. I borrow this term from Michael Riffaterre, "Sémiotique intertextuelle: L'interprétant," in *Rhétoriques sémiotiques* (*Revue d'Esthétique 1–2*) (Paris: UGE, 1979), 128–46.

64. Derrida, *Marges,* 381.

65. For specific studies on these composers and artists see *Collages* (*Revue*

d'Esthétique 3–4) (Paris: UGE, 1978); for Derrida, see Hartman, *Saving the Text.*

66. On this question of reference, see Nelson Goodman, "Routes of Reference," *Critical Inquiry* 8, no. 1 (Autumn 1981): 121–32.

67. Michel Foucault, *L'Ordre du discours* (Paris: Gallimard, 1971), 24.

68. Ibid., 11.

Chapter Four

1. Such writers as Raymond Federman, Alain Robbe-Grillet, and Claude Simon also invent self-conscious narrators. But theirs, unlike those of Beckett, Pinget, and Laporte, are not tormented; rather they are lighthearted and playful.

2. These three types of activity engaged in by Beckett's, Pinget's, and Laporte's self-conscious narrators are typical of self-conscious narrators, from those of Cervantes to Pynchon.

3. Martin Esslin, ed., "Three Dialogues," *Samuel Beckett: A Collection of Critical Essays* (Englewood Cliffs, N.J.: Prentice-Hall, 1965), 16–22.

4. Maurice Blanchot, "Où maintenant? Qui maintenant?" *Nouvelle Revue Française* 2 (October 1953): 678–86.

5. Samuel Beckett, L'Innommable (Paris: Minuit, 1953), and Beckett's own English translation in *Three Novels* (New York: Grove, 1958). Page numbers in the text refer to these two editions. For a discussion of the identity of the narrator in Beckett's trilogy, see my *Structure de la trilogie: Molloy, Malone meurt, L'Innommable* (The Hague: Mouton, 1976).

6. I use Beckett's translation even when it does not render exactly what is written in the French text. Here he does not translate "ce qui se passe ce sont des mots" (what's happening are words).

7. Italics are mine in all the examples I quote in the rest of this section.

8. The importance of speaking, of words, is constantly stressed in Beckett's works, in particular in his plays. See my article *"Endgame* or what talk can do," *Modern Drama* 5 (1979): 291–303.

9. For the influence of German Expressionism on Beckett, see Vivian Mercier, *Beckett/Beckett* (New York: Oxford University Press, 1977), 99.

10. Here Beckett does not translate his neologism or invent another in English. In French, *sucrement* comes from *sucre* (sugar) and is used here by Beckett because of its phonic proximity with *sacrément* (damned, jolly).

11. These transformations and inventions of proverbs are an idiosyncrasy of Beckett's narrators and characters. They are instances of their interest in play, in manipulation, and of their delight in words. See my article "Saying Is Inventing: Gnomic Expressions in *Molloy,"* in *Speech Play,* ed. Barbara Kirshenblatt-Gimblett (Philadelphia: University of Pennsylvania Press, 1976), 163–71.

12. J. D. O'Hara, in his introduction to *Twentieth Century Interpretations of*

Molloy, Malone Dies, The Unnamable (Englewood Cliffs, N.J.: Prentice-Hall, 1970), 21–22, suggests the influence of Hume. Tagliaferri in *Beckett*, 35–46, discusses Beckett and Bruno. For the intertextual relationships that Beckett establishes with Dante, Descartes, and the Bible, see Ruby Cohn, *The Comic Gamut* (New Brunswick, N.J.: Rutgers University Press, 1962); John Fletcher, *The Novels of Samuel Beckett* (New York: Barnes & Noble, 1970); and Hugh Kenner, *Samuel Beckett: A Critical Study* (New York: Grove Press, 1961).

13. Julia Kristeva, *La Révolution du langage poétique* (Paris: Seuil, 1974). Kristeva calls this letting go and opening up of the unconscious and of drives the irruption of the semiotic into the text.

14. Ruby Cohn, *Back to Beckett* (Princeton, N.J.: Princeton University Press, 1973), 111.

15. Robert Pinget, "Pseudo-principes d'esthétique" *Nouveau Roman: Hier, aujourd'hue II* (Paris: UGE, 1972), 311–24.

16. For a general study and bibliographical information on Pinget's novels see Robert M. Henkels, Jr., *Robert Pinget: The Novel as Quest* (University: University of Alabama Press, 1979).

17. Robert Pinget, *Quelqu'un* (Paris: Minuit, 1955). Page numbers in the text refer to this edition. The translations are mine.

18. Nicolas Boileau, *L'Art poétique, Chant I* (Paris: Garnier, 1961), 163.

19. Pierre Bourdieu, *La Distinction* (Paris, Minuit, 1979).

20. Interview with Jean Ristat, "Lire Roger Laporte," *Lettres françaises* 1453 (September 27, 1972): 3–6.

21. Laporte, *Carnets*. Page numbers are cited in the text.

22. Roger Laporte, *Fugue* (Paris: Gallimard, 1970). Page numbers in the text refer to this edition.

23. See J. E. Cirlot, *A Dictionary of Symbols,* 2d ed. (New York: Philosophical Library, 1983), 231.

24. Aristotle, *Rhetoric,* trans. Rhys Robert (Oxford: Oxford University Press, 1946), III, 1405b.

25. The riddle is a very interesting verbal and interactional event. It is a mind activator, since the person asked to provide an answer must make connections between disparate items never before associated. Furthermore, as soon as the answer is provided, the riddle loses its power. It is these two possibilities that are exploited in *Fugue.*

26. See Roger Abrahams, "Introductory Remarks to a Rhetorical Theory of Folklore," *Journal of American Folklore* 81 (1968): 143–58.

27. Ristat, "Lire Roger Laporte," 3.

28. This section has benefited from my reading of the following works: Mathieu Bénézet, *Le Roman de la langue* (Paris: UGE, 1977); Roger Laporte and Bernard Noël, *Deux Lectures de Maurice Blanchot* (Montpellier: Fata Morgana, 1973); Roger Laporte, *Quinze Variations sur un thème biographique* (Paris: Flammarion, 1975); Michel le Guern, *Sémantique de la métaphore et de la métonymie* (Paris: Larousse, 1973).

29. Marc Le Bot, *Figures de l'art contemporain* (Paris: UGE, 1977), 179.

30. Wayne Booth, *The Rhetoric of Fiction* (Chicago: University of Chicago Press, 1970), 212.

31. Maurice Blanchot, *Le Livre à venir* (Paris: Gallimard, 1959), 263.

32. I borrow this notion from a review of Beckett's *Le Dépeupleur* by Anne Fabre-Luce. See *Samuel Beckett: The Critical Heritage,* ed. Lawrence Graver and Raymond Federman (London: Routledge & Kegan Paul, 1979), 315.

Chapter Five

1. Hélène Cixous, "Sorties," in Catherine Clément and Cixous, *La Jeune Née* (Paris: UGE, 1975), 174, 180.

2. Susan Husserl-Kapit, "An Interview with Marguerite Duras," *Signs: Journal of Women in Culture and Society* 1, no. 2 (Winter 1975): 423–34.

3. Monique Wittig, *Les Guérillères,* trans. David Le Vay (New York: Avon, 1973), 112–14; from pp. 162–64 in the original French edition (Paris: Minuit, 1959). Page numbers cited hereafter in the text refer to these two editions.

4. Hélène Cixous, "Le sexe ou la tête?" *Les Cahiers du Grif* 13 (October 1976): 13.

5. David Le Vay translates *les petites filles* as "women," no doubt trying to evoke a feminist perspective. However, the word *femme,* "woman," is never used in Wittig's text. Therefore, following Wittig literally, I have translated *les petites filles* as "little girls," maintaining the denotative and connotative properties of the term that Wittig intended. On the other hand, I do agree with Le Vay's translation of *elles* "they-feminine" as women, since Wittig has chosen the marked feminine form of the third person plural pronoun. This striking feature of her text would be totally missed by translating *elles* into English as "they," thereby losing the contrast so significant in *Les Guérillères* between feminine *elles* and masculine *ils.*

6. The presence of almost exclusively feminine pronouns and feminine names raises our awareness of our normally unconscious grammatical patterning in relation to gender.

7. According to Margaret Crosland, *Women of Iron and Velvet: French Women Writers after George Sand* (New York: Taplinger, 1976), 212. Wittig recognizes having been influenced by Jean-Luc Godard; perhaps in suppressing transitions between different sections and by ending each section arbitrarily, she is practicing textually the jump-cut technique for which Godard is famous on the screen.

8. Raymond Jean, *Pratiques de la littérature* (Paris: Seuil, 1978), 132.

9. Monique Wittig, *Le Corps lesbien* (Paris: Minuit, 1973), and Wittig and Sande Zeig, *Brouillon pour un dictionnaire des amantes* (Paris: Grasset, 1976), display the same types of techniques.

10. Louis Marin, *Utopiques: Jeux d'espaces* (Paris: Minuit, 1973), 88.

11. Here Wittig alludes to the well-known theory of Claude Lévi-Strauss, according to which women are treated as objects of exchange as an aspect of societal marriage rules: see *Les Structures élémentaires de la parenté* (Paris: Presses Universitaires de France, 1945).

12. The English translation maintains the French, probably in order to render the phonic play brought about by the repetition of *plume* and of *ot* in *escargot* and *haricot*.

13. Jean Chevalier and Alain Gheerhbrant in their *Dictionnaire des symboles* (Paris: Laffond, 1982), 868, discuss the symbolism of the snake in the following terms: "It is a first old god that we will find at the beginning in all cosmogeneses, before the religions of the mind dethrone it. It is what animates and what sustains. On the human level, the snake is the double symbol of the soul and of libido."

14. Michel Foucault, *Les Mots et les choses* (Paris: Gallimard, 1966), 9.

15. For some unexplained reason, this postface has been omitted in the English translation.

16. This kind of grafting of many texts within one's own text is also practiced by Philippe Sollers in *Nombres* (Paris: Seuil, 1968), and in *Lois* (Paris: Seuil, 1972); see ch. 2.

17. Natalie Davis, "Women on Top," in *Society and Culture in Early Modern France* (Stanford, Calif.: Stanford University Press, 1975).

18. Judy Chicago, in her book *Through the Flower: My Struggle as a Woman Artist* (Garden City, N.Y.: Doubleday, 1977), 54–69, describes how and why she concentrated on shapes that represent the female sexual anatomy in order to challenge male superiority.

19. For studies of the properties of oral texts, see Ruth Finnegan, *Oral Poetry* (Cambridge: Cambridge University Press, 1977), and Paul Zumthor, *Introduction à la poésie orale* (Paris: Seuil, 1983).

20. For an illustrated presentation of Waurà women and of their myth, see *Lost Empires* (Washington, D.C.: National Geographic Society, 1982): 316.

21. The myth of the women in control exists in several countries: see Type F in Stith Thompson, *The Types of the Folktale,* Communication No. 184 (Helsinki: Folklore Fellows, 1961), 112.

22. Pierre Clastres, *La Société contre l'état* (Paris: Minuit, 1974), and Joel Sherzer, *Kuna Ways of Speaking: An Ethnographic Perspective* (Austin: University of Texas Press, 1983).

23. Other pertinent studies on Wittig include Erika Ostrowsky, "A Cosmogony of O: Wittig's *Les Guérillères,*" in *Twentieth Century French Fiction,* ed. George Stambolian (New Brunswick, N.J.: Rutgers University Press, 1975): 241–51; Lynn Higgins, "Nouvelle nouvelle autobiographie: Monique Wittig's *Le Corps lesbien,*" *Sub-stance* 14 (1976): 160–66.

24. For a complete bibliography, see Carol J. Murphy, *Alienation and Absence in the Novels of Marguerite Duras* (Lexington, Ky.: French Forum, 1982).

25. Marguerite Duras and Xavière Gauthier, *Les Parleuses* (Paris: Minuit, 1974), 67–68.

26. Marguerite Duras, *L'Amour* (Paris: Gallimard, 1971). Page numbers in the text refer to this edition.

27. Duras explains that she realized long after having invented the name S. Thala that it resembles the name Thalassa, which is the Greek word for sea. For a discussion of the importance of the sea in Duras's novels, see Marguerite Duras et Michèle Porte, *Les Lieux de Marguerite Duras* (Paris: Minuit, 1977), 77–91.

28. Deleuze, *Milles Plateaux,* 213.

29. Hubert Nyssen, "Marguerite Duras: Un Silence peuplé de phrases" *Synthèses* (August–September 1967): 254–55.

30. See Duras and Gauthier, *Les Parleuses; Marguerite Duras* (Paris: Albatros, 1975); Duras and Porte, *Les Lieux de Marguerite Duras*; and Duras's two works *Un Barrage contre le Pacifique* (Paris: Gallimard, 1950), and *L'Eden cinéma* (Paris: Gallimard, 1975), which are transpositions of the author's own experiences.

31. *Marguerite Duras,* 84.

32. Ibid., 86.

33. For an excellent study of George Eliot's and Madame de Lafayette's characters, see Nancy K. Miller, "Emphasis Added: Plots and Plausibilities in Women's Fiction," *PMLA* 96, no. 1 (January 1981): 36–48.

34. Claudine Hermann, *Les Voleuses de langue* (Paris: Des femmes, 1976), 139–41.

35. Gombrich, *Art and Illusion,* 331.

36. Henri Maldiney, *Regard Parole Espace* (Paris: L'Age d'Homme, 1973), 166–67.

37. Interview with Christiane Makward, *Sub-Stance* 13 (1976): 28.

38. Ibid., 35.

39. Hélène Cixous, *Souffles* (Paris: Des femmes, 1975). Page numbers in the text refer to this edition. Many of Cixous's other creative and critical works are listed in the bibliography.

40. Cixous, "Le Sexe ou la tête?" 15. In the last clause of this passage, Cixous coins the word *ille* which combines the masculine pronoun *il* and the feminine pronoun *elle.* Hence my translation *heshe.*

41. Ibid., 8.

42. Ibid., 15.

43. Jean Vuarnet, *Extases féminines* (Paris: Arthaud, 1980), 26.

44. Luce Irigaray, *Speculum de l'autre femme* (Paris: Minuit, 1974); and *Ce Sexe qui n'en est pas un* (Paris: Minuit, 1977).

45. Duras and Gauthier, *Les Parleuses,* 8. In my translation I have used the phrase "well-seated words" to render Gauthier's "mots bien assis."

46. Hermann, *Les Voleuses de langue,* 139–41.

47. Hélène Cixous, Madeleine Gagnon, and Annie Le clerc, *La Venue à l'écriture* (Paris: UGE, 1977), 62.

48. Annis Pratt, *Archetypal Patterns in Women's Fiction* (Bloomington: Indiana University Press, 1981), 11.

49. As quoted by Miller, "Emphasis Added," 40.

50. Lisa Appignanesi, *Femininity and the Creative Imagination* (New York: Barnes & Noble, 1973), 14–15.

51. Lyotard, *La Condition postmoderne.*

52. Quoted by Nancy K. Miller in her "Women's Autobiography in France: for a Dialectics of Identification," in *Women and Language in Literature and Society,* ed. Sally McConnell-Ginet et al. (New York: Praeger, 1980): 258–73.

53. Kristeva, *La Révolution du langage poétique.*

54. I am indebted for these remarks to Pratt's *Archetypal Patterns.*

Chapter Six

1. Gilles Deleuze, *Rhizome* (Paris: Minuit, 1976).

2. Barthes, *S/Z,* 61–62, pp. 54–56 in Miller's translation.

3. Catherine Clément, "De la méconnaissance: Fantasme, texte, scène," *Langages* 31 (1973): 36–52.

4. I concur here with David Carroll, who argues this point brilliantly in *The Subject in Question* (Chicago: University of Chicago Press, 1982).

5. Wittgenstein, *Philosophical Investigations,* 11.

6. Robert Blanché, Structures intellectuelles (Paris: Vrin, 1969), 110.

7. See, for instance, Joel Sherzer, *Kuna Ways of Speaking;* and Zumthor, *Introduction à la poésie orale.*

8. Kristeva, *Desire in Language,* 20.

9. Modernism and avant-garde European literary movements of the 1920s such as Dada and Surrealism, in their effort to subvert conventions and to attack conformism, had already introduced changes in modes of representation by means of typographical innovations and montage. But then these experimentations, while pushed aside by literature (they are nonexistent in Existentialism), were appropriated and exploited by capitalism to market its goods, starting in the 1950s. Postmodernism brings back to literature these textual manipulations and makes them part of a strategy to deconstruct logocentrism, to introduce multiplicity and fragmentation.

10. On this question, see Jean-Marie Benoist, *La Révolution structurale* (Paris: Grasset, 1975); and Clifford Geertz, "Blurred Genres: The Refiguration of Social Thought," *American Scholar* 49 (Spring 1980): 165–82.

11. Iannis Xenakis, "Entretien: En quête de l'inoui," *La Quinzaine Littéraire* 353 (August 1981): 36.

12. See Paul Davies, *Other Worlds, A Portrait of Nature in Rebellion: Space, Superspace, and the Quantum Universe* (New York: Simon & Schuster, 1980).

13. Lyotard, *La Condition postmoderne,* 97.

14. Ilya Prigogine, "Probing into Time," *Discovery* 5, no. 1. (September 1980): 5–7.

15. Umberto Eco, *L'Opera aperta* (Milano: Bompiani, 1967), 42.

16. Marjorie Perloff, *The Poetics of Indeterminacy* (Princeton, N.J.: Princeton University Press, 1981), 42.

17. Lyotard, *La Condition postmoderne*, 8.

18. Gilbert Lascaut, "Treize Murs peints," *La Quinzaine Littéraire* 379 (October 1982): 21–22.

Bibliography

All the French primary texts and critical works are listed in the original French published version. In those cases in which I have cited English translations, these are listed as well.

Abrahams, Roger. "Introductory Remarks to a Rhetorical Theory of Folklore." *Journal of American Folklore* 81 (1968): 143–58.
Appignanesi, Lisa. *Femininity and the Creative Imagination.* New York: Barnes & Noble, 1973.
Aristotle. *Rhetoric.* Translated by Rhys Robert. Oxford: Oxford University Press, 1946.
Austin, J. L. *How to Do Things with Words.* New York: Oxford University Press, 1965.
Barthes, Roland. "Drame, Poème, Roman." In *Théorie d'ensemble,* 25–40. Paris: Seuil, 1968.
———. *Essais critiques.* Paris: Seuil, 1964.
———. *Critical Essays.* Translated by Richard Howard. Evanston, Ill.: Northwestern University Press, 1972.
———. *Mythologies.* Paris: Seuil, 1957.
———. *Mythologies.* Translated by Annette Lavers. New York: Hill & Wang, 1975.
———. *Le Plaisir du texte.* Paris: Seuil, 1973.
———. "Rhétorique de l'image." *Communication* 4 (1967): 40–51.

————. *Sollers écrivain.* Paris: Seuil, 1979.

————. *S/Z.* Paris: Seuil, 1970.

————. *S/Z.* Translated by Richard Miller. New York: Hill and Wang, 1970.

Bateson, Gregory. *Steps to an Ecology of Mind.* New York: Ballantine, 1972.

Beckett, Samuel. *L'Innommable.* Paris: Minuit, 1953.

————. *Three Novels.* New York: Grove Press, 1958.

Bénézet, Mathieu. *Le Roman de la langue.* Paris: UGE, 1977.

Benoist, Jean-Marie. *La Révolution structurale.* Paris: Grasset, 1975.

Benveniste, Emile. *Problèmes de linguistique générale.* Paris: Gallimard, 1966.

Blanché, Robert. *Structures intellectuelles.* Paris: Vrin, 1969.

Blanchot, Maurice. *L'Entretien infini.* Paris: Gallimard, 1969.

————. *Le Livre à venir.* Paris: Gallimard, 1959.

————. "Où maintenant? Qui maintenant?" *Nouvelle Revue Française* 2 (October 1953): 678–86.

Boileau, Nicolas. "Chant 1." In *L'Art poétique.* Paris: Garnier, 1961.

Booth, Wayne. *The Rhetoric of Fiction.* Chicago: University of Chicago Press, 1970.

Bothorel, Nicole, et al. *Les Nouveaux Romanciers.* Paris: Bordas, 1976.

Bourdieu, Pierre. *La Distinction.* Paris: Minuit, 1979.

Brooke-Rose, Christine. *A Rhetoric of the Unreal.* Cambridge: Cambridge University Press, 1981.

Buffum, Imbrie. *Studies in the Baroque from Montaigne to Rotrou.* New Haven, Conn.: Yale University Press, 1957.

Burgess, Anthony. Introduction to *A Shorter Finnegans Wake.* New York: Viking, 1968.

Butor, Michel. *Degrés.* Paris: Gallimard, 1962.

————. *L'Emploi du temps.* Paris: Minuit, 1956.

————. *Illustrations.* Paris: Gallimard, 1964.

————. *Illustrations II.* Paris: Gallimard, 1969.

————. *Illustrations III.* Paris: Gallimard, 1973.

————. *Matière de rêves.* Paris: Gallimard, 1975.

————. *Matière de rêves II.* Paris: Gallimard, 1976.

————. *Matière de rêves III.* Paris: Gallimard, 1977.

————. *Mobile.* Paris: Gallimard, 1962.

————. *Mobile.* Translated by Richard Howard. New York: Simon & Schuster, 1963.

————. *La Modification.* Paris: Minuit, 1957.

————. *Passage de Milan.* Paris: Minuit, 1954.

————. *Répertoire I.* Paris: Gallimard, 1960.

————. *Répertoire II.* Paris: Minuit, 1964.

————. *Répertoire III.* Paris: Minuit, 1968.

————. *Répertoire IV.* Paris: Minuit, 1974.

————. *Réseau aérien.* Paris: Gallimard, 1962.

Carroll, David. *The Subject in Question*. Chicago: University of Chicago Press, 1982.

Caruso, Paolo. "Michel Butor." *Aut Aut* 68 (March 1982): 168.

Chevalier, Jean, and Alain Gheerhbrant. *Dictionnaire des symboles*. Paris: Laffond, 1982.

Chicago, Judy. *Through the Flower: My Struggle as a Woman Artist*. Garden City, N.Y.: Doubleday, 1977.

Cirlot, J. E. *A Dictionary of Symbols*. 2d ed. New York: Philosophical Library, 1971.

Cixous, Hélène. *Angst*. Paris: Des femmes, 1977.

———. *Les Commencements*. Paris: Grasset, 1970.

———. *Dedans*. Paris: Grasset, 1969.

———. *L'Exil de James Joyce*. Paris: Grasset, 1968.

———. *Illa*. Paris: Des femmes, 1980.

———. *Introduction à Lewis Carroll*. Paris: Aubier, 1975.

———. *La*. Paris: Gallimard, 1976.

———. *Neutre*. Paris: Grasset, 1972.

———. *Le Nom d'Oedipe*. Paris: Des femmes, 1978.

———. *Portrait de Dora*. Paris: Des femmes, 1976.

———. *Portrait du soleil*. Paris: Denöel, 1973.

———. *Prénoms de personne*. Paris: Seuil, 1974.

———. *Préparatifs de noces au delà de l'abîme*, Paris: Des femmes, 1978.

———. "Le Rire de la Méduse." *L'Arc* 61 (Winter 1975): 39–54.

———. "Le Sexe ou la tête?" *Les Cahiers du Grif* 13 (October 1976): 5–15.

———. *Souffles*. Paris: Des femmes, 1975.

———. *Le Troisième Corps*. Paris: Grasset, 1970.

Cixous, Hélène; Madeleine Gagnon; and Annie Leclerc. *La Venue à l'écriture*. Paris: UGE, 1977.

Clastres, Pierre. *La Société contre l'état*. Paris: Minuit, 1974.

Clément, Catherine. "De la méconnaissance: Fantasme, texte, scène." *Langages* 31 (1973): 36–52.

Clément, Catherine, and Hélène Cixous. *La Jeune Née*. Paris: UGE, 1975.

Collages (Revue d'Esthétique 3–4). Paris: UGE, 1978.

Cohn, Ruby. *Back to Beckett*. Princeton, N.J.: Princeton University Press, 1973.

———. *The Comic Gamut*. New Brunswick, N.J.: Rutgers University Press, 1962.

Corredor, Eva. "Théorie de la fiction et fiction théorique." *French Review* 54, no. 4 (March 1981): 540–50.

Crosland, Margaret. *Women of Iron and Velvet: French Women Writers after George Sand*. New York: Taplinger, 1976.

Dällenback, Lucien. *Le Récit spéculaire*. Paris: Seuil, 1977.

Davies, Paul. *Other Worlds, A Portrait of Nature in Rebellion: Space, Superspace, and the Quantum Universe*. New York: Simon & Schuster, 1980.

Davis, Natalie. "Women on Top." In *Society and Culture in Early Modern France*. Stanford, Calif.: Stanford University Press, 1975.

Deleuze, Gilles. *Milles Plateaux*. Paris: Minuit, 1980.

———. *Rhizome*. Paris: Minuit, 1976.

Deleuze, Gilles, and Félix Guattari. *L'Anti-Oedipe*. Paris: Minuit, 1972.

Derrida, Jacques. "La Différance." In *Théorie d'ensemble*, 41–66. Paris: Seuil, 1968.

———. *La Dissémination*. Paris: Seuil, 1972.

———. *Marges de la philosophie*. Paris: Minuit, 1972.

———. "Structure, Sign, and Play in the Discourse of the Human Sciences." In *The Languages of Criticism and the Sciences of Man: The Structuralist Controversy*, ed. Richard Macksey and Eugenio Donato, 247–65. Baltimore, Md.: Johns Hopkins University Press, 1970.

———. *La Vérité en peinture*. Paris: Flammarion, 1978.

Dictionnaire des oeuvres érotiques. Paris: Mercure de France, 1971.

Dorflès, Gillo. *Kitsch*. New York: Bell, 1968.

Duras, Marguerite. *L'Amante anglaise*. Paris: Cahiers du Théatre National Populaire, 1968.

———. *L'Amour*. Paris: Gallimard, 1971.

———. *Un Barrage contre le Pacifique*. Paris: Gallimard, 1950.

———. *Le Camion*. Paris: Gallimard, 1977.

———. *L'Eden cinéma*. Paris: Gallimard, 1978.

———. *Hiroshima mon amour*. Paris: Gallimard, 1960.

———. *L'Homme assis dans le couloir*. Paris: Minuit, 1980.

———. *Moderato cantabile*. Paris: Minuit, 1958.

———. *Le Ravissement de Lol V. Stein*. Paris: Gallimard, 1964.

———. *Véra Baxter ou les plages de l'Atlantique*. Paris: Albatros, 1980.

———. *Le Vice-Consul*. Paris: Gallimard, 1965.

Duras, Marguerite, and Xavière Gauthier. *Les Parleuses*. Paris: Minuit, 1974.

Duras, Marguerite, and Michelle Porte. *Les Lieux de Marguerite Duras*. Paris: Minuit, 1977.

DuVerlie, Claud. "Interview with Claude Simon." *Sub-Stance* 8 (1974): 3–20.

Eco, Umberto. *L'Opera aperta*. Milano: Bompiani, 1967.

Ellman, Richard. *James Joyce*. New York: Oxford University Press, 1965.

Esslin, Martin. *Samuel Beckett: A Collection of Critical Essays*. Englewood Cliffs, N.J.: Prentice-Hall, 1965.

Fardeau, Patrice. "Manif." *France Nouvelle* 1690 (April 1978): 44.

Federman, Raymond, ed. *Surfiction: Fiction Now . . . and Tomorrow*. Chicago: Swallow Press, 1975.

Finnegan, Ruth. *Oral Poetry*. Cambridge: Cambridge University Press, 1977.

Fletcher, John. *The Novels of Samuel Beckett*. New York: Barnes & Noble, 1970.

Foucault, Michel. *Les Mots et les choses*. Paris: Gallimard, 1966.

————. *L'Ordre du discours.* Paris: Gallimard, 1971.

Foster, Hal, ed. *The Anti-Aesthetics: Essays on Postmodern Culture.* Port Townsend, Wash.: Bay Press, 1983.

Francastel, Pierre. *Peinture et société.* Paris: Gallimard, 1965.

Freud, Sigmund. *Beyond the Pleasure Principle.* New York: Norton, 1961.

Friedrich, Paul. *Language, Context, and the Imagination.* Stanford, Calif.: Stanford University Press, 1979.

Gallop, Jane. *The Daughter's Seduction: Feminism and Psychoanalysis.* Ithaca, N.Y.: Cornell University Press, 1982.

Gardiner, Alan. *The Theory of Proper Names,* 2d ed. Oxford: Oxford University Press, 1957.

Geertz, Clifford. "Blurred Genres: The Refiguration of Social Thought." *American Scholar* 49 (Spring 1980): 165–82.

————. "Thick Description: Toward an Interpretative Theory of Culture." In *The Interpretation of Cultures,* 3–32. New York: Basic, 1973.

Genette, Gérard. *Figures III.* Paris: Seuil, 1972.

————. *Introduction à l'architexte.* Paris: Seuil, 1979.

————. *Palimpsestes.* Paris: Seuil, 1982.

Goffman, Erving. *Frame Analysis.* New York: Harper & Row, 1974.

Gombrich, E. H. *Art and Illusion.* Princeton, N.J.: Princeton University Press, 1972.

Goodman, Nelson. "Routes of Reference." *Critical Inquiry* 8, no. 1 (Autumn 1981): 121–32.

Goody, Jack. *The Domestication of the Savage Mind.* Cambridge: Cambridge University Press, 1977.

Graver, Lawrence, and Raymond Federman, eds. *Samuel Beckett: The Critical Heritage.* London: Routledge & Kegan Paul, 1979.

Greimas, Algiras J. *Essais de sémiotique poétique.* Paris: Larousse, 1972.

Halliday, Michael A., and Ruqaiya Hasan. *Cohesion in English.* London: Longman, 1976.

Hartman, Geoffrey H. *Saving the Text.* Baltimore, Md.: Johns Hopkins University Press, 1981.

Hassan, Ihab. "Culture, Indeterminacy and Immanence: Margins of the (Postmodern) Age." *Humanities in Society* (Winter 1978): 51–85.

Hayman, David. "Some Writers in the Wake of the *Wake.*" *TriQuarterly* 38 (Winter 1977): 3–38.

————. Sollers interview. *Iowa Review* 5, no. 4 (1974): 101.

Heath, Stephen. *The Nouveau Roman.* Philadelphia: Temple University Press, 1972.

Henkels, Robert M., Jr. *Robert Pinget: The Novel as Quest.* University: University of Alabama Press, 1979.

Henric, Jacques. *Maurice Roche par les autres.* Paris: L'Athanor, 1978.

Hermann, Claudine. *Les Voleuses de langue.* Paris: Des femmes, 1976.

Higgins, Lynn. "Nouvelle nouvelle autobiographie: Monique Wittig's *Le Corps lesbien.*" *Sub-Stance* 14 (1976): 160–66.

Hjelmslev, Louis. *Prolegomena to a Theory of Language*. Rev. trans. Madison: University of Wisconsin Press, 1961.

Holquist, Michael, and Walter Reed. "Six Theses on the Novel and Some Metaphors." *New Literary History* 11 (1979–80): 413–23.

Husserl-Kapit, Susan. "An Interview with Marguerite Duras." *Signs: Journal of Women in Culture and Society* 1, no. 2 (Winter 1975): 423–34.

Irigaray, Luce. *Ce Sexe qui n'en est pas un*. Paris: Minuit, 1977.

———. *Speculum de l'autre femme*. Paris: Minuit, 1974.

Jakobson, Roman. "Linguistics and Poetics." In *Style in Language*, ed. Thomas Sebeok, 350–77. Cambridge, Mass.: MIT Press, 1964.

Jean, Raymond. *Pratiques de la littérature*. Paris: Seuil, 1978.

Jenny, Laurent. "La stratégie de la forme." *Poétique* 27 (1976): 257–81.

Kenner, Hugh. *Sameul Beckett: A Critical Study*. New York: Grove Press, 1961.

Kristeva, Julia. *Desire in Language: A Semiotic Approach to Literature and Art*, ed. Leon S. Roudiez. New York: Columbia University Press, 1980.

———. "Le Mot, le dialogue, et le roman." In *Semiotiké*, 143–73. Paris: Seuil, 1969.

———. *Polylogue*. Paris: Seuil, 1980.

———. *La Révolution du langage poétique*. Paris: Seuil, 1974.

———. *Semiotiké*. Paris: Seuil, 1969.

———. *Le Texte du roman*. Paris: Seuil, 1970.

Lamblin, Bernard. "Vanitas: La Symbolique de l'objet." In *Pour l'objet* (*Revue d'Esthétique 3–4*), 197–232. Paris: UGE: 1979.

Laporte, Roger. *Carnets*. Paris: Hachette, 1979.

———. *Fugue*. Paris: Gallimard, 1970.

———. *La Veille*. Paris: Gallimard, 1963.

———. *Une Voix de fin silence I*. Paris: Gallimard, 1966.

———. *Pourquoi? Une Voix de fin silence II*. Paris: Gallimard, 1967.

———. *Quinze Variations sur un thème biographique*. Paris: Flammarion, 1975.

Laporte, Roger, and Bernard Noël. *Deux Lectures de Maurice Blanchot*. Montpellier: Fata Morgana, 1973.

Lascaut, Gilbert. "Treize Murs peints." *La Quinzaine Littéraire* 379 (October 1982): 21–22.

Le Bot, Marc. *Figures de l'art contemporain*. Paris: UGE, 1977.

Le Guern, Michel. *Sémantique de la métaphore et de la métonymie*. Paris: Larousse, 1973.

L'Espace et la lettre. Cahiers Jussieu 3. Paris: UGE, 1977.

Lévesque, Claude. *L'Etrangeté du texte*. Paris: UGE, 1978.

Lévi-Strauss, Claude. *Les Structures élémentaires de la parenté*. Paris: Presses Universitaires de France, 1945.

Lodge, David. *The Modes of ModernWriting*. Lodnon: Edward Arnold, 1977.

Lost Empires. Washington, D. C.: National Geographic Society, 1982.

Lyotard, François. *La Condition postmoderne*. Paris: Minuit, 1979.

MacCannel, Dean. *The Tourist.* New York: Schocken Books, 1976.

Magazine littéraire 65 (1972).

Makward, Christiane. "Interview with Hélène Cixous." *Sub-Stance* 13 (1976): 19–37.

Maldiney, Henri. *Regard Parole Espace.* Paris: L'Age d'homme, 1973.

Marguerite Duras. Paris, Albatros, 1975.

Marks, Elaine, and Isabelle de Courtivron, eds. *New French Feminisms.* New York: Schocken, 1981.

Marin, Louis. *Utopiques: Jeux d'espaces.* Paris: Minuit, 1973.

Mercier, Vivian. *Beckett / Beckett.* New York: Oxford University Press, 1977.

Miller, Nancy K. "Emphasis Added: Plots and Plausibilities in Women's Fiction." *PMLA* 96, no. 1 (January 1981): 36–48.

———. "Women's Autobiography in France: For a Dialectics of Identification." In *Women and Language in Literature and Society,* ed. Sally McConnell-Ginet et al., 258–73. New York: Praeger, 1980.

Murphy, Carol J. *Alienation and Absence in the Novels of Marguerite Duras.* Lexington, Ky.: French Forum, 1982.

Nouveau Roman: Hier, aujourd'hui I. Paris: UGE, 1972.

Nouveau Roman: Hier, aujourd'hui II. Paris: UGE, 1972.

Nyssen, Hubert. "Marguerite Duras: Un Silence peuplé de phrases." *Synthèses* (August–September 1967): 254–55.

O'Hara, J. D. Introduction to *Twentieth Century Interpretations of Molloy, Malone Dies, The Unnamable.* Englewood Cliffs, N.J.: Prentice-Hall, 1970.

Ostrowsky, Erika. "A Cosmogony of O: Wittig's *Les Guérillères.*" In *Twentieth Century French Fiction,* ed. George Stambolian, 241–51. New Brunswick, N.J.: Rutgers University Press, 1975.

La Parodie (*Cahiers du 20ème* siècle 6). Paris: Klincksieck, 1976.

Perloff, Marjorie. *The Poetics of Indeterminacy.* Princeton, N.J.: Princeton University Press, 1981.

Pinget, Robert. *Baqa.* Paris: Minuit, 1958.

———. *Cette Voix.* Paris: Minuit, 1975.

———. *Entre Fantoine et Agapa.* Paris: Minuit, 1951.

———. *L'Inquisitoire.* Paris: Minuit, 1962.

———. *Mahu ou le materiau.* Paris: Minuit, 1952.

———. *Quelqu'un.* Paris: Minuit, 1955.

Pratt, Annis. *Archetypal Patterns in Women's Fiction.* Bloomington: Indiana University Press, 1981.

Praz, Mario. *Mnemosyne: The Parallel between Literature and the Visual Arts.* Princeton, N.J.: Princeton University Press, 1970.

Prigogine, Ilya. "Probing into Time." *Discovery* 5, no. 1 (September 1980): 5–7.

Proust, Marcel. *A la recherche du temps perdu: Noms de pays.* Paris: Gallimard, 1954.

Raillard, Georges. "Le rythme des choses." *Critique* 414 (November 1981): 1167–80.

Rambures, Jean-Louis de. Sollers interview. *Le Monde,* November 29, 1974.

Rhétoriques sémiotiques (Revue d'esthétique 1–2). Paris: UGE, 1979.

Ricardou, Jean. *Nouveaux Problèmes du roman.* Paris: Seuil, 1978.

———. *L'Observatoire de Cannes.* Paris: Minuit, 1965.

———. *Problèmes du nouveau roman.* Paris: Seuil, 1967.

———. *Révolutions minuscules.* Paris: Gallimard, 1971.

———, ed. *Claude Simon: Colloque de Cerisy.* Paris: UGE, 1975.

Riffatterre, Michael. *La Production du texte.* Paris: Seuil, 1979.

Rimbaud, Arthur. *The Illuminations.* Translated by Enid Rhodes Peschel. New York: Oxford University Press, 1973.

Ristat, Jean. "Lire Roger Laporte." *Lettres françaises* 1453 (September 27, 1972): 3–6.

Robbe-Grillet, Alain. *Dans le labyrinthe.* Paris: Minuit, 1959.

———. *Les Gommes.* Paris: Minuit, 1953.

———. *La Jalousie.* Paris: Minuit, 1957.

———. *La Maison de rendez-vous.* Paris: Minuit, 1965.

———. *La Maison de rendez-vous.* Translated by Richard Howard. New York: Grove, 1966.

———. *Projet pour une révolution à New York.* Paris: Minuit, 1970.

Roche, Maurice. *Camar(a)de.* Paris: Seuil, 1982.

———. *Circus.* Paris: Seuil, 1972.

———. *Codex.* Paris: Seuil, 1974.

———. *Compact.* Paris: Seuil, 1965.

———. *Macabré.* Paris: Seuil, 1976.

———. *Maladie mélodie.* Paris: Seuil, 1980.

———. *Mémoire.* Paris: Belfond, 1976.

———. *Monteverdi.* Paris: Seuil, 1960.

———. *Opéra bouffe.* Paris: Seuil, 1975.

———. *Testament. Livre/cassette.* Paris: Cercles, 1979.

Roudaut, Jean. *Michel Butor ou le livre futur.* Paris: Gallimard, 1966.

Roudiez, Léon. *French Fiction Today: A New Direction.* New Brunswick, N.J.: Rutgers University Press, 1972.

Sanches, Mary, and Barbara Kirshenblatt-Gimblett. "Children's Traditional Speech Play and Child Language." In *Speech Play,* ed. Barbara Kirshenblatt-Gimblett, 65–110. Philadelphia: University of Pennsylvania Press, 1976.

Sartre, Jean-Paul *La Nausée.* Paris: Gallimard, 1938.

———. *Nausea.* Translated by Robert Baldick. Harmondsworth, Eng.: Penguin, 1969.

Searle, John. "Proper Names." *Mind* 67, no. 266 (1958): 166–73.

———. *Speech Acts.* Cambridge: Cambridge University Press, 1969.

Sherzer, Dina. "*Endgame* or what talk can do." *Modern Drama* 5 (1979): 291–303.

———. "Saying Is Inventing: Gnomic Expressions in Molloy." In *Speech*

Play, ed. Barbara Kirshenblatt-Gimblett, 163–71. Philadelphia: University of Pennsylvania Press, 1976.

———. *Structure de la Trilogie: Molloy, Malone meurt, L'Innommable.* The Hague: Mouton, 1976.

Sherzer, Dina, and Joel Sherzer. "Literature in San Blas: Discovering the Kuna *Ikala.*" *Semiotica* 6 (1972): 182–99.

Sherzer, Joel. *Kuna Ways of Speaking: An Ethnographic Perspective.* Austin: University of Texas Press, 1983.

Simon, Claude. *Les Corps conducteurs.* Paris: Minuit, 1971.

———. *Orion aveugle.* Paris: Skira, 1970.

———. *Triptyque.* Paris: Minuit, 1973.

———. *Triptych.* Translated by Helen R. Lane. New York: Viking, 1976.

Spitzer, Leo. "Quelques Aspects de la technique des romans de Michel Butor." In *Etudes de style,* 482–531. Paris: Gallimard, 1970.

Sollers, Philippe. *Uni Curieuse Solitude.* Paris: Seuil, 1958.

———. *Le Défi.* Paris: Seuil, 1957.

———. *Drame.* Paris: Seuil, 1965.

———. *L'Ecriture et l'expérience des limites.* Paris: Seuil, 1968.

———. *Femmes.* Paris: Gallimard, 1982.

———. *H.* Paris: Seuil, 1973.

———. *Logiques.* Paris: Seuil, 1969.

———. *Lois.* Paris: Seuil, 1972.

———. *Nombres.* Paris: Seuil, 1968.

———. *Le Parc.* Paris: Seuil, 1961.

Tagliaferri, Aldo. *Beckett et la surdétermination littéraire.* Paris: Payot, 1977.

Thom, René. *Structural Stability and Morphogenesis.* Reading, Mass.: W. A. Benjamin, 1975.

Thomas, Jean-Jacques. "Lecture / Montage / Espace." *Stanford French Review* 1982: 87–100.

Thompson, D'Arcy. *On Growth and Form.* Cambridge, Mass.: Cambridge University Press, 1961.

Thompson, Stith. *The Types of the Folktale.* Communication no. 184. Helsinki: Folklore Fellows, 1961.

Uspenski, Boris. "Structural Isomorphism of Verbal and Visual Art." *Poetics* 5 (1972): 5–39.

Vaillant, George. *The Aztecs of Mexico.* New York: Doubleday, 1944.

Vuarnet, Jean. *Extases féminines.* Paris: Arthaud, 1980.

Whorf, Benjamin. *Language, Thought and Reality.* Cambridge, Mass.: MIT Press, 1956.

Wittgenstein, Ludwig. *Philosophical Investigations.* New York: Macmillan, 1968.

Wittig, Monique. *Le Corps lesbien.* Paris: Minuit, 1973.

———. *Les Guérillères.* Paris: Minuit, 1959.

———. *Les Guérillères.* Translated by David Le Vay. New York: Avon, 1973.

Wittig, Monique, and Sande Zeig. *Brouillon pour un dictionnaire des amantes*. Paris: Grasset, 1976.

Xenakis, Iannis. "Entretien: En quête de l'inouï." *La Quinzaine Littéraire* 353 (August 1981): 36.

Yates, Frances. *The Art of Memory*. Chicago: University of Chicago Press, 1966.

———. *Giordano Bruno and the Hermetic Tradition*. Chicago: University of Chicago Press, 1964.

Zumthor, Paul. *Introduction à la poésie orale*. Paris: Seuil, 1983.

Index